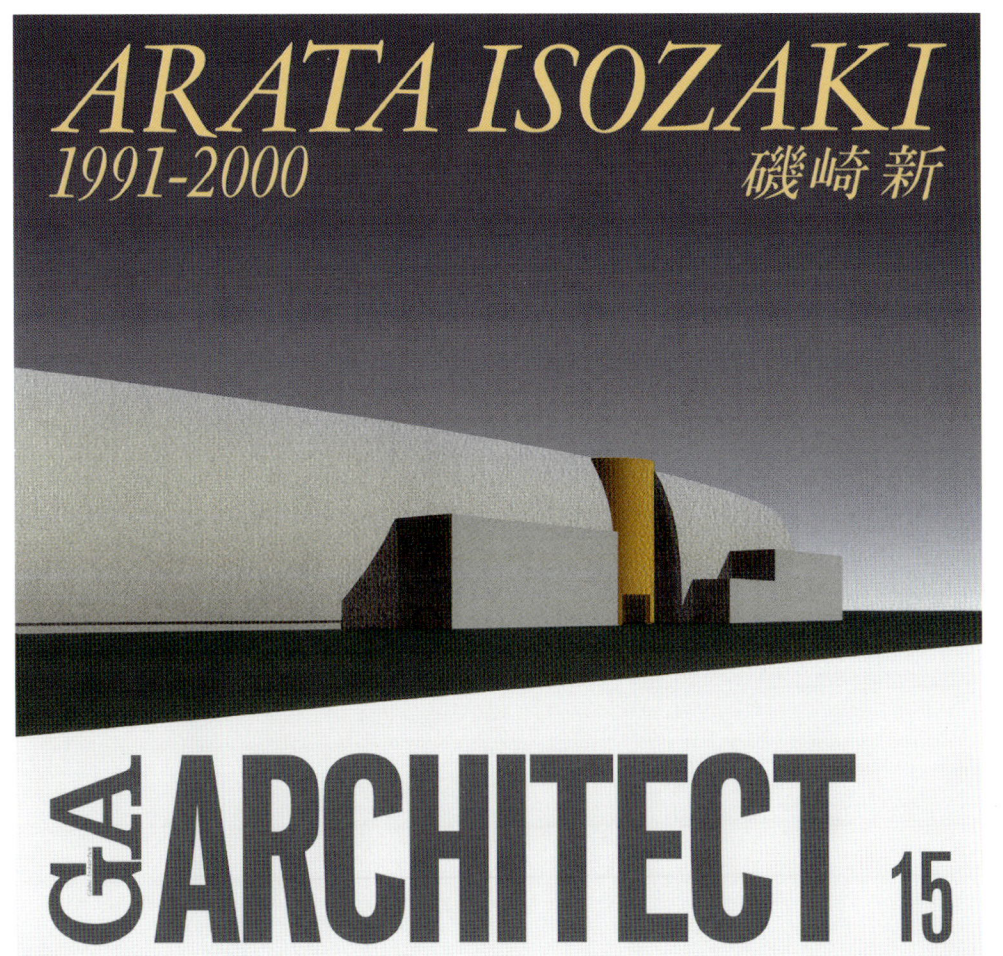

GA ARCHITECT 15

磯崎 新 3 1991-2000

TEXTS: Arata Isozaki
WORKS: Team Disney Building／B-Con Plaza／Toyonokuni Libraries for Cultural Resources／Kyoto Concert Hall／Nagi Museum of Contemporary Art／Nagi Town Library／Nara Centennial Hall／DOMUS; Interactive Museum La Coruna／Bass Museum of Art／Okayama West Police Station／Shizuoka Perfoming Arts Center/Daendo／Shizuoka Performing Arts Center／Ohio's Center of Science and Industry(COSI)／The Museum of Modern Art, Gunma Contemporary Art Wing／Gunma Astronomical Observatory／The Akiyoshidai International Art Village／Art Plaza／The Man-made Island Project, "Mirage"／Shenzhen International Trade Plaza／"Art and Fashion"／Yamanaka／Yamaguchi Cultural Complex／The New Exit for the Uffizi, Project for Piazza Castellani／and others

論文・作品解説：磯崎新
作品：ティーム・ディズニー・ビルディング／ビーコン・プラザ／豊の国ライブラリー／京都コンサートホール／奈義町現代美術館・奈義町立図書館／なら100年会館／ラ・コルーニャ人間科学館／バス・ミュージアム／岡山西警察署／静岡県コンベンション・アーツセンター＜グランシップ＞／静岡県舞台芸術センター／野外劇場＜有度＞，本部棟／オハイオ21世紀科学工業センター／群馬県立近代美術館現代美術棟／県立ぐんま天文台／秋吉台国際芸術村／アートプラザ／海市計画／深圳国際公易広場／タイム・アンド・ファッション／フィレンツェ・ビエンナーレ '96／やま中／山口市文化交流プラザ／ウフィツィ美術館新玄関プロジェクト／他

Size: 300×307mm／264 total pages, 96 in color
paperback: ¥6,648, hard cover: ¥9,333

GA ARCHITECT 16

安藤忠雄 vol.3 1994-2000 / TADAO ANDO 1994-2000

CRITICISM: Williams J. R. Curtis
WORKS: Chikatsu-Asuka Historical Museum, Osaka／Garden of Fine Art, Kyoto／Suntory Museum／Rokko Housing III／FABRICA (Benetton Communication Research Center)／Eychaner/Lee House／Nariwa Museum／Awaji-Yumebutai／Naoshima Contemporary Art Museum, Annex／Meditation Space, UNESCO／TOTO Seminar House／Town House in Hirano (Nomi House)／Daylight Museum／Church of The Light, Sunday School／Komyo-ji Temple／and others
PROJECTS: Pulitzer Foundation for the Arts／Sayamaike Historical Museum／Tate Gallery of Modern Art／Penthouse in Manhattan／Hyogo Prefectural Museum of Modern Art+Kobe Waterfront Plaza／Modern Art Museum of Fort Worth／The Museum of World Cultures on the River Rhine／and others

論文：ウィリアム・J・R・カーティス
作品：大阪府立近つ飛鳥博物館／京都府立陶板名画の庭／サントリーミュージアム／六甲の集合住宅III／FABRICA（ベネトン・アートスクール）／アイキャナー／リー邸／成羽町美術館／淡路夢舞台／直島コンテンポラリーアートミュージアム・アネックス／ユネスコ瞑想空間／TOTOセミナーハウス／平野区の町屋（能見邸）／織田廣喜ミュージアム／光の教会日曜学校／南岳山光明寺／他
プロジェクト：ピューリッツァー美術館／大阪府立狭山池博物館／テートギャラリー現代美術館国際設計競技応募案／マンハッタンのペントハウス／兵庫県立新美術館＋神戸市水際広場／フォートワース現代美術館／ライン世界文化博物館／他

Size: 300×307mm／276 total pages, 48 in color　¥6,648

表記価格には消費税は含まれておりません。

素材空間

20世紀の建築は，様々な素材の登場により，新しい建築様式が生まれました。21世紀を迎えるにあたって，建築デザインを素材面から考えてみようと，この企画を立案しました。

建築以外の航空・車両・エレクトロニクスといった分野では，ここ十数年間に，大変な進歩を遂げています。この雑誌では，ほかの産業で開発されている材料も含めて，建築に応用できる素材の発見と，現在，一般的に使用されている建築材料についても，研究・改良されていく様子をリポートしていきます。

近刊

Japanese text only　Size: 300×228mm

特集 GLASS 素材空間 02
透明素材の系譜と未来への挑戦

■素材空間へ
質料としての素材考／谷川渥
透明ということ／榮久庵憲司
■連載
記憶に残る素材とディテール
／松村秀一
素材ノート／石山修武
素材探訪／杉本賢司
新素材の現場／①FRPとは何か？

特集：ガラスの可能性
■ガラス建築 50選
■ガラス建築概観
／鈴木博之
■半透明建築の系譜
／岡部憲明
■ガラス技術発展史
／池内清治
■発想と実現のガラス建築
／横田暉生
■構造家にとってガラスとは何か
／アラン・バーデン
■ガラス建築の可能性
／岡村仁＋仁藤喜徳
■環境工学から見たガラスの魅力と罠
／近藤靖史
■エッセイ・インタヴュー
／葉祥栄，赤坂喜顕，他
■ガラス工場・研究所訪問

GA JAPAN 50
ENVIRONMENTAL DESIGN　5-6/2001

50　新［現代建築を考える ○と×］宮城県迫桜高等学校
批評座談会：小嶋一浩・山本理顕・二川幸夫

作品：
小嶋一浩＋三瓶満真／C+A／宮城県迫桜高等学校　原広司／東京大学駒場Ⅱ地区／柏地区キャンパス
黒川紀章／日本赤十字九州国際看護大学　堀場弘＋工藤和美／K&H／福岡市立博多小学校・奈良屋公民館
石田敏明／印西消防署牧ノ原分署　隈研吾／県南総合防災センター
日本設計／しものせき水族館「海響館」　古市徹雄／福島県ハイテクプラザ会津若松技術支援センター
久米設計／ふくしま森の科学体験センター（ムシテックワールド）

連載：
GA SCHOOL「造物主義論Ⅱ」磯崎新
GA SCHOOL「モダンストラクチャーの原型」佐々木睦朗
［建築家登場］⑮石田敏明

GA広場：
「見えない建築—カルダー美術館設計コンペ案」安藤忠雄
「トリノ・ピエモンテ州庁舎コンペの審査より」渡辺誠
「音から環境をデザインする」庄野泰子
「列島リポート」　「世界の現場より」

Japanese text only
Size: 300×228mm　184 total pages, 64 in color　¥2,333

表記価格には消費税は含まれておりません。

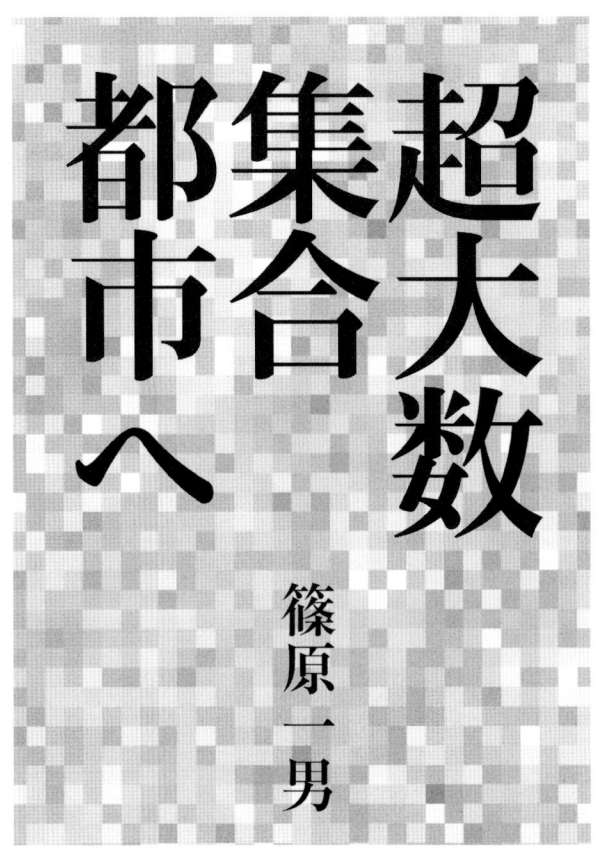

超大数集合都市へ　篠原一男

アフリカ・ヨーロッパ・南北アメリカ・日本という地域軸と，古代から現代までの2000年を超える時間軸を，縦横に織り上げることによって論じられる「都市」。

2001年1月発売　　Japanese text only　Size：210×148mm
160 total pages 32 in color　¥1,900（予価）

建築のエッセンス　齋藤裕

GA JAPANで好評を博した同名タイトルの連載をもとに，加筆，単行本化。時代や風土を越えて建築のエッセンスを抽出・再解釈し，我々が忘れかけている建築の本質にせまる。

Japanese text only　Size：210×148mm
320 total pages 32 in color　¥2,476

GA JAPAN 別冊①
20世紀の現代建築を検証する○と×

鉄・ガラス・コンクリートの出現から，ミース・コルビュジエ・ライトの巨匠時代を経て，現代日本建築にいたるまで。歴史家と建築家による20世紀の横断。

磯崎　新
鈴木博之

Japanese text only　Size：300×228mm
192 total pages 72 in color　¥2,800

1851-1919 ① 近代建築の黎明

第1章：ガラス，鉄，鋼，そしてコンクリート　1775-1915
第2章：シカゴ派の建築——都市と郊外　1830-1915
第3章：アール・ヌーヴォーの構造と象徴主義　1851-1914
第4章：オットー・ワグナーとワグナー派　1894-1912
第5章：工業生産と文化の危機　1851-1910

Japanese text only
Size：210×148mm　224 total pages 48 in color　¥2,300

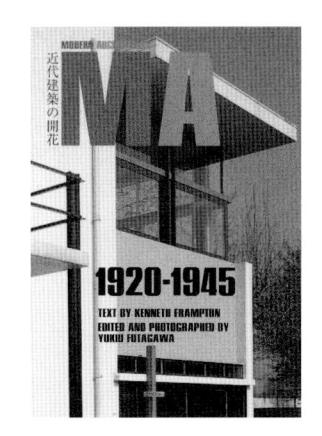

1920-1945 ② 近代建築の開花

第6章：北ヨーロッパの風土建築としての煉瓦造近代建築：オーストリア，ドイツ，オランダ　1914-1935
第7章：古典主義の伝統とヨーロッパのアヴァンギャルド：フランス，ドイツ，スカンジナヴィア　1912-1937
第8章：ヨーロッパの芸術と建築における千年王国的な衝撃：ロシアとオランダ　1913-1922
第9章：地方都市と共同都市計画：建築とアメリカの運命　1913-1945
第10章：インターナショナル・モダニズムと国民的自覚　1919-1939

Japanese text only
Size：210×148mm　256 total pages 48 in color　¥2,300

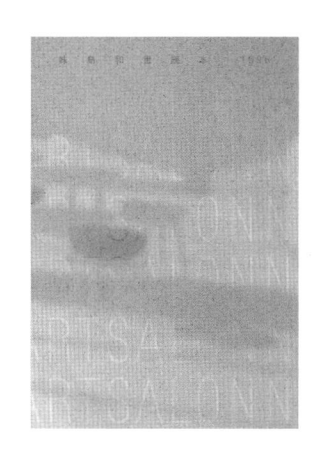

妹島和世読本——１９９８

収録作品　PLATFORM I, II, III／再春館製薬女子寮／カステルバジャック・スポーツ・ショップ／那須野ヶ原ハーモニーホール公開設計競技優秀案／パチンコパーラーI, II, III／森の別荘／Y-HOUSE／中原中也記念館公開設計競技応募案／横浜港国際客船ターミナル設計競技入選案／せんだいメディアテーク公開設計競技応募案／長岡文化創造フォーラム指名提案競技優秀案／調布駅北口交番／アパートメントのプロトタイプ／ハウジングスタディ／岐阜県営北方住宅／S-HOUSE／マルチメディア工房／熊野古道なかへち美術館／K本社屋／牛久新駅駅前利便施設／O資料館／世界都市博覧会・警消センター／KAZUYO SEJIMA 12 PROJECTS展／他

Japanese text only
Size：210×148mm　336 total pages 42 in color　¥2,800

隈研吾読本——１９９９

サイバーからリアル，メガからミクロ，アカデミズムからストリート，建築家・隈研吾の境界を越えて横断する思考と重層するアクティビティーを，インタヴューと対談を交えて解明する。

収録作品　伊豆の風呂小屋／バーバリアンコロニー／M2／亀老山展望台／水／ガラス／檮原町地域交流施設／日本美術館構想／ガラス／影／ヴェネツィア・ビエンナーレ日本館／川／フィルター／森舞台／愛知万博2005／淡路サービスエリア／エコ・パーティクル／北上川・運河交流館　水野洞窟／森／スラット／慰霊公園／臨海副都心計画／スーパーストリート構想／他

Japanese text only
Size：210×148mm　224 total pages 64 in color　¥2,333

表記価格には消費税は含まれておりません。

GA DO

Global Architecture

GA DOCUMENT 65
Publisher: *Yukio Futagawa*
Editor: *Yoshio Futagawa*

Published in May 2001
©*A.D.A. EDITA Tokyo Co., Ltd.*
3-12-14 Sendagaya, Shibuya-ku,
Tokyo, 151-0051 Japan
Tel. 03-3403-1581
Fax.03-3497-0649
e-mail: info@ga-ada.co.jp
www.ga-ada.co.jp

Logotype Design: *Gan Hosoya*

Printed in Japan by
Dai Nippon Printing Co., Ltd.

All rights reserved.

Copyright of Photographs:
©*GA photographers*

65

GA DOCUMENT 65
発行：二川幸夫
編集：二川由夫

2001年5月11日発行
エーディーエー・エディタ・トーキョー
東京都渋谷区千駄ヶ谷3-12-14
電話(03)3403-1581(代)
ファクス(03)3497-0649
e-mail: info@ga-ada.co.jp
www.ga-ada.co.jp

ロゴタイプ・デザイン：細谷巖

印刷・製本：大日本印刷株式会社

禁無断転載

ISBN4-87140-165-0 C1352

取次店
トーハン・日販・大阪屋
栗田出版販売・誠光堂
西村書店・中央社・太洋社

A.D.A. EDITA Tokyo

GA INTERNATIONAL 2001

TADAO ANDO
Born in Osaka, Japan, 1941
Establish Tadao Ando Architect & Associates in Osaka, 1968

34

PETER EISENMAN
Born in Newark, New Jersey, USA, 1932
Graduate from:
Cornell University, B. Arch., 1955
Columbia University, M.S. Arch., 1960
Cambridge University, M.A., 1962 and Ph.D., 1963
At Present, Eisenman Architects, New York, New York

40

NORMAN FOSTER
Born in Manchester, England, 1935
Graduate from University of Manchester in 1961 and
Yale University (M. Arch.) in 1962
Establish private practice in 1963
At present, Foster and Partners, London, Berlin, Hong kong, Singapore

86

FRANK O. GEHRY
Born in Toronto, Canada, 1929
Graduate from University of Southern California in 1951 and
Harvard Graduate School of Design in 1957
Establish Frank O. Gehry and Associates in Los Angeles, 1962

28

ZAHA M. HADID
Born in Baghdad, Iraq, 1950
Degree in mathematics, American University of Beirut, 1971
Graduate from Architectural Association, London, 1974
Joined Office for Metropolitan Architecture (OMA), 1977
Establish private practice in London, 1980

34

HIROSHI HARA
Born in Kanagawa, Japan, 1936
Graduate from University of Tokyo (B. Arch.) in 1959, and receive Ph.D. in 1964
Establish Hiroshi Hara + Atelier Φ in Tokyo, 1970

54

STEVEN HOLL
Born in Bremerton, Washington, USA, 1947
Graduate from University of Washington (B. Arch.) in 1970
Post-graduates studies at Architectural Association, London, 1976
Establish private practice in New York, 1976

20

ARATA ISOZAKI
Born in Oita, Japan, 1931
Graduate from University of Tokyo (B. Arch.) in 1954
Establish Arata Isozaki & Associates in Tokyo, 1963

70

TOYO ITO
Born in Seoul, Korea, 1941
Graduate from University of Tokyo (B.Arch.) in 1965
Establish Toyo Ito & Associates in Tokyo, 1971

94

LEGORRETA+LEGORRETA
Ricardo Legorreta
Born in Mexico City, Mexico, 1931
Graduate from National University of Mexico in 1953
Establish Legorreta Arquitectos in Mexico, 1963

102

MECANOO

Francine Houben
Born in Sittard, the Netherlands,1955
Graduate from Delft University of Technology in 1984

Henk Döll
Born in Haarlem, the Netherlands, 1956
Graduate from Delft University of Technology in 1984

Chris de Weijer
Born in Wageningen, the Netherlands, 1956
Graduate from Delft University of Technoogy in 1983

Establish Mecanoo in Rotterdam, 1984

37

RICHARD MEIER

Born in Newark, New Jersey, USA, 1934
Graduate from Cornell University (B. Arch.) in 1957
Establish private practice in New York, 1963
At present, Richard Meier & Partners Architects, New York/Los Angeles

46

MORPHOSIS

Thom Mayne
Born in Los Angeles, California, USA, 1944
Graduate from Southern California Institute of Architecture (B. Arch.) in 1968
Receive M. Arch. from Harvard University in 1978
Establish Morphosis in Santa Monica, 1974

64

ERIC OWEN MOSS

Born in Los Angeles, California, USA, 1943
Graduate from UCLA (B.A.) in 1965
Receive M. Arch. from University of California, Barkeley in 1968
and from Harvard University Graduate School of Design in 1972
Establish Eric Owen Moss Architects in Culver City, California, 1976

74

JEAN NOUVEL

Born in Fumel, France, 1945
Receive Architecte DPLG from École des Beaux-Art in 1972
Co-founder of the French architects' "Mars 1976" in 1976
Founder and artistic director of the "Biennale d'Architecture" in 1980
At present, Architectures Jean Nouvel, Paris

8

DOMINIQUE PERRAULT

Born in Clermont-Ferrand, France, 1953
Receive Architecte DPLG from UP6 Paris, École des Beaux-Art in 1978
Certificate of advanced studies, École des Ponts et Chaussées, Paris, 1979
Receive Master in historical studies from
École des Hautes Études en Sciences Sociales, Paris, 1980
Establish private practice in Paris, 1981

98

RENZO PIANO

Born in Genoa, Italy, 1937
Graduate from School of Architecture, Milan Polytechnic in 1964
Collaborate with Richard Rogers from 1971 (Piano & Rogers); from 1977 with
Peter Rice (Atelier Piano & Rice) and from 1980 with
Richard Fitzgerald in Houston.
At present, Renzo Piano Building Workshop, Genoa, Paris and Berlin

90

CHRISTIAN DE PORTZAMPARC

Born in Casablanca, Morocco, 1944
Graduate from Ecole Normale Supérieure des Beaux-Arts, Paris, 1969
Establish private practice in Paris, 1970

80

SHIN TAKAMATSU

Born in Shimane, Japan, 1948
Graduate from Kyoto University (B. Arch) in 1969
Establish Shin Takamatsu Architects & Associates in Kyoto, 1980

59

BERNARD TSCHUMI

Born in Lausanne, Switzerland, 1944
Graduate from EHT in Zurich, 1969
Establish private practice in Paris and New York, 1981
Dean of Graduate School of Architecture, Planning and Preservation,
Columbia University, New York, 1984-
At present, Bernard Tschumi Architects, Paris/New York

48

JEAN NOUVEL

BARCELONE TORRE AGBAR

Barcelona, Spain Design: 1999– Construction: 2001–

©Artefactory

It's not a tower, a sky scraper in its American sense: it's a unique emergence in the middle of a rather calm city. But not a nervous and slender vertical line like spires or steeples that generally punctuate horizontal cities. No, it's rather a fluid mass that would have perforated the ground, a geyser with a permanent and well-balanced pressure. The surface of the building evokes water: smooth, continuous but also vibrant and transparent since its matter can be read as a coloured and uncertain depth, luminous and with nuances. This architecture comes from the earth but does not support the weight of stone. Although it could be a distant echo of old Catalan formal obsessions carried by the mysteries of wind close by Montserrat. The uncertainties of matter and of light make the AGBAR campanile vibrate on the Barcelona Skyline. Distant mirage, night and day. Precise milestone of the new entrance of the Diagonal coming from the Las Glorias place.

 The singular object becomes the new symbol of the international metropolis and one of its best representatives.

Jean Nouvel

これはタワーではなく、アメリカ的感覚におけるスカイスクレーパーである。どちらかといえば平穏な都市の真ん中に上昇する特異物体である。しかし、水平に広がる都市に通例差し挟まれている尖塔や塔状の建物のような、神経質で細い垂直線ではない。それはむしろ、地面を穿つ流体性のマッス、恒久的な、よく均衡のとれた圧力で吹き出す間欠泉と言えようか。その建物の表面は水を喚起させる。滑らかに広がっているが、脈動し透明である。その構成物質は、色彩をまとい、不確かな深度を持ち、明るく輝き、微妙な色調や陰影を備えたものとして見えるはずだからだ。この建築は大地から現れるが、石の重さを支えてはいない。それはまた、モンセラート付近の風の神秘に運ばれた、古いカタロニア人が抱いていた形態に対する妄想の、遠い反響かもしれない。その物質と光が備える不安定さが、"AGBAR鐘楼"をバルセロナのスカイライン上で、生き生きと振動させる。夜となく昼となく瞬く遙かなミラージュ。ラス・グロリアス広場から続くディアゴナル通りの新しい入り口を示す明確な里程標。

 この特異物体はバルセロナという国際的なメトロポリスの新しい象徴、この都会を最も代表するものとなる。

(ジャン・ヌヴェル)

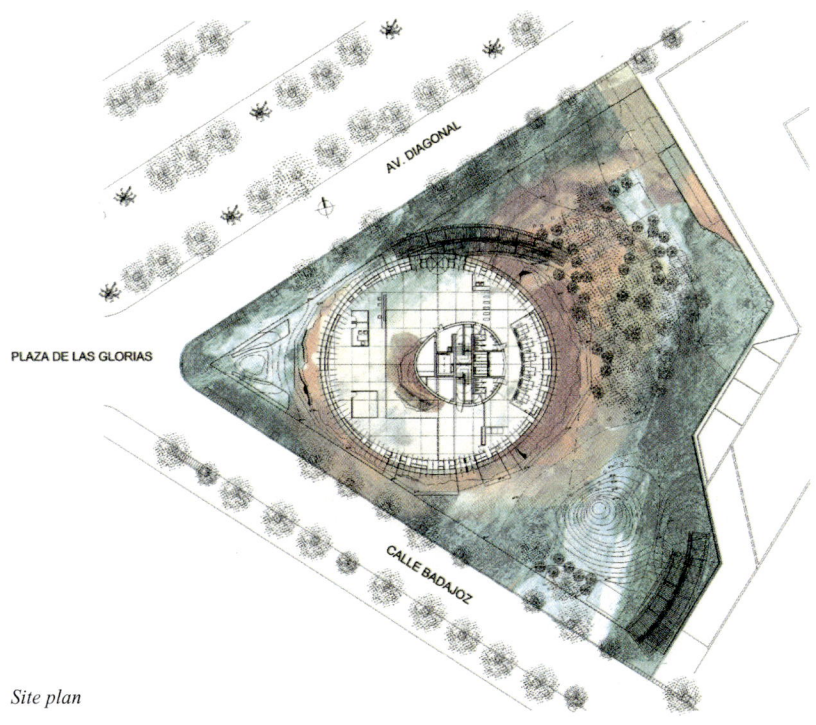

Site plan

Sections

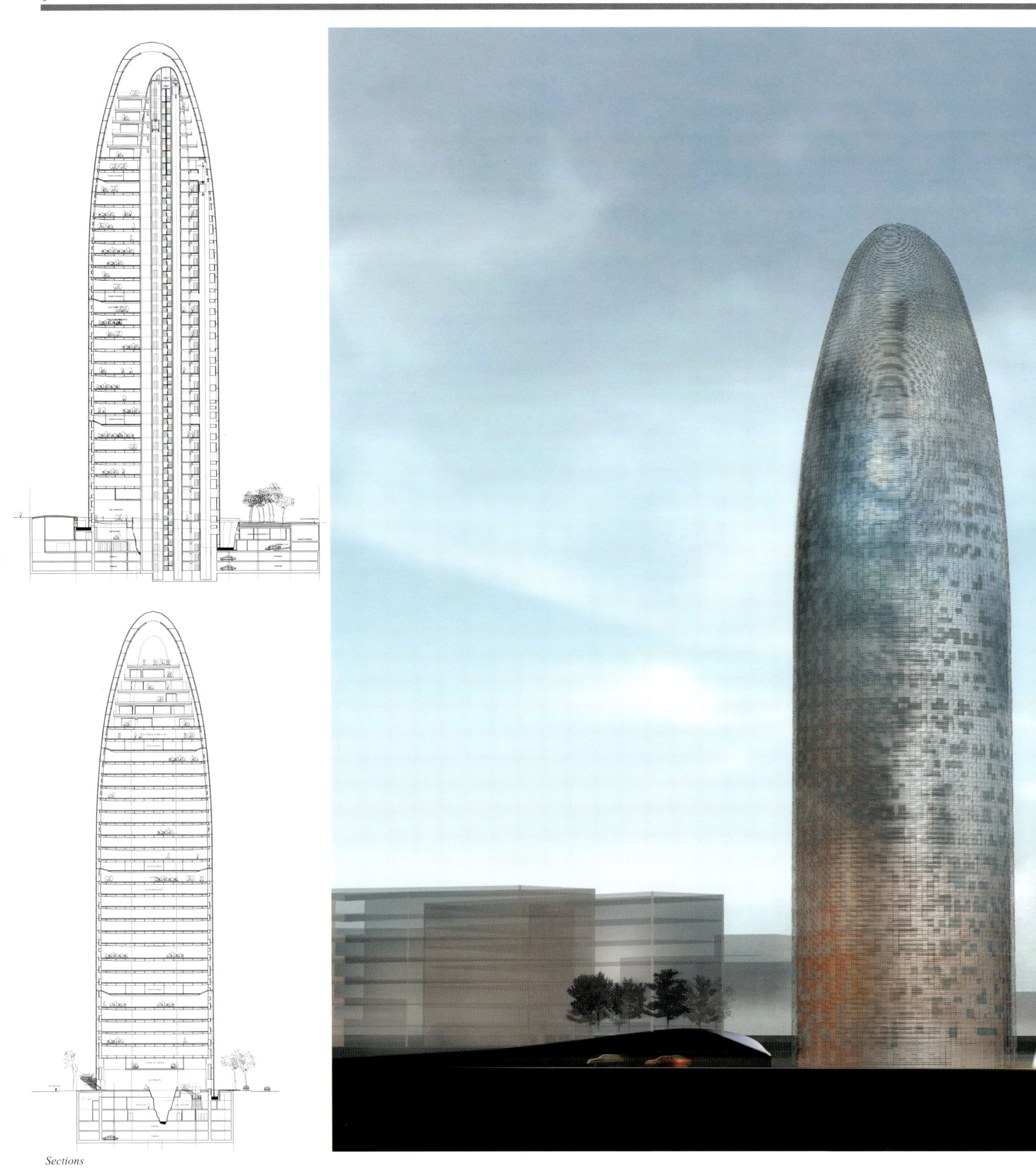

©*Artefactory*

Basement first floor

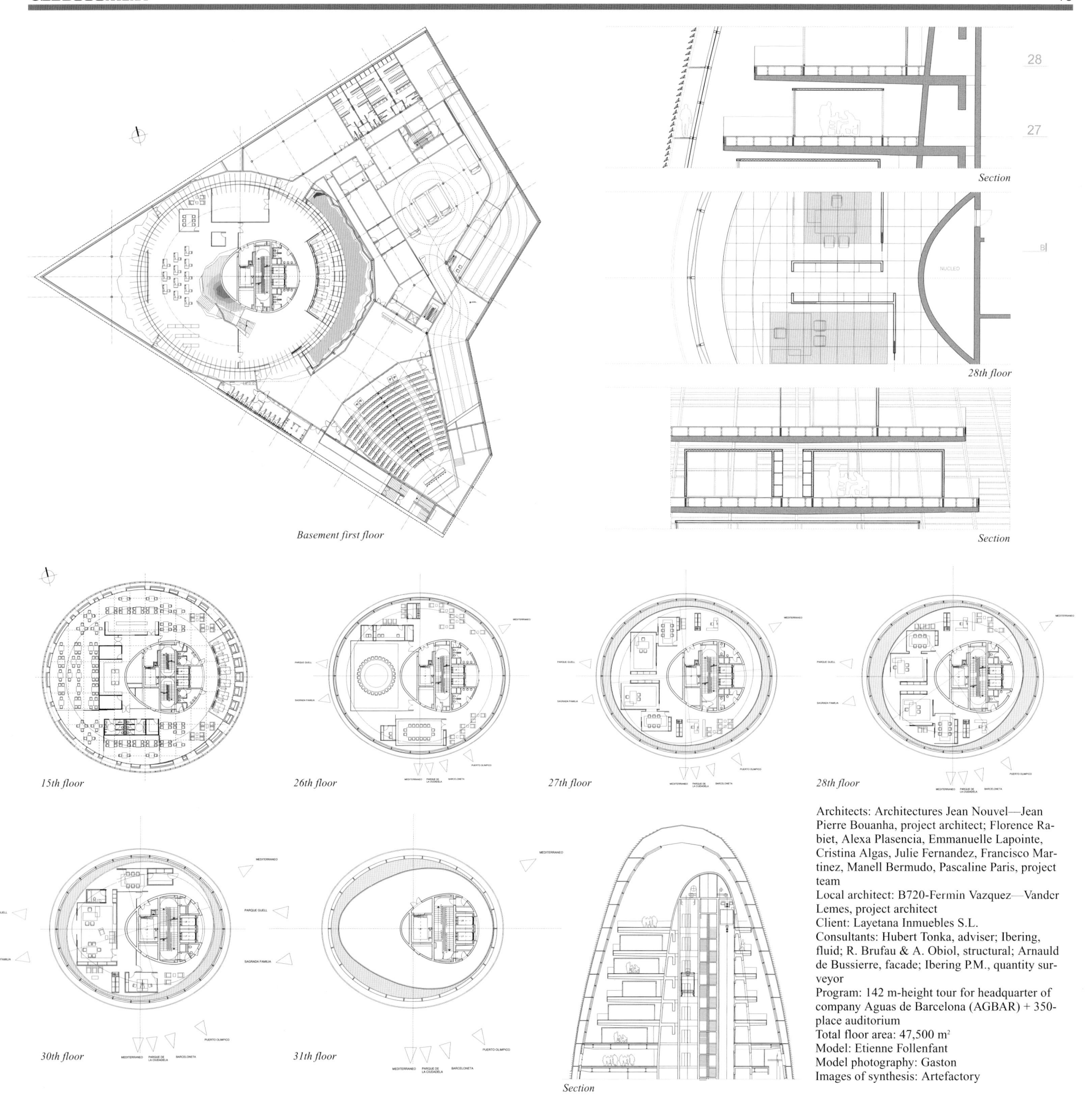

Section

28th floor

Section

15th floor

26th floor

27th floor

28th floor

30th floor

31st floor

Section

Architects: Architectures Jean Nouvel—Jean Pierre Bouanha, project architect; Florence Rabiet, Alexa Plasencia, Emmanuelle Lapointe, Cristina Algas, Julie Fernandez, Francisco Martinez, Manell Bermudo, Pascaline Paris, project team
Local architect: B720-Fermin Vazquez—Vander Lemes, project architect
Client: Layetana Inmuebles S.L.
Consultants: Hubert Tonka, adviser; Ibering, fluid; R. Brufau & A. Obiol, structural; Arnauld de Bussierre, facade; Ibering P.M., quantity surveyor
Program: 142 m-height tour for headquarter of company Aguas de Barcelona (AGBAR) + 350-place auditorium
Total floor area: 47,500 m²
Model: Etienne Follenfant
Model photography: Gaston
Images of synthesis: Artefactory

GA PROJECT

ESTE — N-E — NORTE — N-O — OESTE — S-O — SUR — S-E

ascensores | MEDITERRANEO | PARQUE GÜELL | SAGRADA FAMILIA | PUERTO OLIMPICO | MEDITERRANEO | ascensores

ESTE — N-E — NORTE — N-O — OESTE — S-O — SUR — S-E

ZAHA M. HADID

SCIENCE CENTER WOLFSBURG

Wolfsburg, Germany Design: 2000–01 Construction: 2001–03

The Magic Box
The Science Center, the first of its kind in Germany, appears as a mysterious object, giving rise to curiosity and discovery. The visitor is faced with a degree of complexity and strangeness, which is ruled however by a very specific system of structural organization.

Located on a very special site in the City of Wolfsburg it is set both as the endpoint of a chain of important cultural buildings (by Aalto, Scharoun) as well as being a connecting link to the north bank of the Mittelland Kanal—Volkswagen's Car Town.

Multiple threads of pedestrian and vehicular movement are pulled through the site both on an artificial ground landscape and inside and through the building, effectively composing an interface of movement-paths.

Volumetrically, the building is structured in such a way that it maintains a large degree of transparency and porosity on the ground since the main volume—the Exhibition—is raised thus covering an outdoor public plaza with a variety of commercial and cultural functions which reside in the structural concrete cones.

An artificial crater like landscape is developed inside the open exhibition space allowing diagonal views to the different levels of the exhibition-scape, while volumes, which protrude, accommodate other functions of the science center. A glazed public wormhole-like extension of the existing bridge flows through the building allowing views to and from the exhibition space.

マジック・ボックス
この科学センターは，この種の建物としてはドイツで初めてのものであり，不思議な物体として登場し，好奇心や発見したいという気持ちを誘発させるだろう。来館者は相当複雑で奇妙なものに直面するが，それは，非常に精密な構造システムによって規定されている。

敷地はヴォルフスブルク市でも，特別な性格をもつ場所にあり，文化的に重要な建物（アアルトとシャロウン設計）が立ち並ぶ道筋の終点であると同時に，フォルクスワーゲンの車の街，ミッテルラント・カナルの北河岸と結ぶ道筋でもある。

歩行者と自動車の動きに対応した多種多様な道筋が，景観構成した風景，建物のなか，その両方の面から敷地のなかに引き込まれ，動きの，つまり道のインターフェイスを効果的に構成している。

容積的に，建物は，かなりの透明性と地上面の空隙率を維持するように構成されている。というのは，中心となるヴォリュームである展示空間は，持ち上げられているからである。こうして，屋外の公共広場は，コンクリート構造の円錐形のなかに配置される様々な商業・文化施設に上を覆われる。

人工的なクレーターのような風景が，開放的な展示空間の内部に展開され，展示空間を構成する多様なレベルを対角方向に見せてくれる。一方，上に突き出したヴォリュームには科学センターのその他の機能が収容される。既存ブリッジの延長部である，虫食い穴に似たガラス張りのパブリック・スペースは建物のなかを流れて行き，展示空間をあちらこちらから見せてくれる。

Underside view

Competition Design: Zaha M. Hadid
Architects: Zaha Hadid with mayer baehrle—Christos K Passas, project architect; Sara Klomps, Silvia Forlati, Guenter Barzcik, Helmut Kinzler, Liam Young, Lida Charsouli, David Salazar, David Gerber, Jan Huebener, Gianluca Racana, Enrico Kleinke, Patrik Schumacher, Markus Dochantschi, project team; Christos Passas, Janne Westermann, Chris Dopheide, Stanley Lau, Eddie Can, Yoash Oster, Jan Hubener, Caroline Voet, competition team
Consultants: Adams Kara Taylor (London)—Hanif Kara, Paul Scott, structural; Tokarz Freirichs Leipold (Hanover)—L. Leipold, structural; Buro Happold (London-Berlin)—Ewan McLeod, Peter Roberts, mechanical; NEK (Braunschweig)—S. Wachtel, mechanical; Hanscomb GmbH (Berlin)—M. Sauerborn, cost consultant; OVI Inc. (New York)—E. Peiniger, J. Sundin, lighting (concept), Faehlke & Dettmer (Hannover), lighting (design), Zaha M. Hadid, landscape
Model photography: David Grandorge

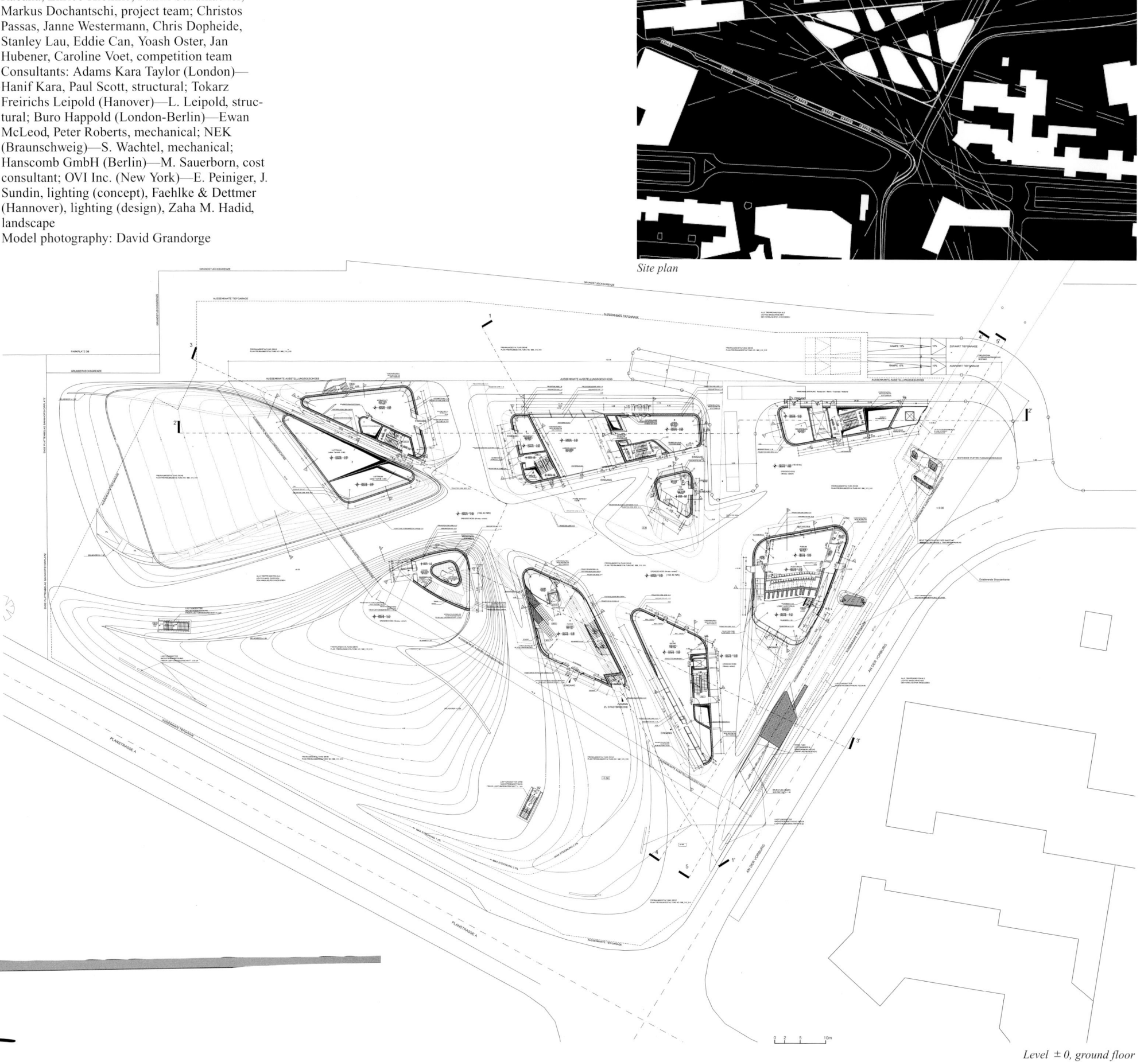

Site plan

Level ± 0, ground floor

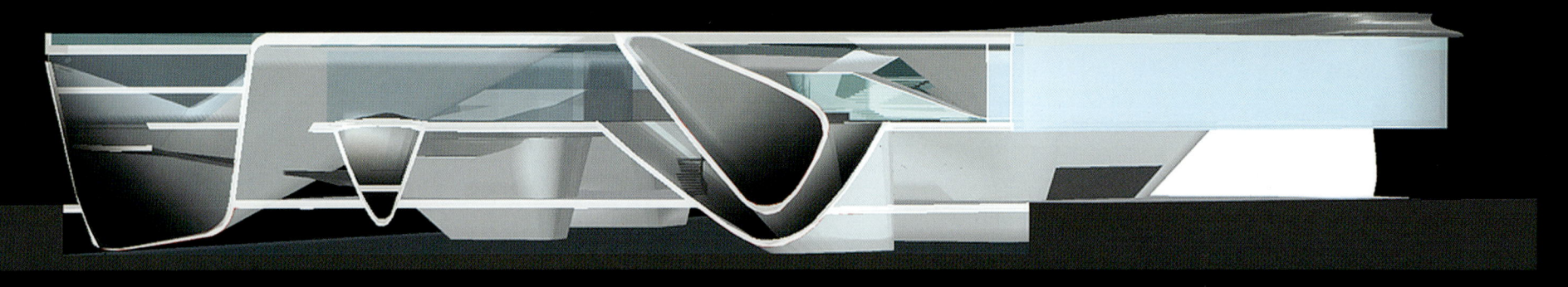

Section

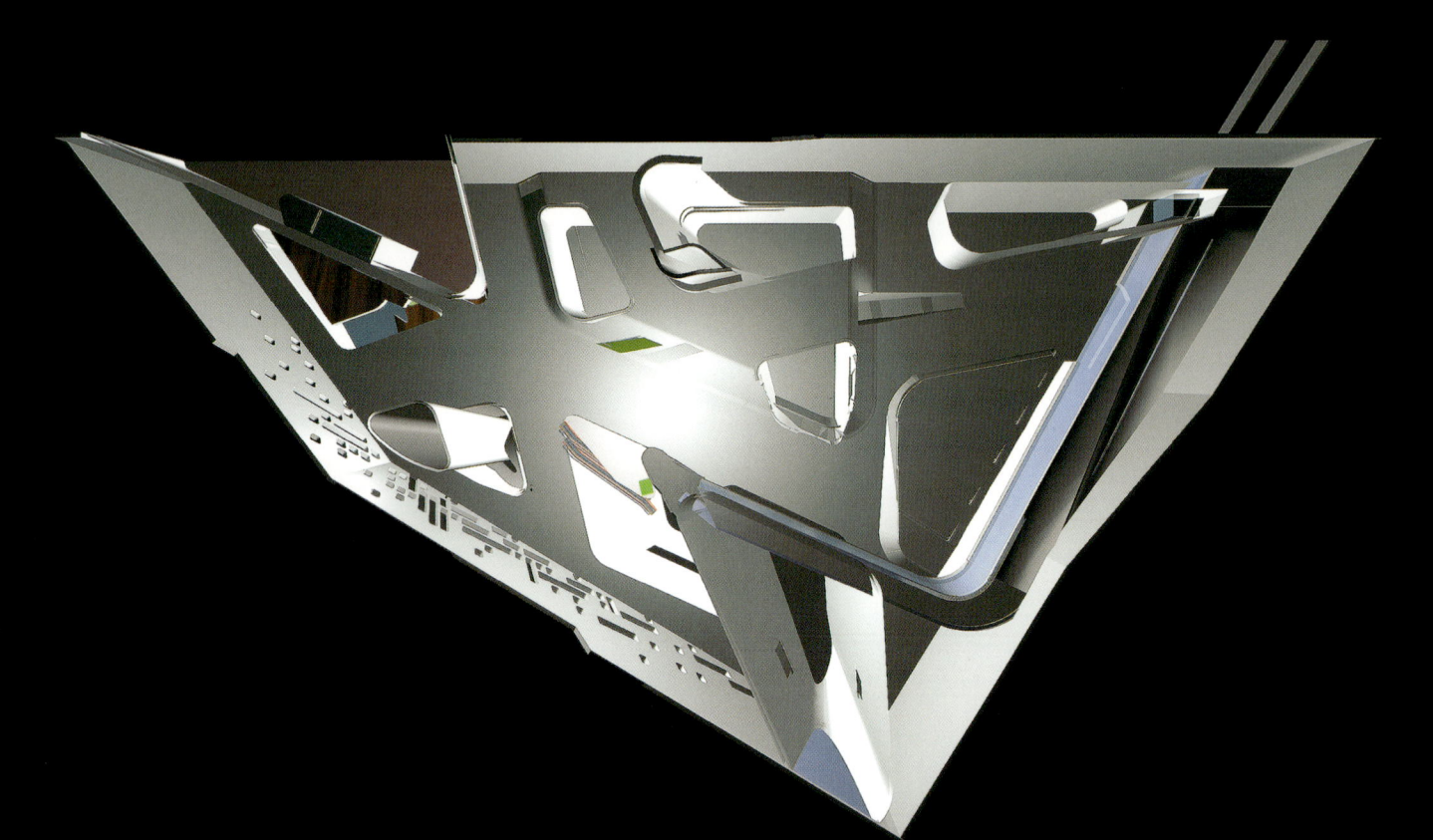

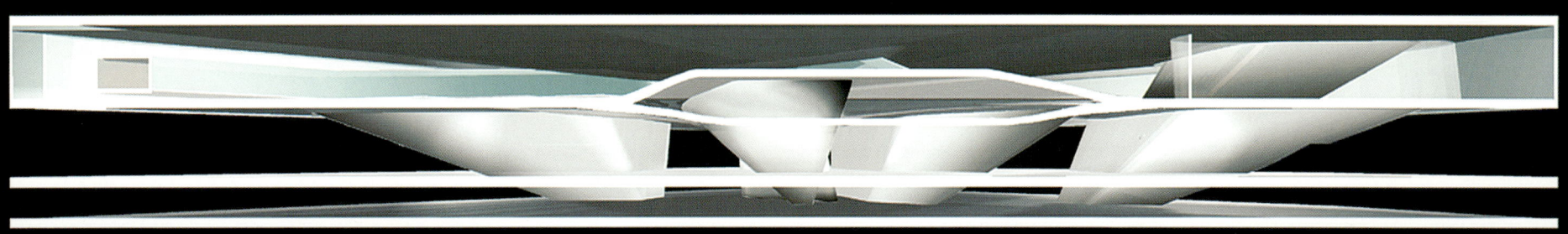

Section

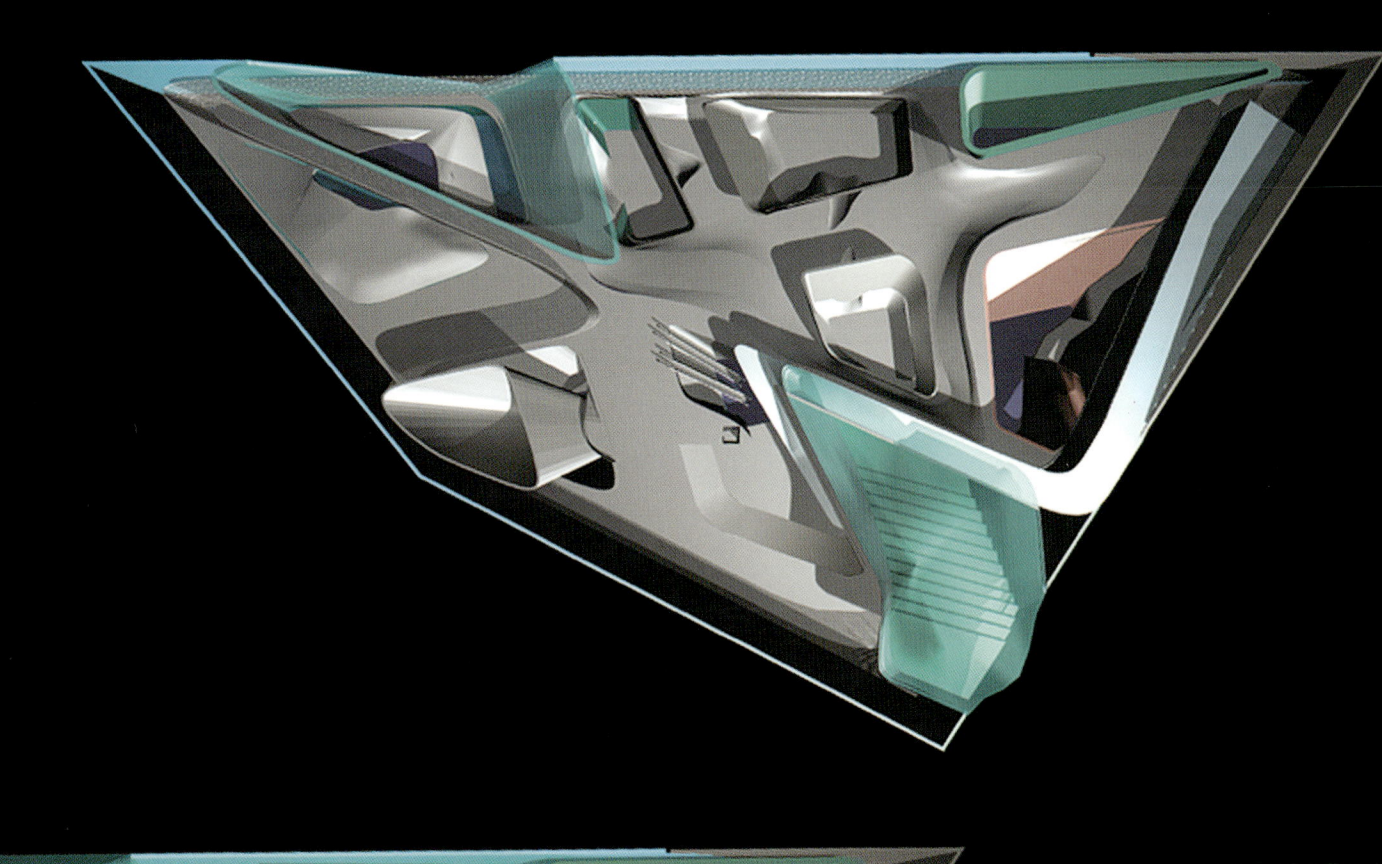

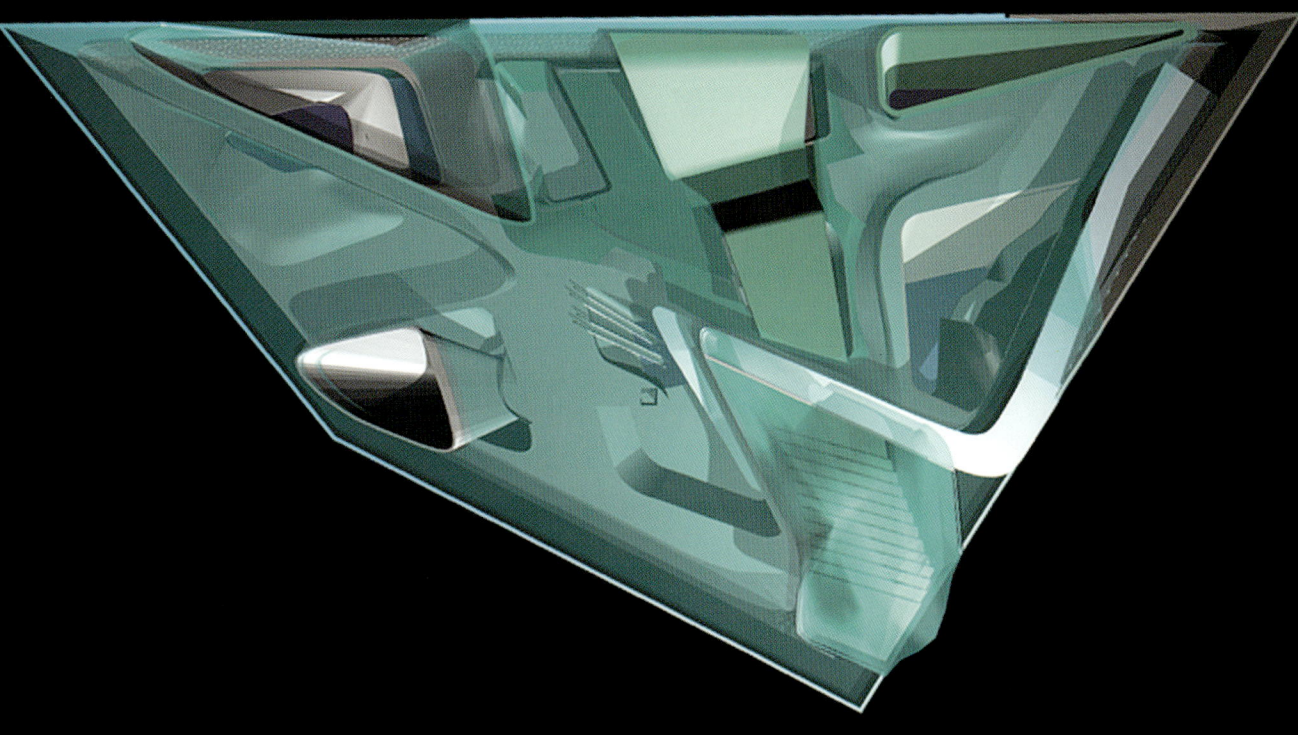

Level +10.25m

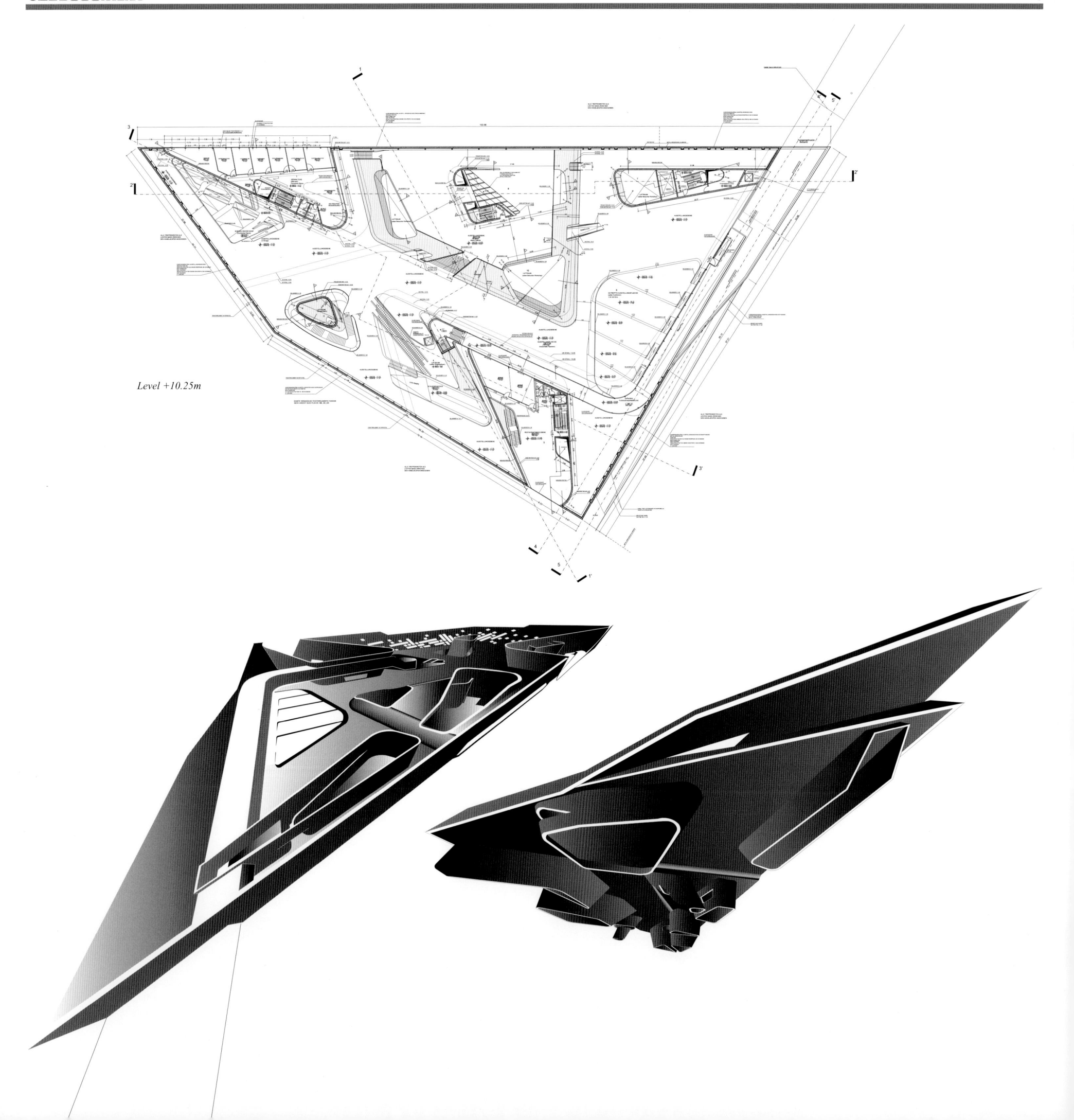

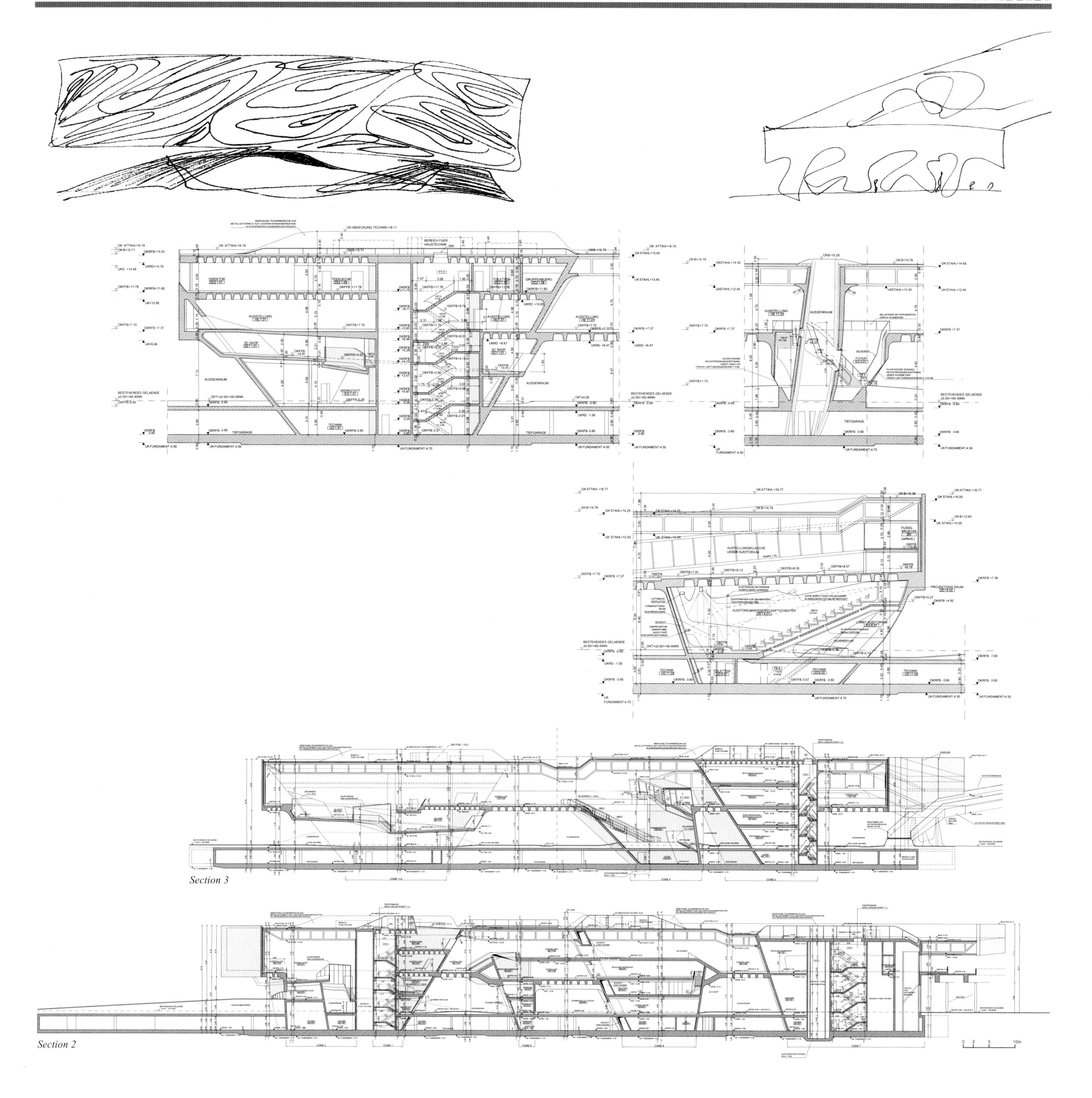

Section 3

Section 2

GA DOCUMENT

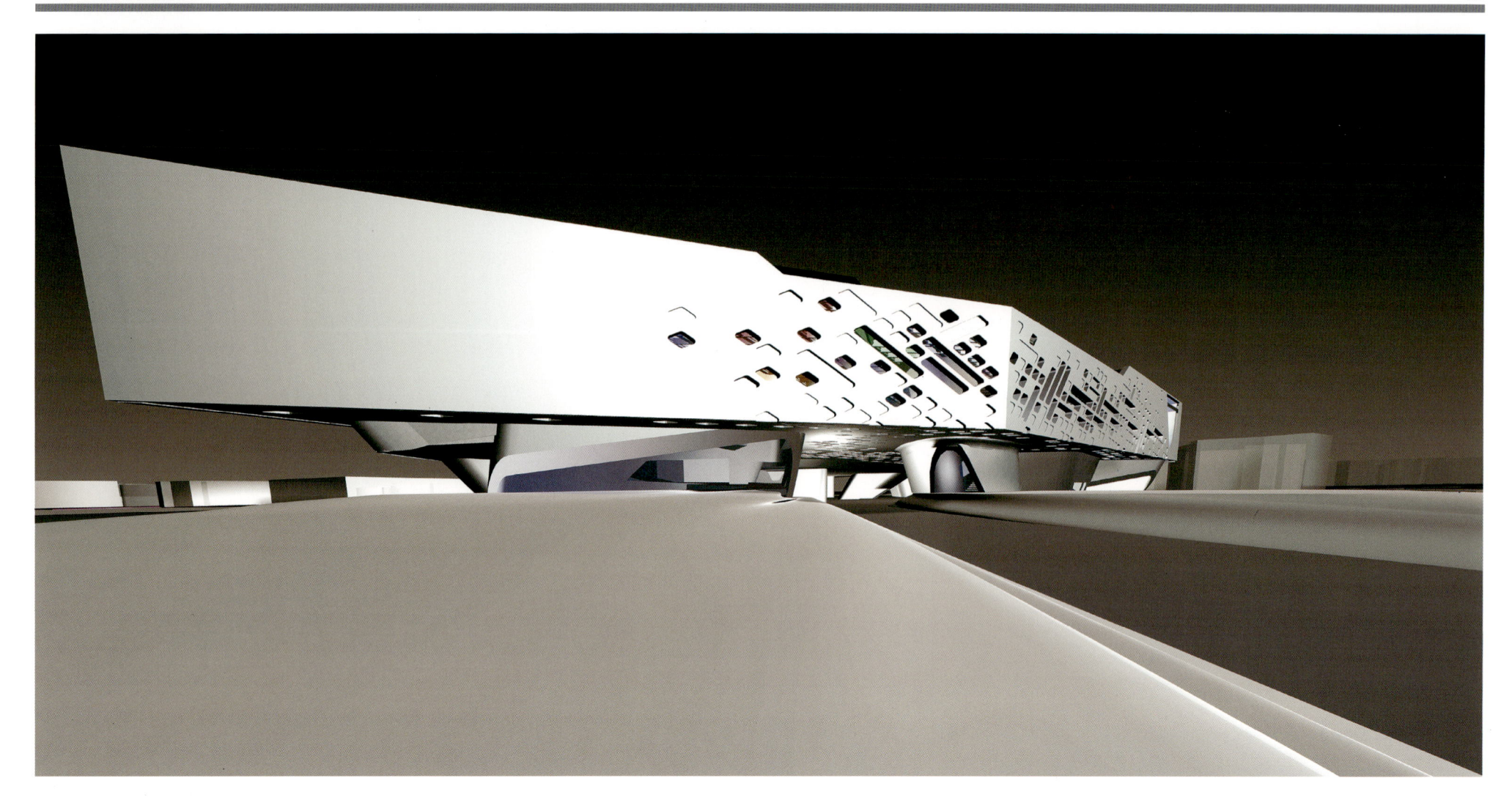

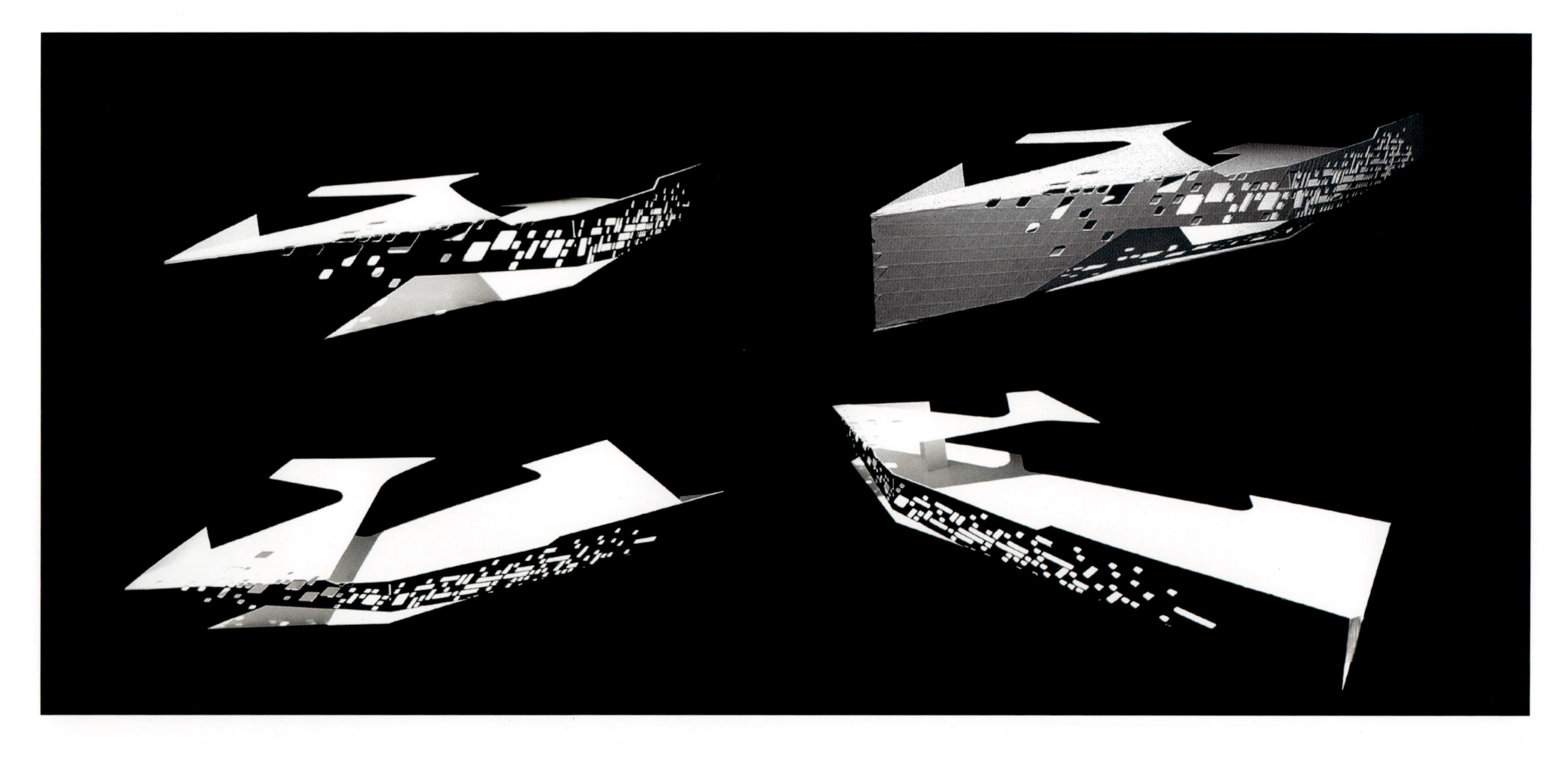

19　　GA PROJECT

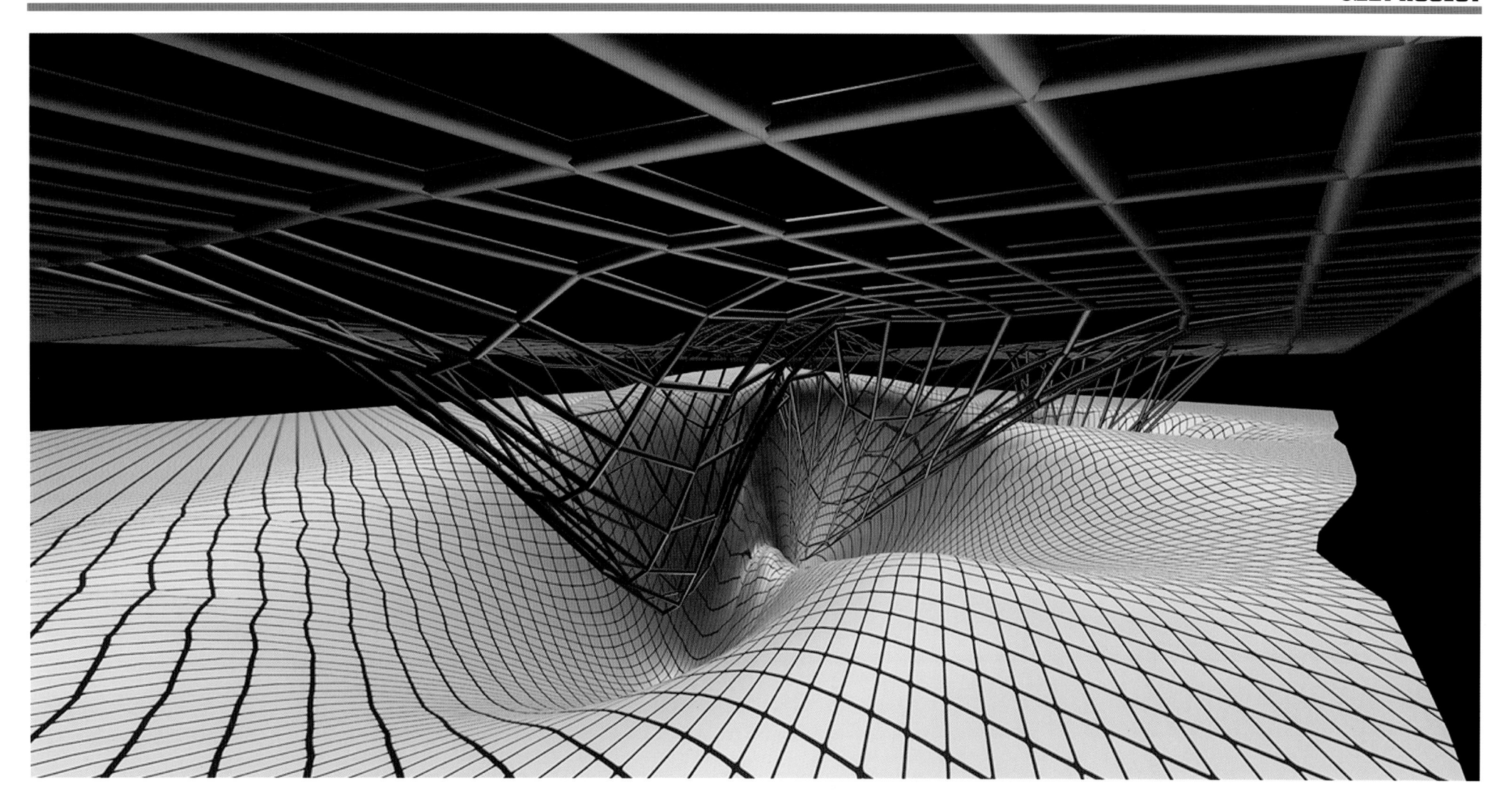

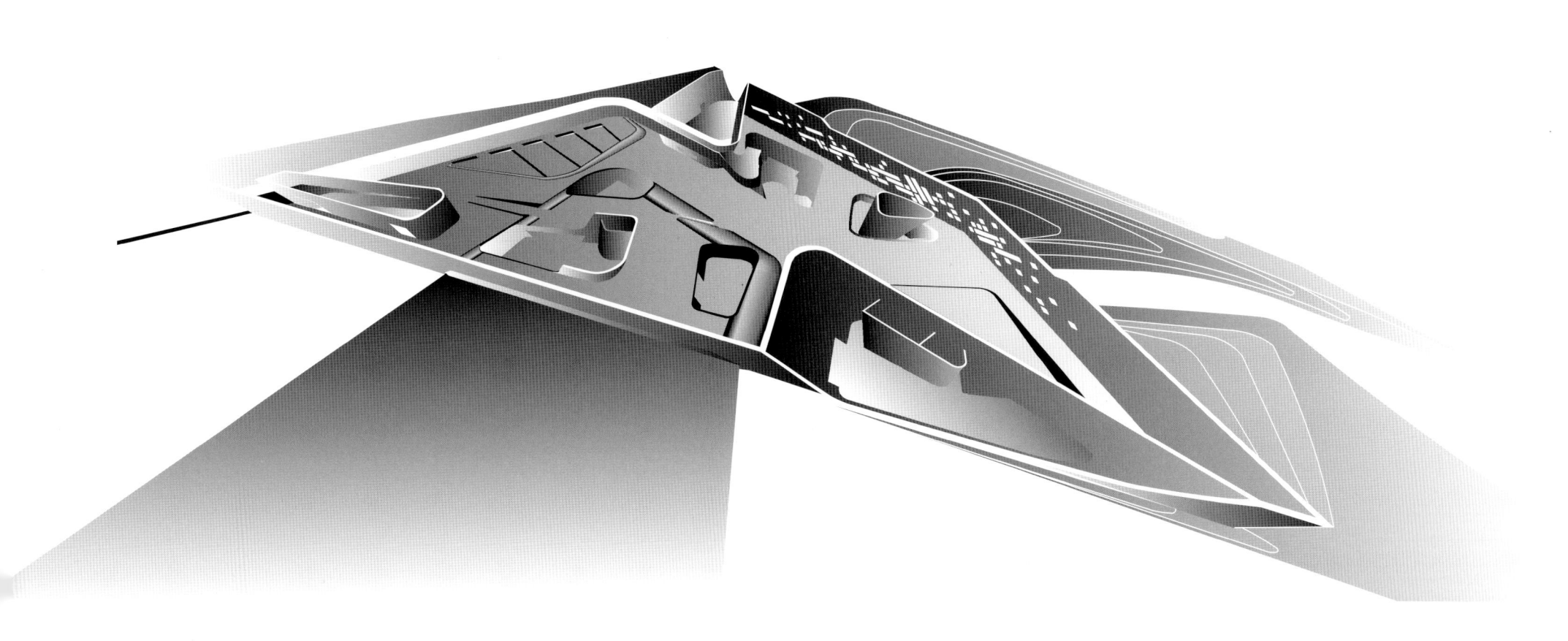

STEVEN HOLL

MUSÉE DES CONFLUENCES
Lyon, France Design: 2001(competition)

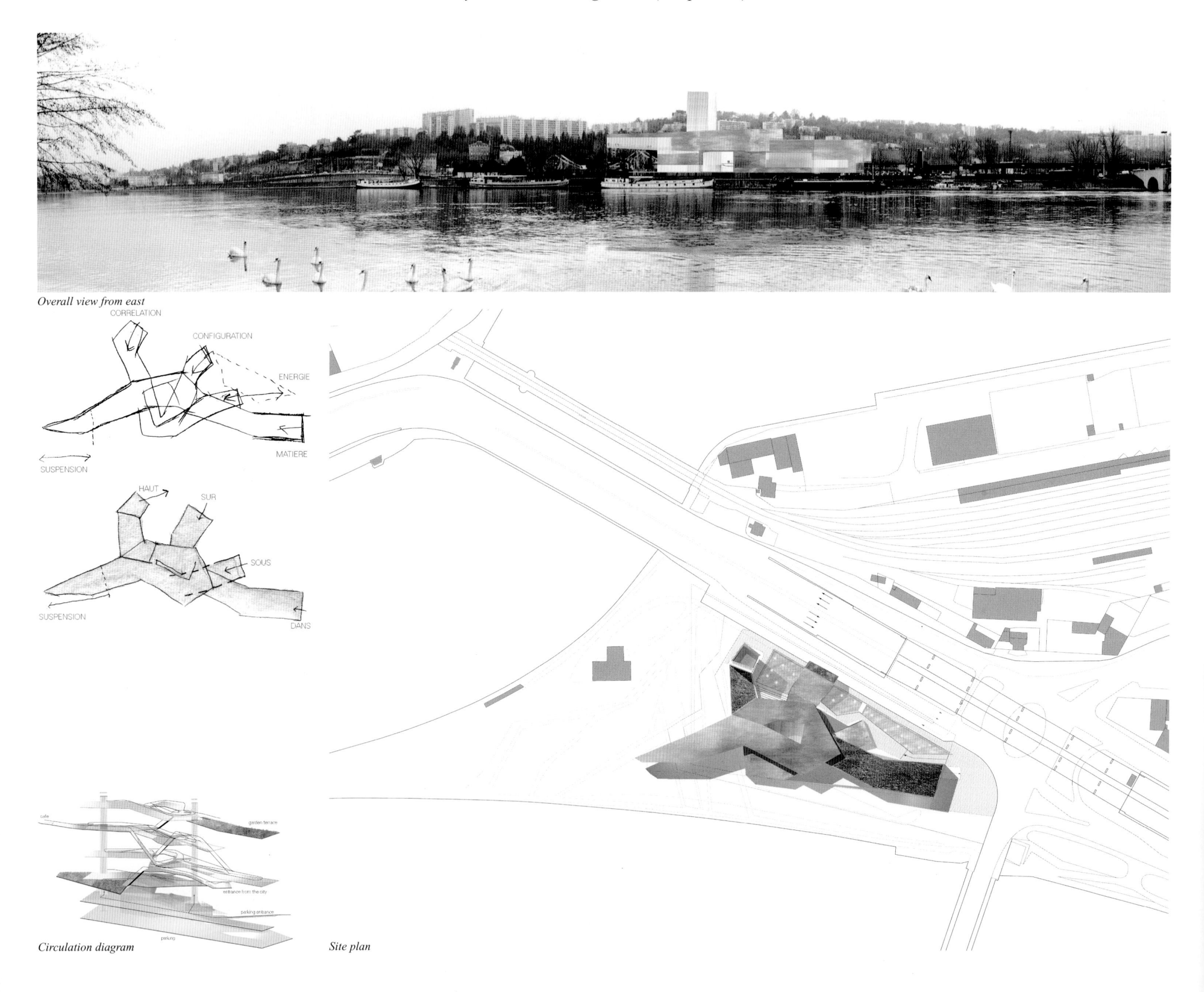

Overall view from east

Circulation diagram

Site plan

Site
The unique aspects of the site. Its thinness and tapering off, the wide space of flow of the converging Rhone and Soane Rivers, the horizontality and organic turbulence are all aspects responded to in the building section of the new museum.

Program
The ambitious program: interpretive global balance and shifts in balance, the great cycles of nature, dynamic programs in culture and science, different points of interpretation and access lead us to a multifaceted concept linking all these properties and potentials.

Concept
The convergence of four geophysical aspects:
1. Matter: the in and out of physical exhibition materials
2. Energy: the main entry hall of public flow
3. Configuration: the auditorium and main orientation
4. Correlation: the education tower-classrooms for study and deeper evaluation.

敷地
敷地が持つ独特の様相。幅の狭い先細がりの土地，互いに近寄って行くローヌ川とソーヌ川の流れの広い空間，水平性と有機的な乱流，これらのすべてに，新しいミュージアムの建築構成のなかで応答する。

プログラム
野心的なプログラム。地球規模の均衡とその転換についての解説，自然の大循環，文化と科学分野の動的なプログラム，多様な解説方法とアクセスが，これらの属性や可能性のすべてを連結する多面的なコンセプトに私たちを導く。

コンセプト
地球物理学的な4つの様相を集合する。
1）物質：物理的な展示材料全体。
2）エネルギー：一般の人が流入するメイン・エントランス・ホール。
3）各要素の配置：オーディトリアムと主要方位。
4）相互関係：学習とさらに深い考察のためのエデュケーション・タワー＝教室。

Third floor

Second floor

Architects: Steven Holl Architects—Steven Holl, principal-in-charge; Timothy Bade, project architect; Makram El-Kadi, Annette Goderbauer, Ziad Jammeladine, Matt Johnson, Christian Wassmann, project team
Associate architect: Pierre Vurpas & Associes—Pierre Vurpas and Brigitte Scharff
Consultants: Jacobs Serete—Philippe Averty, structural
Collaborator: Guy Nordenson and Associates

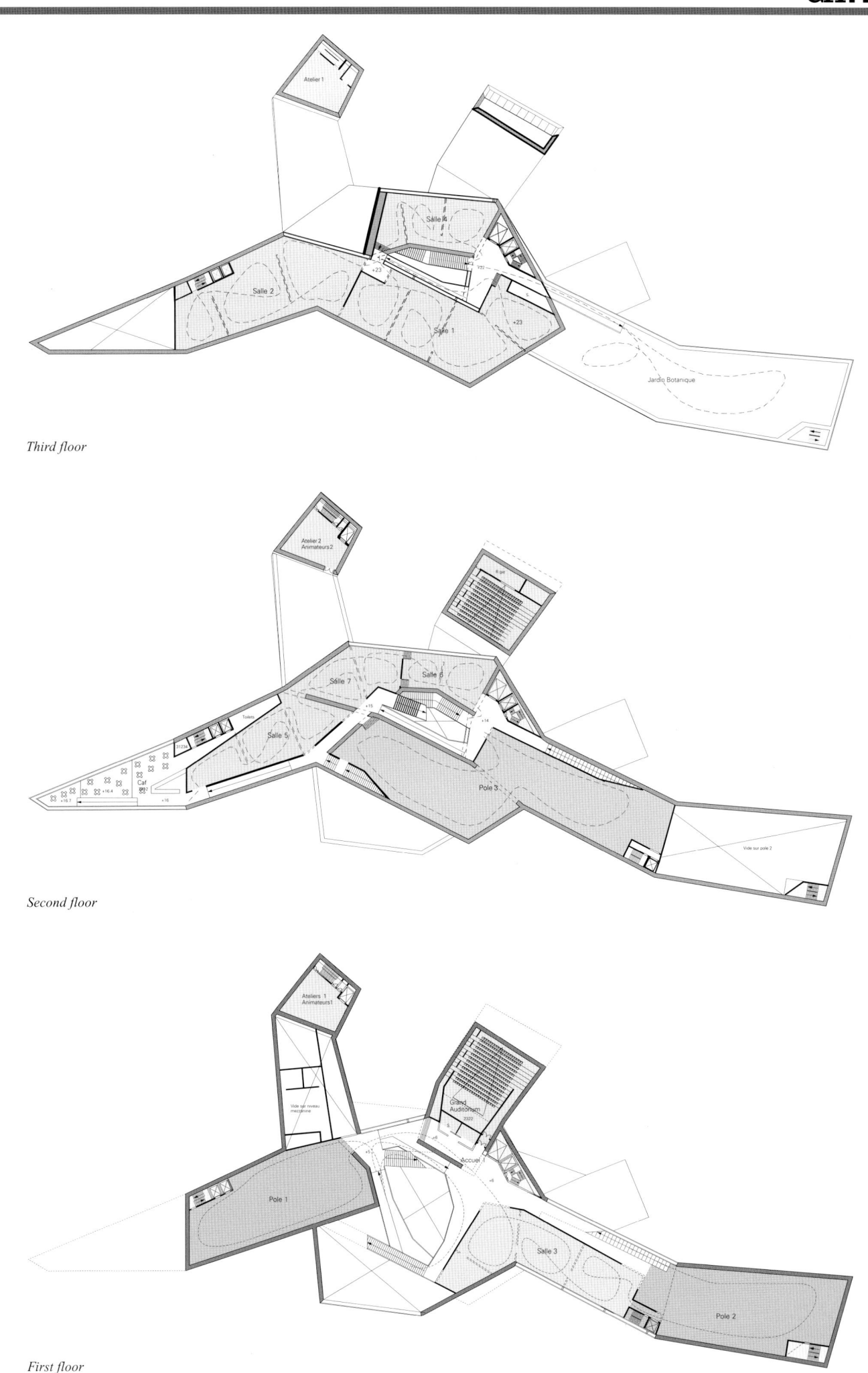

First floor

Aerial view

Sketch: night view

West elevation

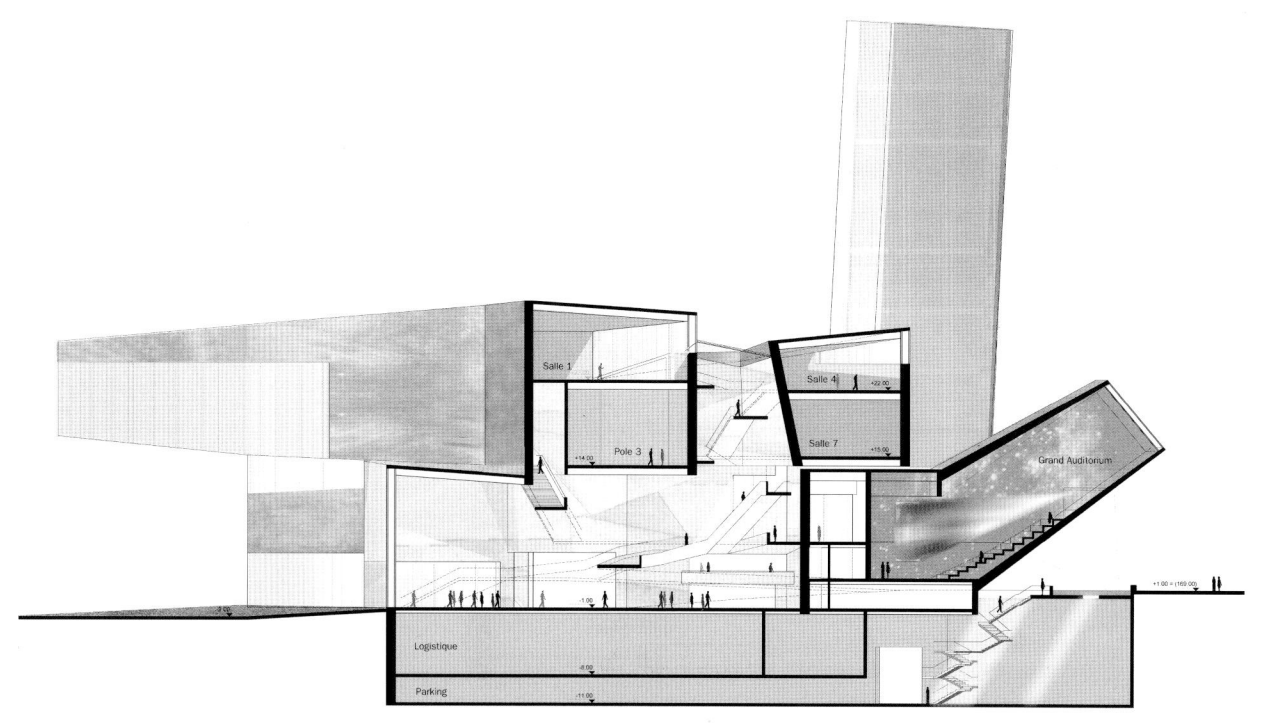

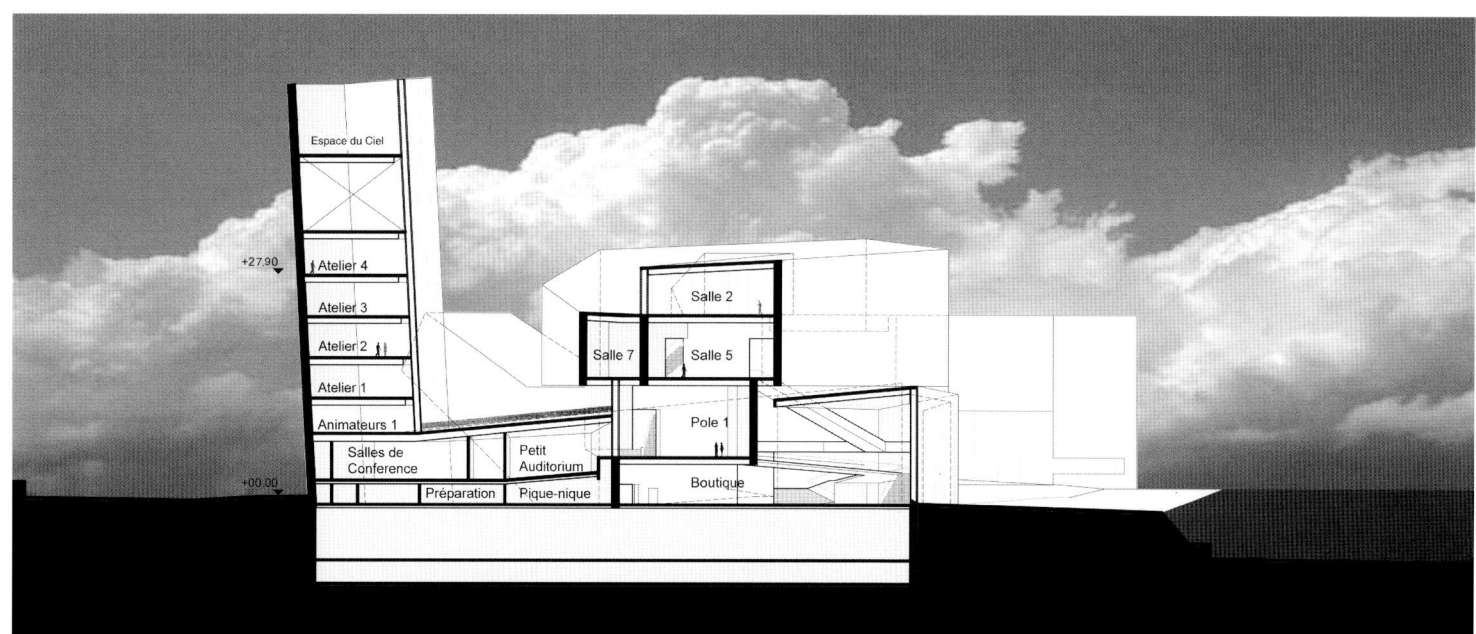

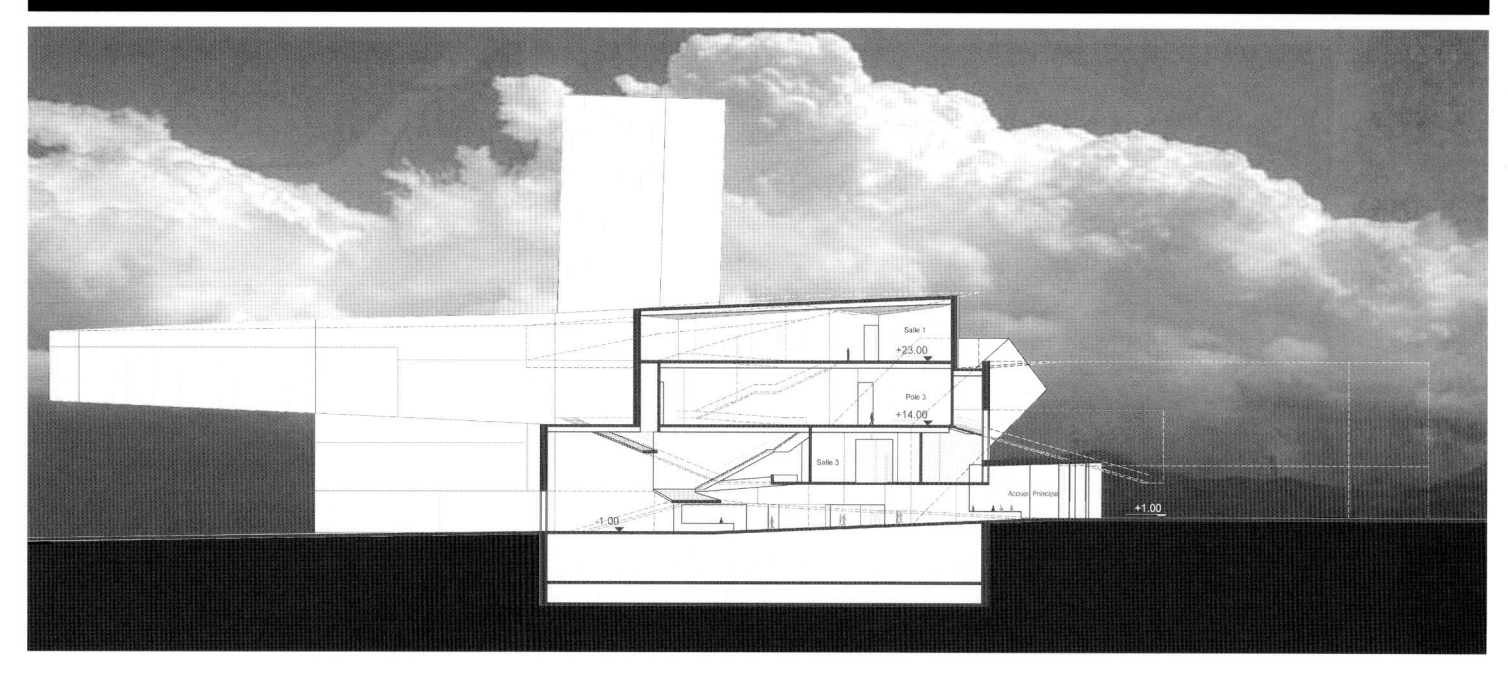

Sections

Gallery perspective

Entrance hall

The building's geometry moves toward horizontal vectors like that of the rivers... "metamorphosis of water" linked with the earth, that is with rock reduced to very small fragments and mixed with all sorts of debris, vegetable and animal. All of it reduced to particles minute and layered, bedded down, that nonetheless stand upright, flourish. —Francis Ponge

Climactic and environmental responsive design characterize the different elevations: south with passive solar glass, a reflecting pond at the entrance which doubles as the evaporative cooling reservoir and brings light to the parking garage. Thermal roof insulation in the form of roof garden, solar cells and attention to all aspects of the chemical make-up of the building materials.

The steel framed structure utilizes standard sections due to new computer programs producing each joint effortlessly in complex geometries.

The building skin is a special golden patina copper alloy with a natural patina's positive response to typical urban air pollution. Glass walls are double with an energy recycling of the inner air space.

We envision a dynamic reshaping of the gardens around the new museum in the horizontal spirit of its merging geometry.

The four vectors of matter, energy, configuration and correlation are analogous to conformational analysis in chemical physics with matter as the organic molecules, configuration as the order in which the atoms are joined together, and energy varying in free rotation about double bonds. The deeper ideas and interrogation of thought systems is implied in correlation.

These four vectors join in a central horizontal turbulence from which a suspended taper emerges horizontally cantilevered above with the flowing rivers reflected on its underside.

It is an open concept of flowing within the architecture with spaces in liquid discourse. Interior passages should intervene and cross-cut. Exhibitions are held within parentheses walls bounded by intersecting potential. The building sections aim at relationships working at the root level, where things and formulations merge.

Suspended "Cafe de la Pointe"

建物のジオメトリーは2つの川のように水平方向に向かって進む……地と結ばれた"水の変容"。つまり極小の断片に還元された岩，あらゆる種類の残骸，野菜や動物などとの混成。そのすべてが，微少の粒子へ縮小され，積み重なり，横たわる。にもかかわらずそれは直立し，成長する。
——フランシス・ポンジュ

気候や環境に敏感に反応したデザインが，多様な立面構成を特徴づける。南面は，パッシヴ・ソーラー・グラス。エントランスに位置するリフレクティング・プールは，蒸発作用による冷却用貯水池であり，駐車場に外光を送るという二重の役割を持つ。屋根は屋上庭園によって断熱。太陽電池，建築材料の化学的組成が備えるあらゆる特徴に留意する。

各ジョイントの複雑な幾何学形態を簡単に製作する，新しいコンピュータ・プログラムのために，鉄骨枠組構造には標準接合部材を利用する。

建物の被膜は，独特の，緑青を帯びた金色の銅合金で，都市に典型的な大気汚染への積極的対応として自然の錆をつける。二重のガラス壁は内側の空気層によりエネルギーを再利用するためである。

新しいミュージアムの周りに，その合流するジオメトリーに漲る水平性のなかで，庭をダイナミックに再形成することを思い描く。

物質，エネルギー，配置，相互関係の4つのベクトルは，物理化学における対立的な分析方法に似ている。生物分子としての物質，原子が結合するなかにおける秩序としての配置，二重結合を取り巻く自由な回転のなかで変動するエネルギー。深化されたアイディアと思考方式である質疑は，相互関係のなかに暗示される。

これら4つのベクトルは，中央で発生する水平の乱流のなかに加わる。そこから，宙吊りになった，先細の形が現れ出て，その下面に姿を映す2つの川の流れの上に水平に片持ちで差し出される。

それは，流動性の話法に基づいたスペースを持つ建築のなかの，流れという開放系のコンセプトである。内部通路は介入し横断して行くはずだ。展覧会は交差の可能性に拘束された，挿入句的な壁の内側で開かれる。建物断面は，状況と系統的論述が合流する基礎レベルで作用する関係性に照準を合わせる。

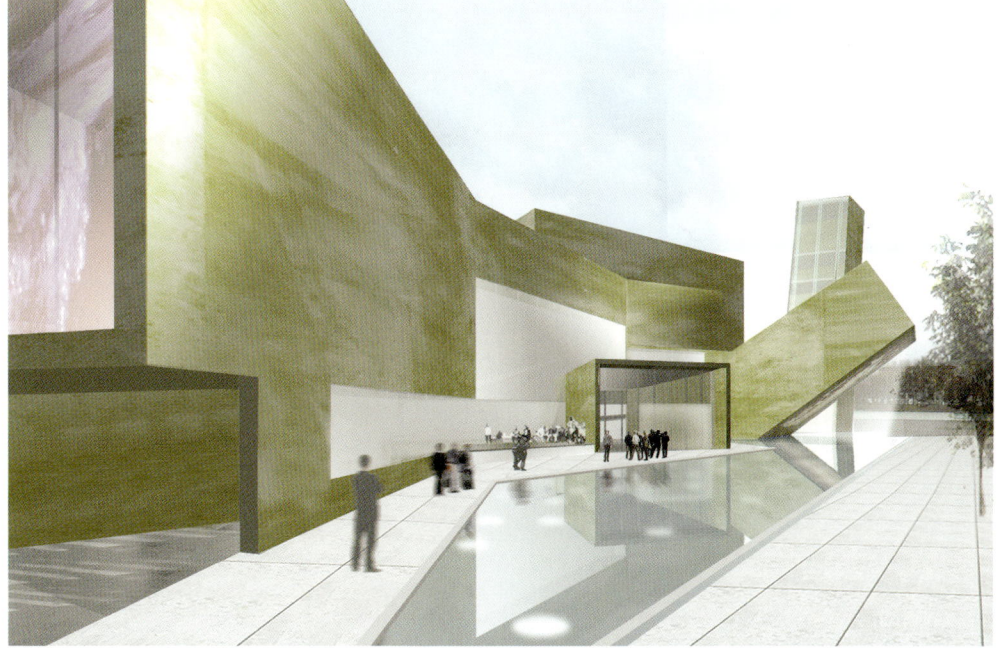

Entrance from city

FRANK O. GEHRY

PERFORMING ARTS CENTER AT BARD COLLEGE
New York, New York, U.S.A. Design: 1997–2000 Construction: 2000–02

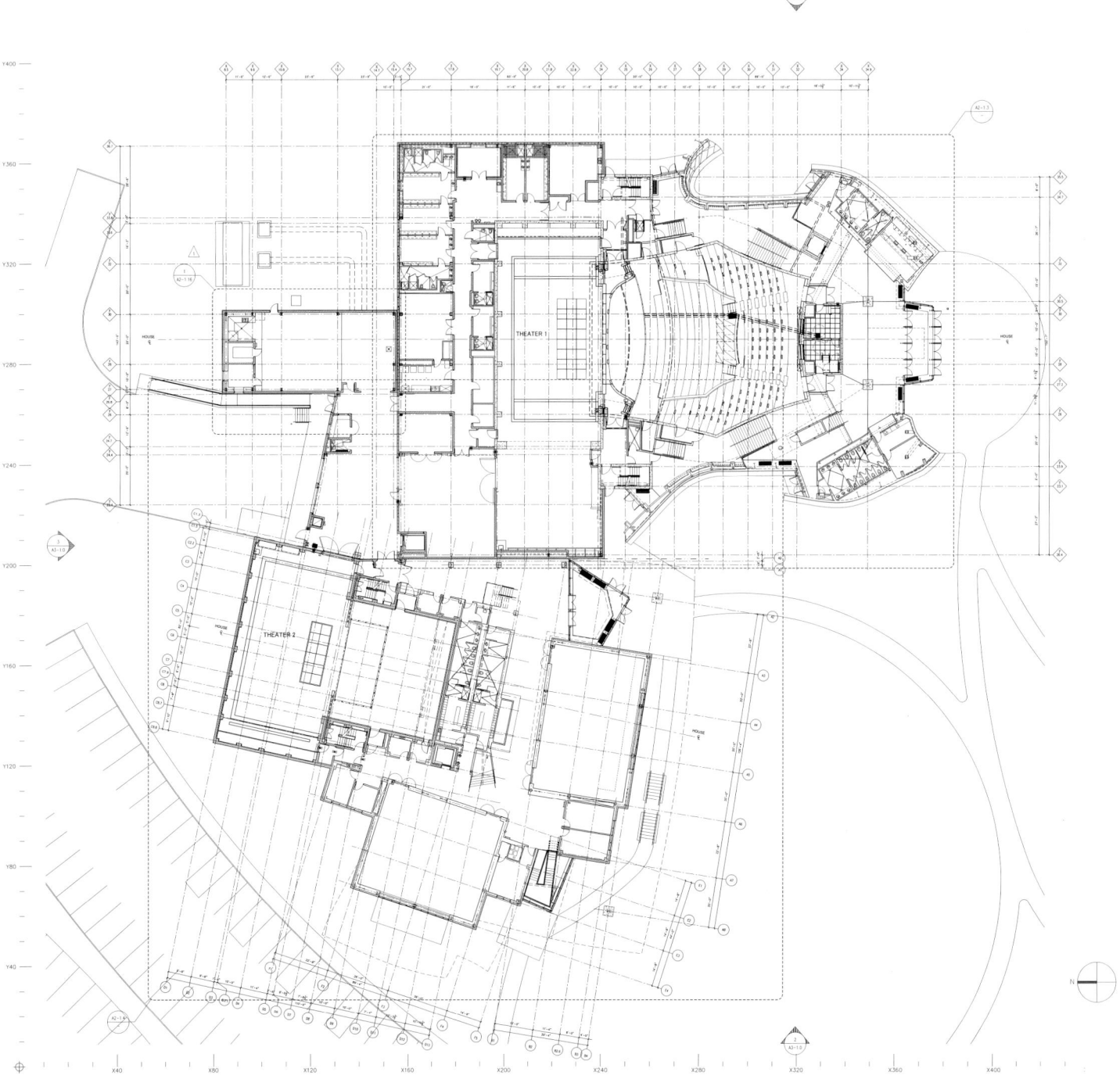

The Performing Arts Center at Bard College provides spaces for dance, drama, opera and music performances. The 105,000 square foot building, which contains two multi-purpose performance theaters, is located on the Bard College campus in a beautiful area of tall trees and open lawns.

Theater 1 features an 85 foot wide by 40 foot deep stage with a full flying system for scenery. A concert shell and fore-stage lift allows conversion for symphonic music performance. The high ceiling and overall shape of the theater provides characteristics that will be excellent for all performance types. Theater 1 has 800 seats in an orchestra section and two balcony sections. By seating the audience only in the orchestra section, a feeling of intimacy is provided for smaller student productions intended for audiences of 400-500 people. Alternately, by placing additional seating on the stage, the capacity of Theater 1 can be increased to 1000, providing a space in which the student body and faculty can assemble for lectures or other major events. Theater 1 features a wood ceiling and concert shell. The house walls are concrete, providing the mass necessary for excellent acoustical reflections. The highly sculptural exterior of Theater 1 responds to the theater's internal organization. A sail-like canopy clad in stainless steel panels projects out over the box office and lobby. The stainless steel panels loosely wrap around the sides of the theater toward the proscenium, creating two tall, sky-lit gathering areas on either side of the main lobby. The stainless steel panels then flare out at the proscenium creating a sculptural collar-like shape that rests on the simple concrete and plaster form of the stage house. The structure supporting the canopy and the collar-like shape will be exposed and visible from within the main lobby.

Theater 2, a black box theater dedicated to student dance and drama productions, features a full flying system that is slightly smaller than the system featured in Theater 1. Theater 2 has 200 seats. The seats in Theater 2 are retractable, allowing the theater to be re-configured into a large, open performance space. The interior of Theater 2 is clad in solid and perforated painted plywood panels. The exterior of Theater 2 features concrete and plaster walls and an undulating roof clad in stainless steel panels. The sculptural form of the roof responds to the canopy and to the collar-like shape on the exterior of Theater 1. Two dance rehearsal rooms and two drama rehearsal rooms are located adjacent to Theater 2. Glazed skylights integrated into the roof and operable windows allow natural light and ventilation into the rehearsal rooms. Administrative offices, conference rooms, and a secondary lobby and gathering area are also located adjacent to Theater 2.

A number of different exterior materials and finishes were considered for the building. After a lengthy on site review process, a soft, brushed stainless steel was selected for the exterior cladding because of the material's ability to reflect the light and colors of the sky and the surrounding landscape.

Stage level

29

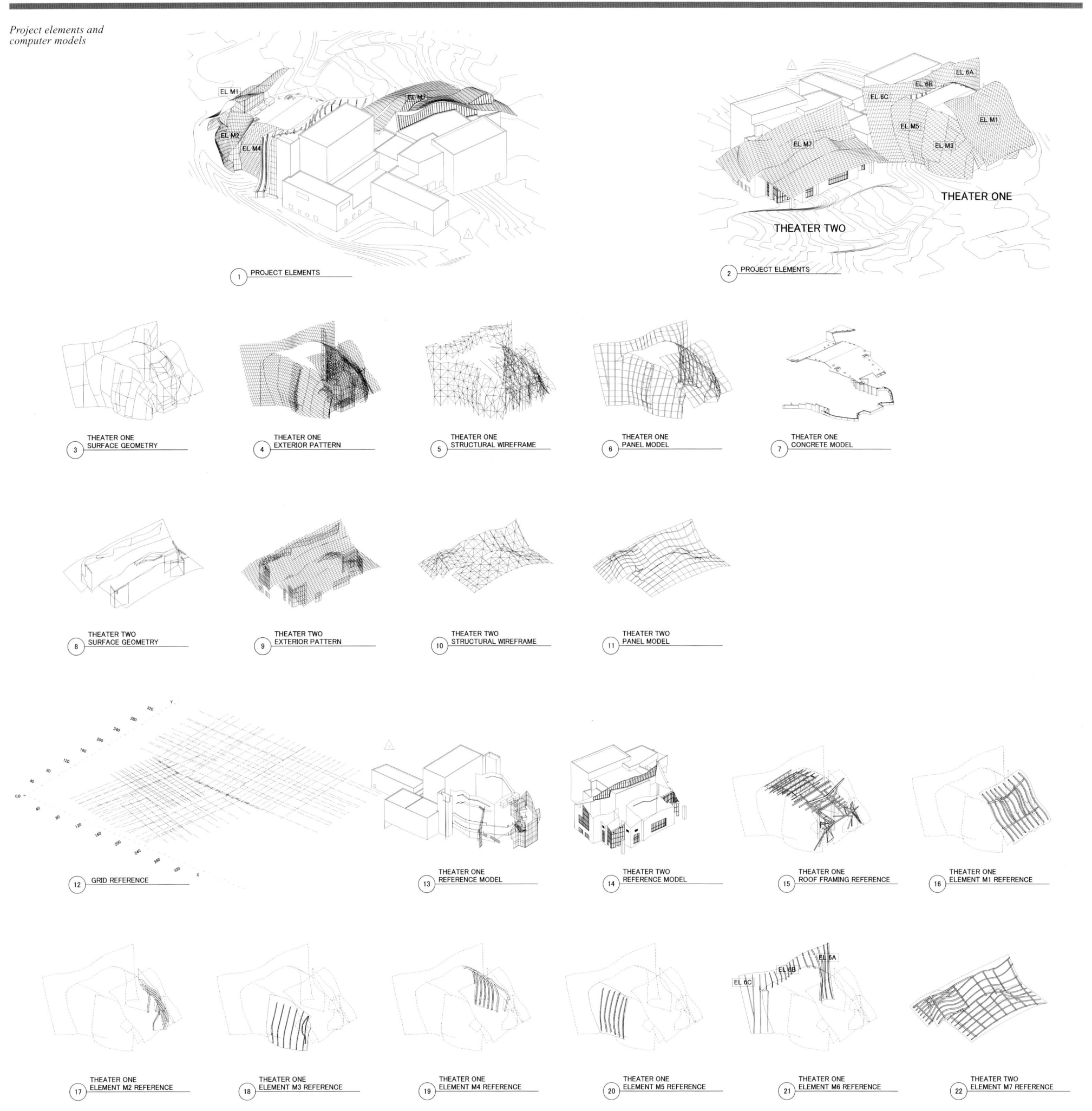

Project elements and computer models

1	PROJECT ELEMENTS
2	PROJECT ELEMENTS
3	THEATER ONE — SURFACE GEOMETRY
4	THEATER ONE — EXTERIOR PATTERN
5	THEATER ONE — STRUCTURAL WIREFRAME
6	THEATER ONE — PANEL MODEL
7	THEATER ONE — CONCRETE MODEL
8	THEATER TWO — SURFACE GEOMETRY
9	THEATER TWO — EXTERIOR PATTERN
10	THEATER TWO — STRUCTURAL WIREFRAME
11	THEATER TWO — PANEL MODEL
12	GRID REFERENCE
13	THEATER ONE — REFERENCE MODEL
14	THEATER TWO — REFERENCE MODEL
15	THEATER ONE — ROOF FRAMING REFERENCE
16	THEATER ONE — ELEMENT M1 REFERENCE
17	THEATER ONE — ELEMENT M2 REFERENCE
18	THEATER ONE — ELEMENT M3 REFERENCE
19	THEATER ONE — ELEMENT M4 REFERENCE
20	THEATER ONE — ELEMENT M5 REFERENCE
21	THEATER ONE — ELEMENT M6 REFERENCE
22	THEATER TWO — ELEMENT M7 REFERENCE

バード・カレッジのパフォーミング・アーツ・センターは，ダンス，演劇，オペラ，音楽などの公演のための空間を提供する。多目的劇場2つを容する10万5千平方フィートの建物は，背の高い木々や広い芝生が広がる，構内の美しい場所に建てられる。

シアター1は，場面転換のためのフライング・システムを完備した，幅85フィート，奥行き40フィートの舞台が目玉である。コンサート・シェルと上げ下ろし可能な張り出し舞台によって，交響楽の演奏舞台にも転換できる。高い天井と劇場全体の形が，あらゆるタイプの公演に優れた適応力を発揮する。座席数はオーケストラ・ピットとバルコニー合わせて800席。観客をオーケストラ・ピットだけに限れば，400人から500人を想定した，学生による小公演に相応しい雰囲気が生まれる。反対に，舞台上に追加の座席を据えれば，収容能力は1000人に増え，講演や大規模なイベントに学生団体や教職員が集まることができる。シアター1の特徴は木造の天井とコンサート・シェルである。壁はコンクリートで，音の反響をよくするために必要なかなりの大きさの厚い面を提供する。シアター1の外形は，内部構成に呼応して非常に彫刻的である。ステンレス・スティール・パネルを張った帆のようなキャノピーが切符売り場とロビーの上に突き出ている。ステンレス・スティール・パネルは劇場側面をプロセニアムに向かって緩やかに包み，メイン・ロビーの両側に天井が高く，スカイライトからの光が注ぐ集いの場をつくりだす。このステンレス・スティール・パネルは次に，プロセニアムのところで朝顔型に広がり，客席を囲むコンクリートとプラスターの単純な形態の上で，彫刻された衿のような形をつくって休止する。キャノピーの支持構造と衿形は露出され，メイン・ロビーからも見える。

シアター2は，ブラック・ボックス・シアターで，学生によるダンスや演劇が上演され，シアター1より少し小さいフライング・システムが完備されている。座席数は200。座席は格納式なので，広く開放してパフォーマンス・スペースに再編できる。内装は，有孔と無孔，2種類の塗装合板で仕上げ，外観は，コンクリートとプラスターの壁にステンレス・スティール・パネルで被覆した波形屋根である。この彫刻的な屋根の形は，シアター1の外観に見えるキャノピーと衿のような形に応答している。ダンスと演劇のリハーサル室が2つずつ，シアター2に隣接して置かれる。リハーサル室には，屋根に組み込まれたガラス張りのスカイライトと開閉できる窓から自然光や風が入る。オフィス，会議室，第2ロビー，集いの場もシアター2に隣接して置かれる。

建物の外壁については，相当数の種類の材料や仕上げが考慮された。敷地について長い検討を重ねた結果，陽射しや，空の色，周囲の風景を映し込める材料ということで，滑らかに磨いたステンレス・スティールが選択された。

West view

Model photos: Whit Preston

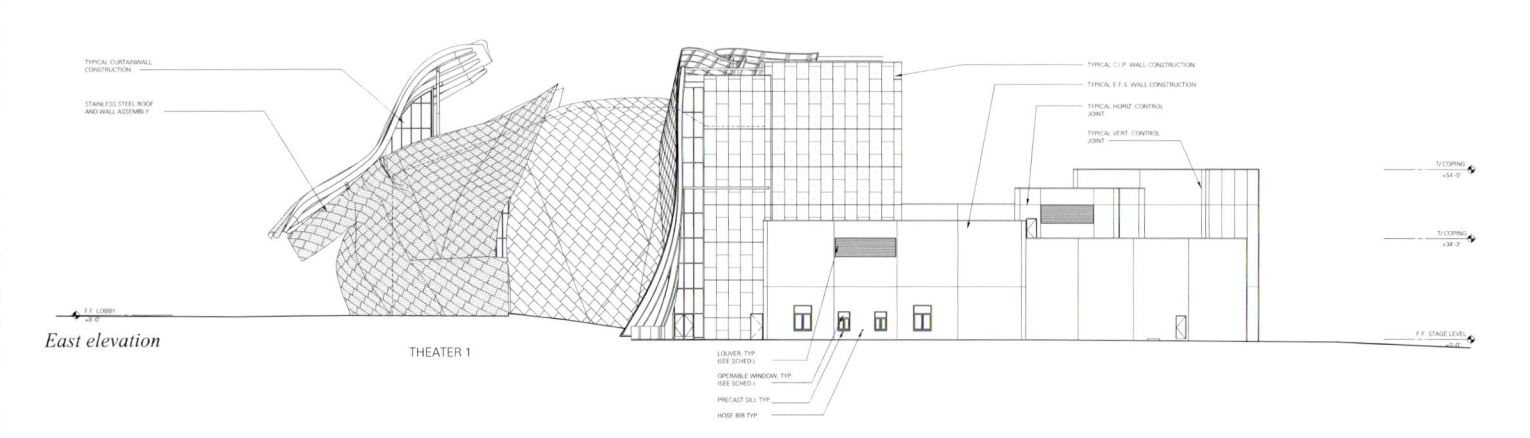

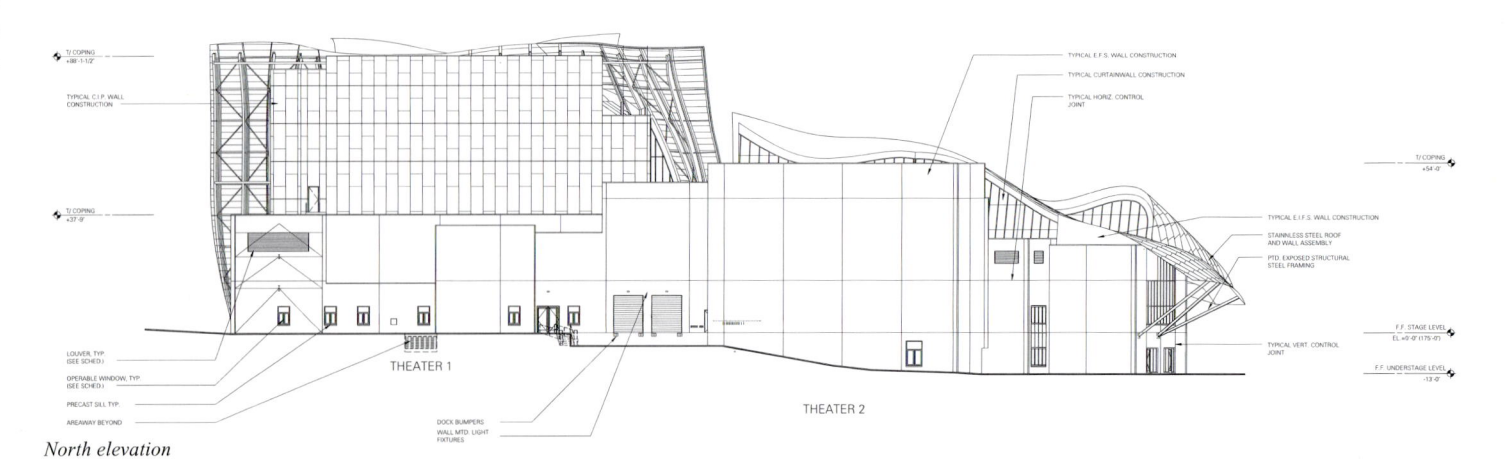

East elevation

North elevation

GA PROJECT

South view

View of main entrance from east

Interior of theater

Model photo: Josh White

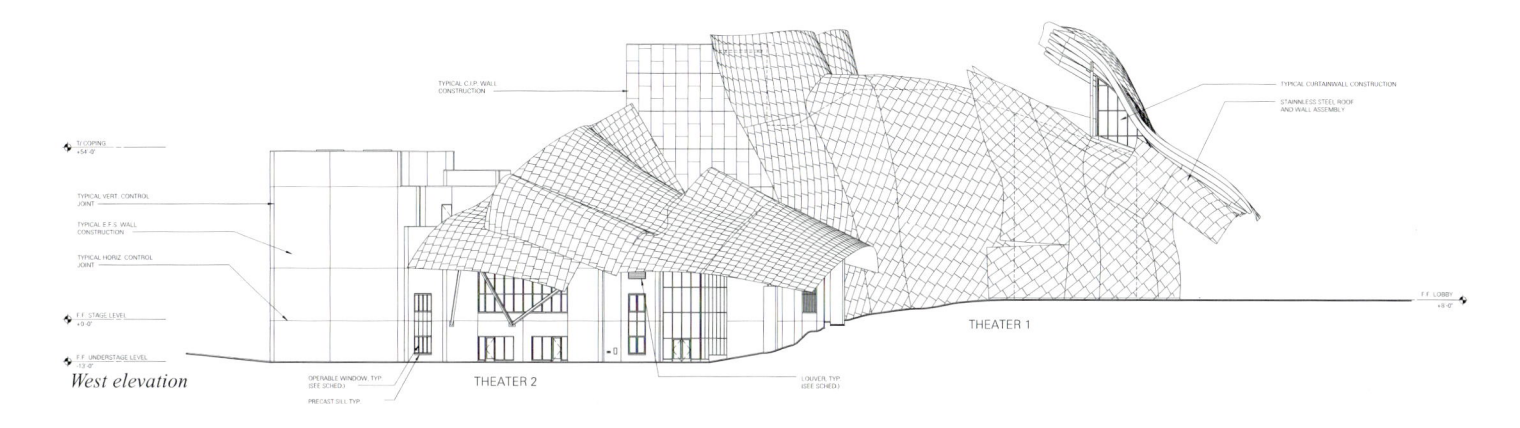

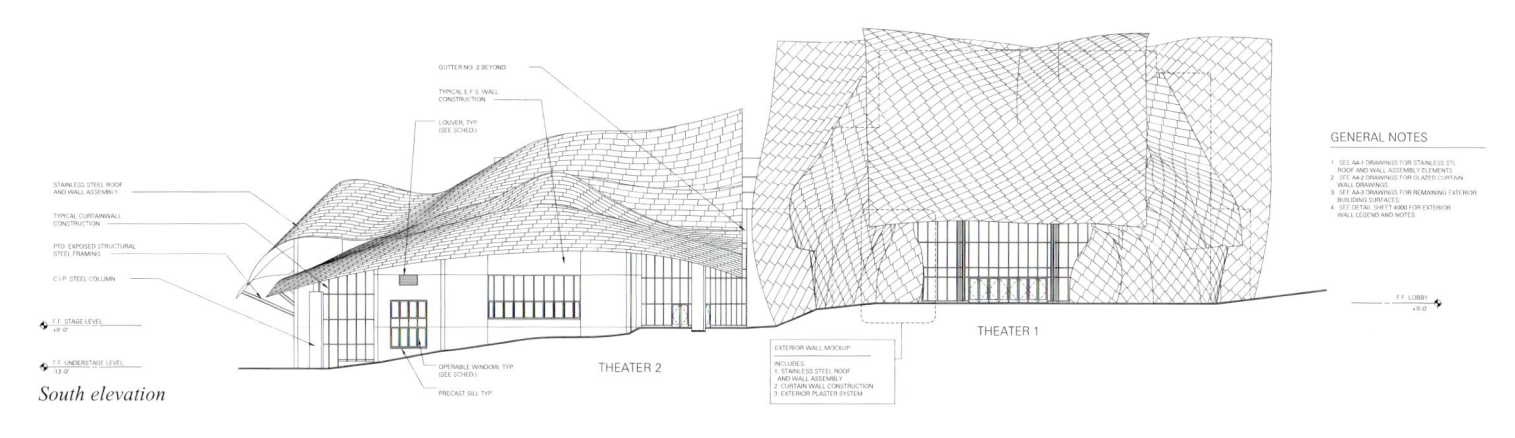

West elevation

South elevation

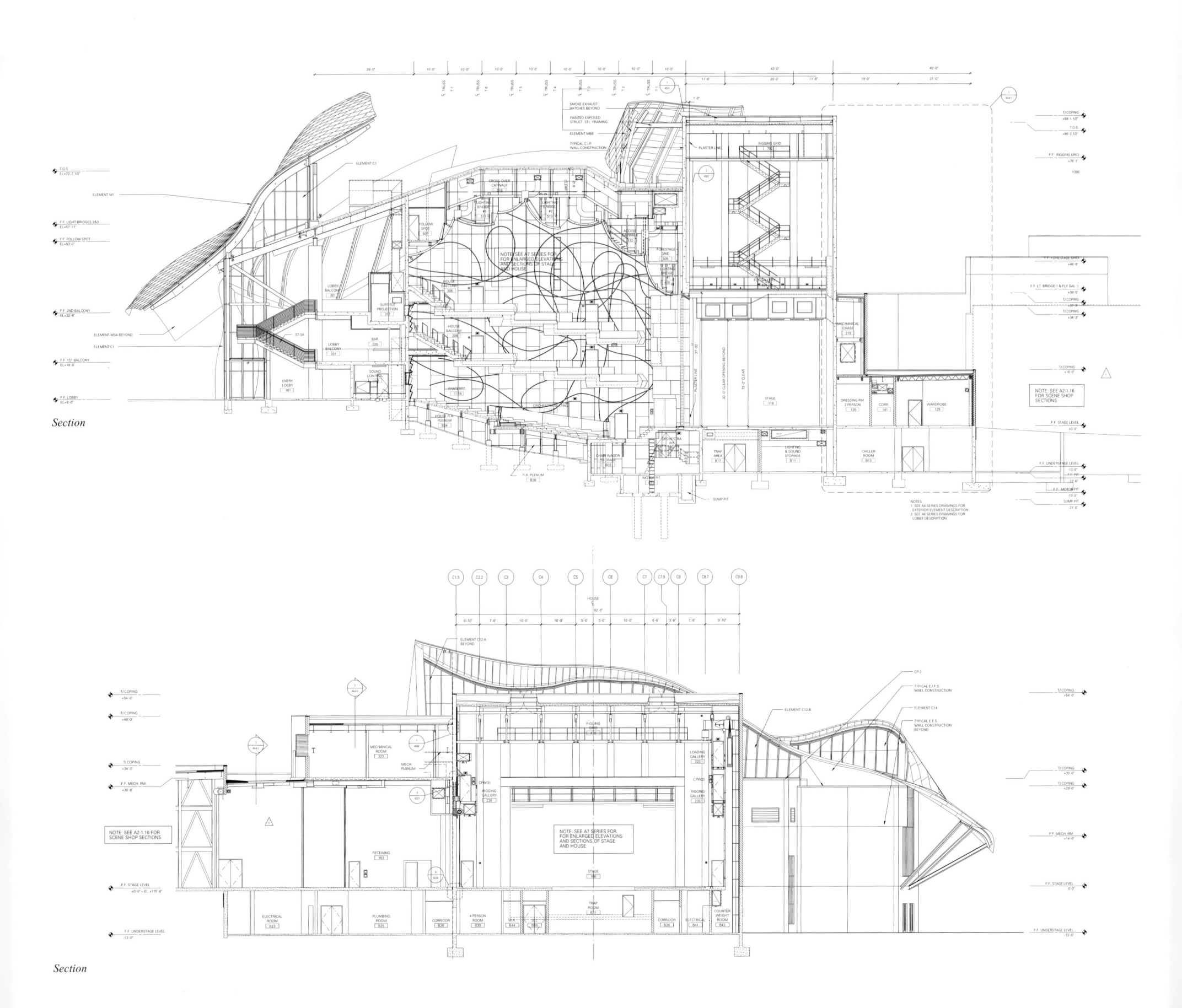

Section

Section

GA PROJECT

Section

Section

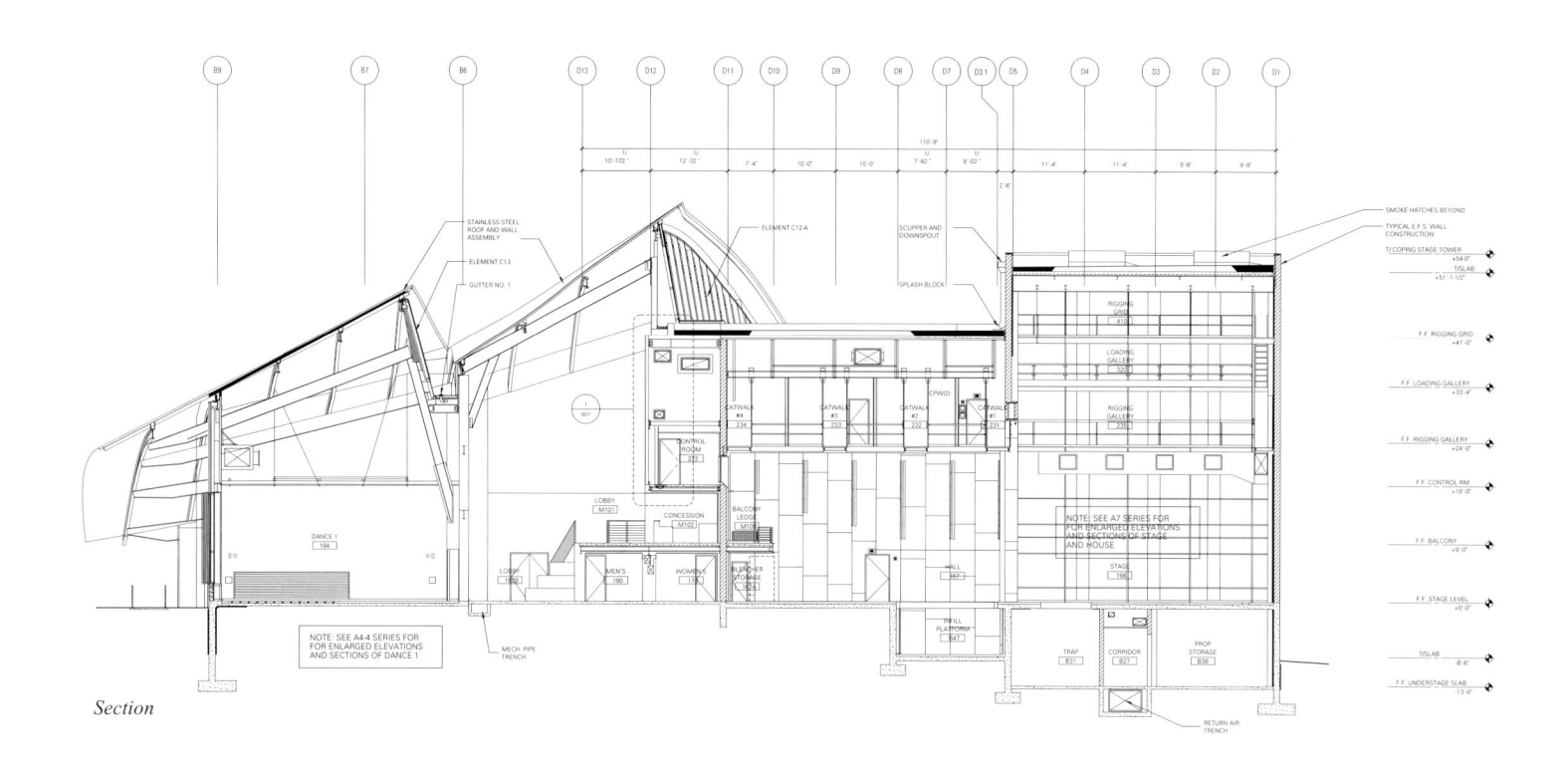

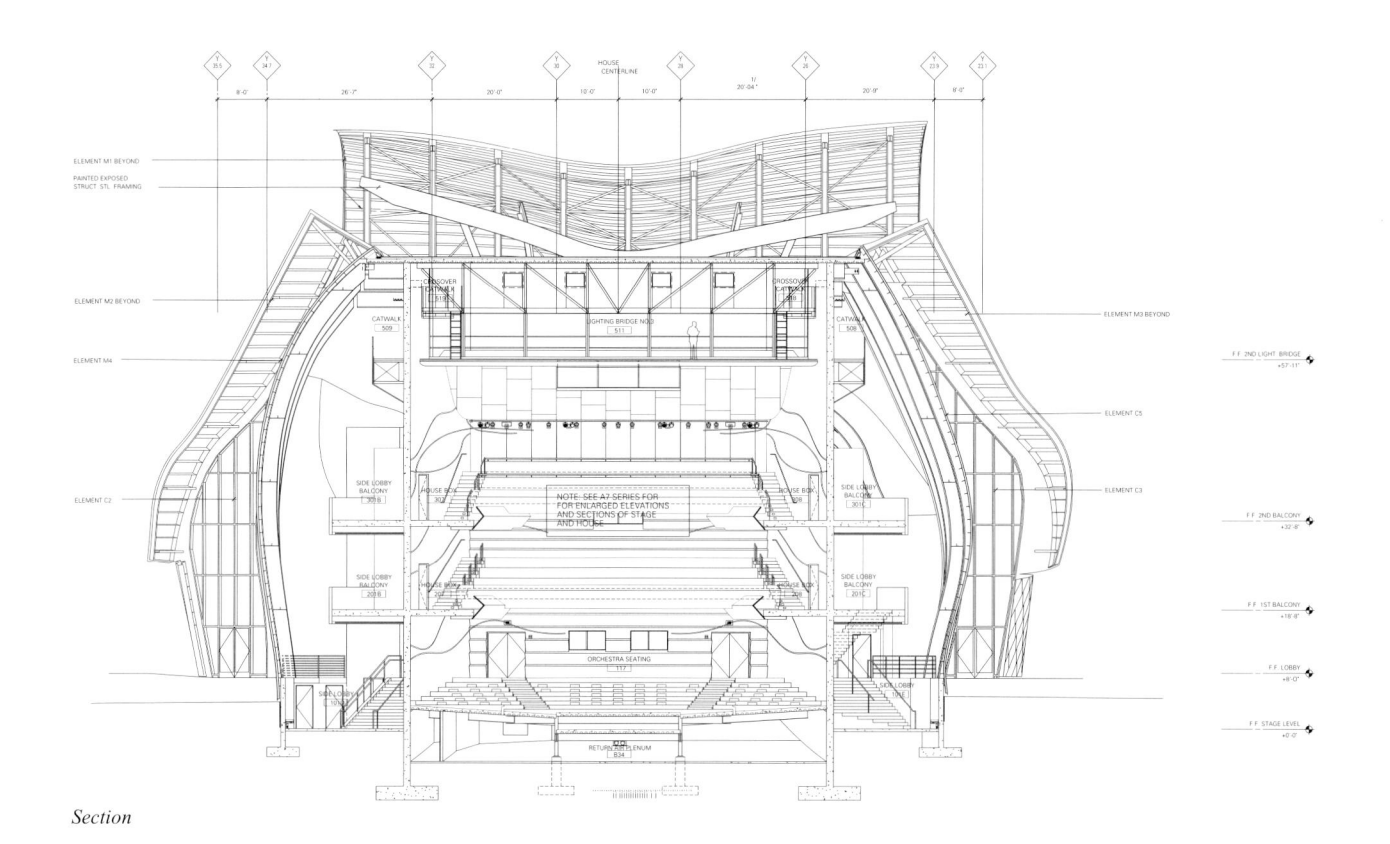

Architects: Frank O. Gehry & Associates—Frank O. Gehry, principal-in-charge; Randy Jefferson, project principal; Craig Webb, project designer; John Bowers, project architect; Suren Ambartsumyan, Guillermo Angarita, David Blackburn, Kirk Blaschke, Earle Briggs, Nida Chesonis, Matt Fineout, Sean Gale, Craig Gilbert, Jeff Guga, James Jackson, Julian Mayes, Chris Mazzier, Frank Medrano, John Murphey, David Pakshong, Yanan Par, Lynn Pilon, David Rodriguez, Tadao Shimizu, Karen Tom, Jose Catriel Tulian, Mok Wai Wan, Yannina Manjarres-Weeks, Adam Wheeler, Brad Winkeljohn, Brian Zamora
Client: Bard College
Consultants: DeSimone Consulting Engineers, structural; Cosentini Associates, consulting engineers; Theatre Projects Consultants, theater; Nagata Acoustics—Yasuhisa Toyota, acoustic; L'Observatoire International, lighting; Olin Partnership, landscape; Morris Associates, civil engineer; Maxim Technologies, geotechnical; Peter Muller, curtain wall
General contractor: Daniel O'Connell's Sons, Inc.

TADAO ANDO

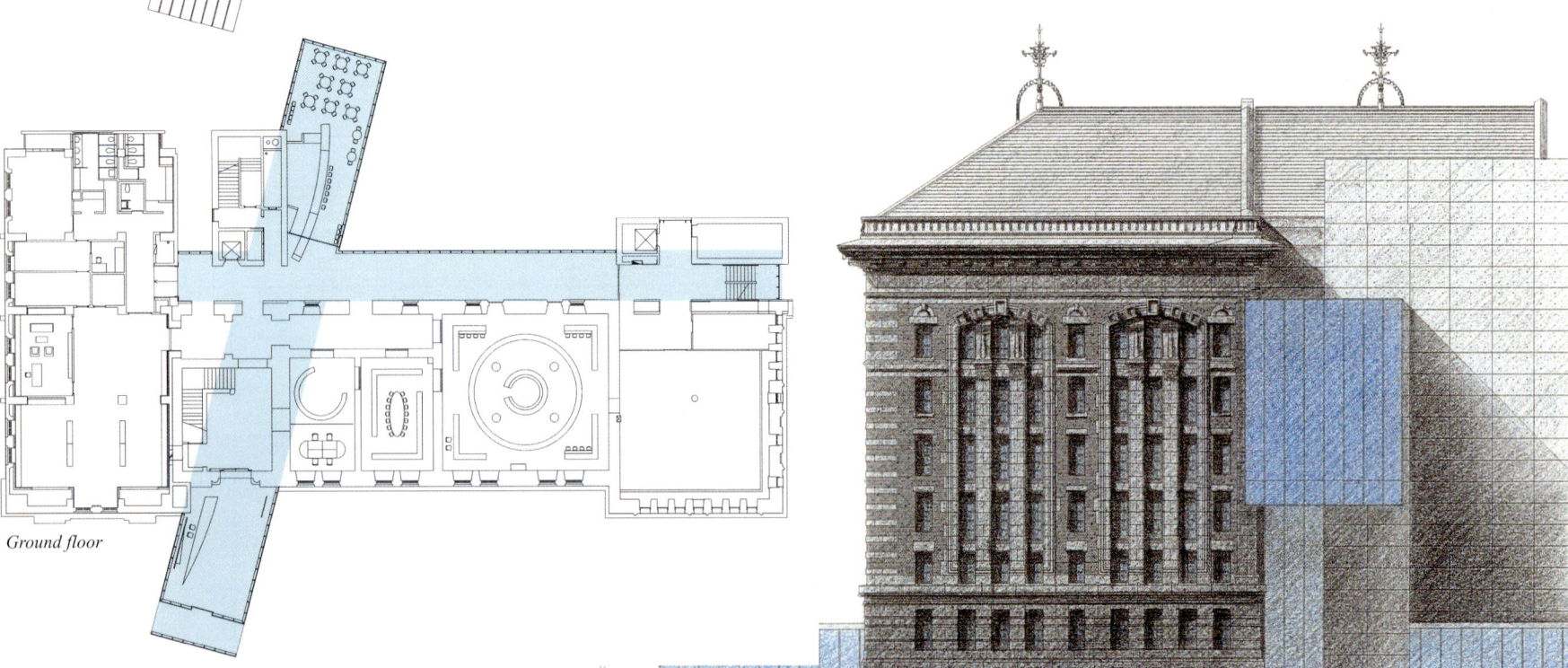

INTERNATIONAL LIBRARY OF CHILDREN'S LITERATURE
Taito, Tokyo, Japan Design: 1997–2000 Construction: 1998–2002

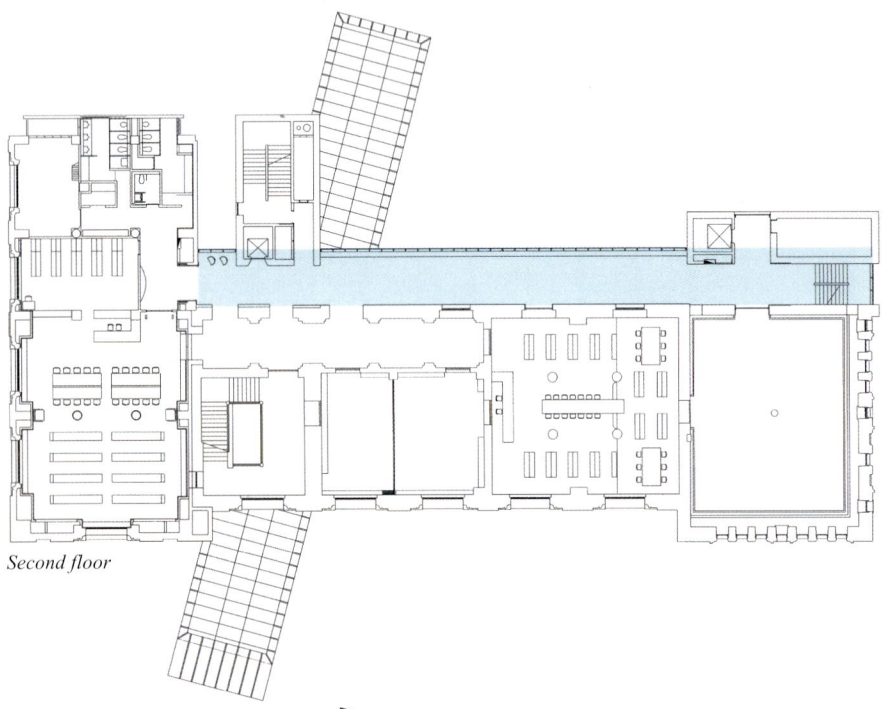

Third floor

Second floor

Ground floor

Inaugurated in 1906, the old Ueno Library, an annex to the National Diet Library, was first conceived as the Imperial Library. The current project is a restoration and revival of this old library as the International Library of Children's Literature. It involves reinforcement of structure, adopting earthquake-resistant methods of construction.

Although its original plan featured a massive Western-style building, the old Ueno Library has never been completed. To this day, only a quarter of this square building which has a hollow square in the center like a doughnut—that is, the side corridor—was finished. It was long known as a unique building whose form may be classified under a certain style of architecture, but lacked for a front entrance. Our approach was to insert a modern, glass box that would point to new possibilities and create space linking, in order to revive the library as a self-contained building. To cope with the library's diversifying functions, introduction of magazines collection and an electronic version of the library is considered, in addition to the existing collection of approx. 400,000 books.

An information base for the children who are to bear the future of the Earth on their shoulders, would be realized in form of a collision between an old building of historical values and a modern box made of glass. I expect that the energy emitted by such clash will be the source of new possibilities.
Tadao Ando

North elevation

明治39年に帝国図書館として竣工した旧国会図書館支部上野図書館を，免震工法を含む耐震補強を施して改修し，新たに国際子ども図書館として活用する計画である。

　旧上野図書館は，当初洋風の巨大なロの字型プランで構想されたにもかかわらず，その1/4，側廊部分だけが完成した状態で現在に至っており，様式的だが正面玄関を持たない特異な建物として知られていた。我々の提案は，そこに現代的なガラスの箱を挿入することで，新しい方向性や空間の繋がりをつくり出し，一つの完結した建物として再生するというものである。図書館という建物の機能の多様化を受けて，図書約40万冊を収蔵するだけでなく，雑誌の収集や電子図書館化の積極的な導入なども考えている。

　次代を担う子どものための情報基地が，文化財級の旧い建物と全く新しいガラスの箱のぶつかり合いというかたちで実現する。その衝突によって生まれるエネルギーが，新たな可能性を生み出していくのではないかと期待している。　　　　（安藤忠雄）

Architects: Tadao Ando Architects & Associates, Nikken Sekkei, Ministry of Land, Infrastructure and Transport
Client: Ministry of Land, Infrastructure and Transport
General cotractor: Konoike
Structural system: steel frame, reinforced concrete
Site area: 5,433.0 m²
Total floor area: 6,740.0 m²

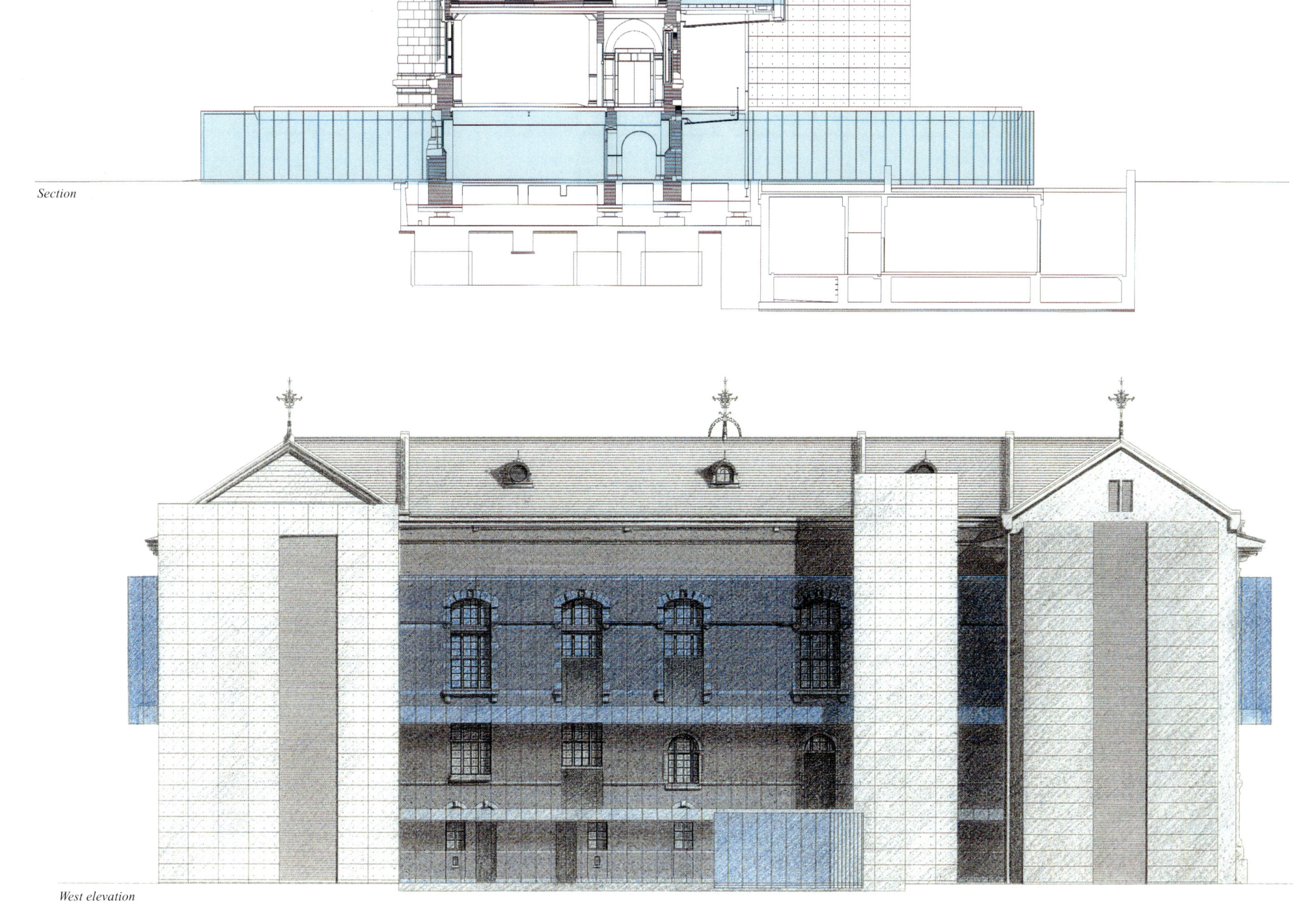

Section

West elevation

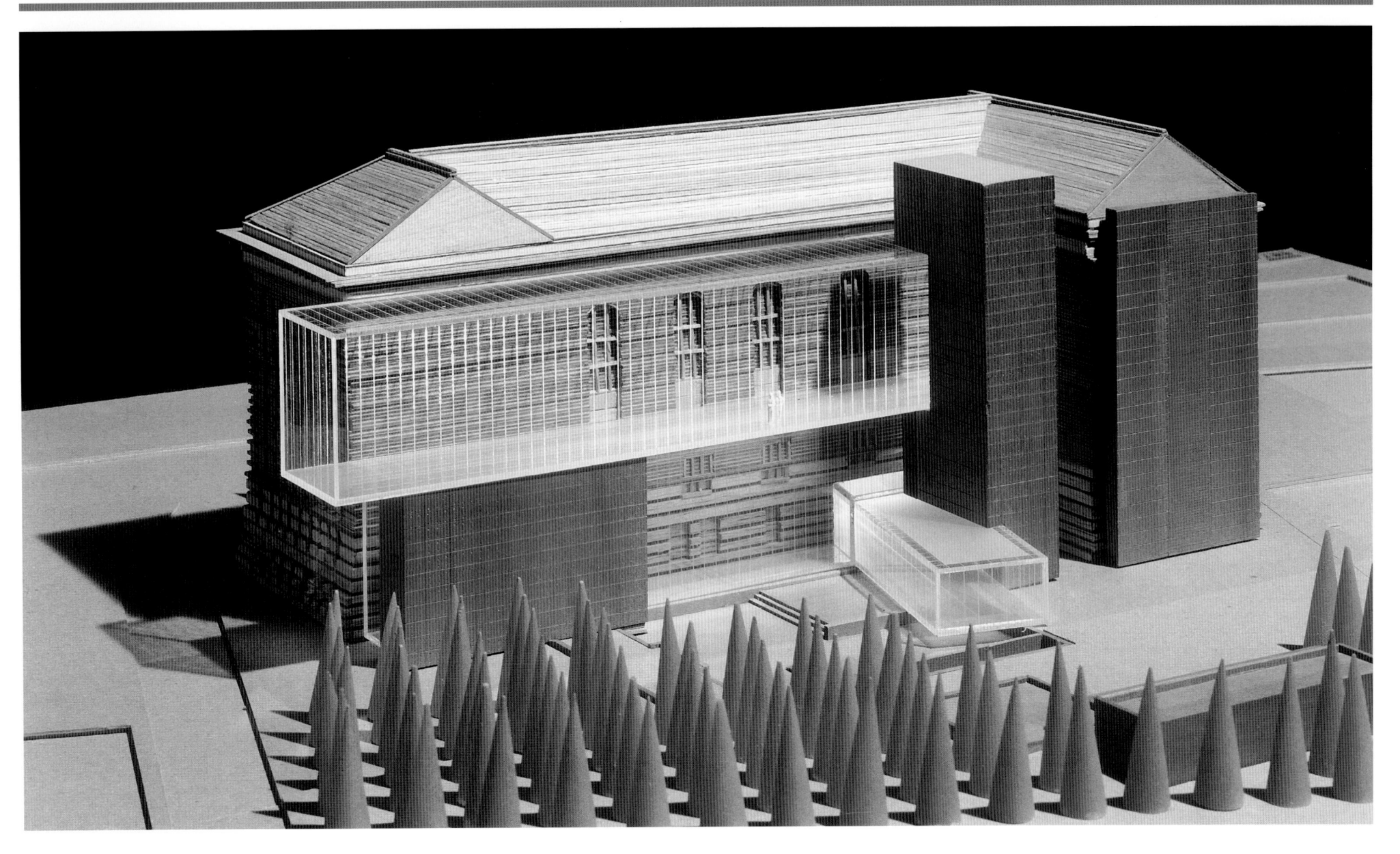

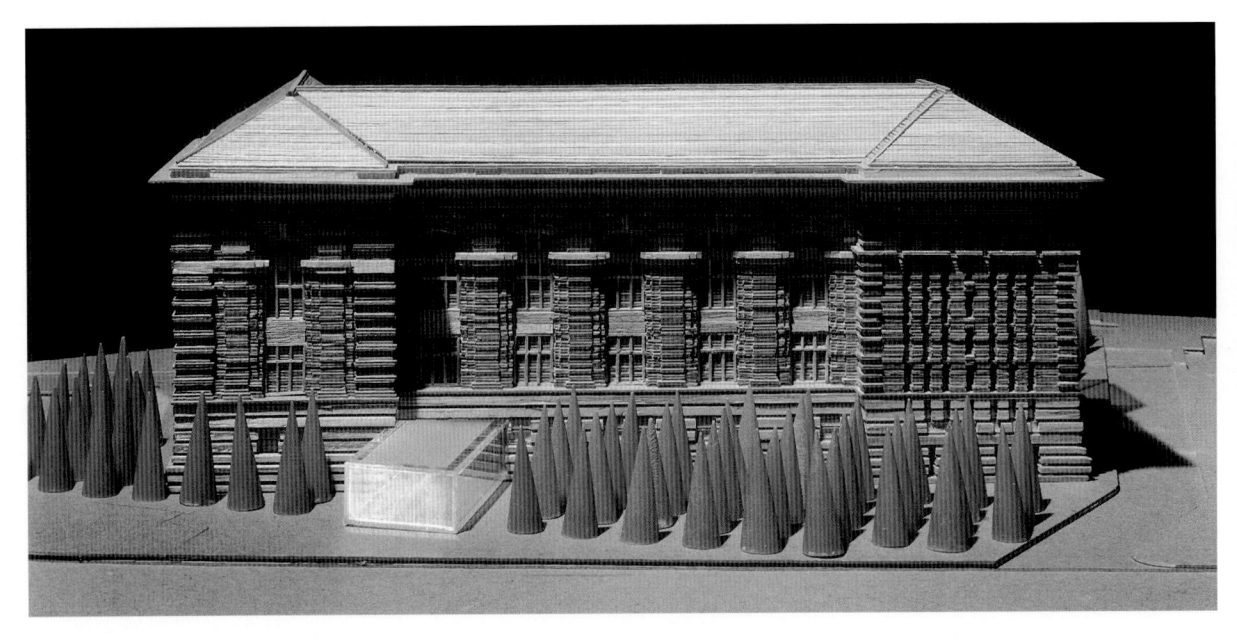

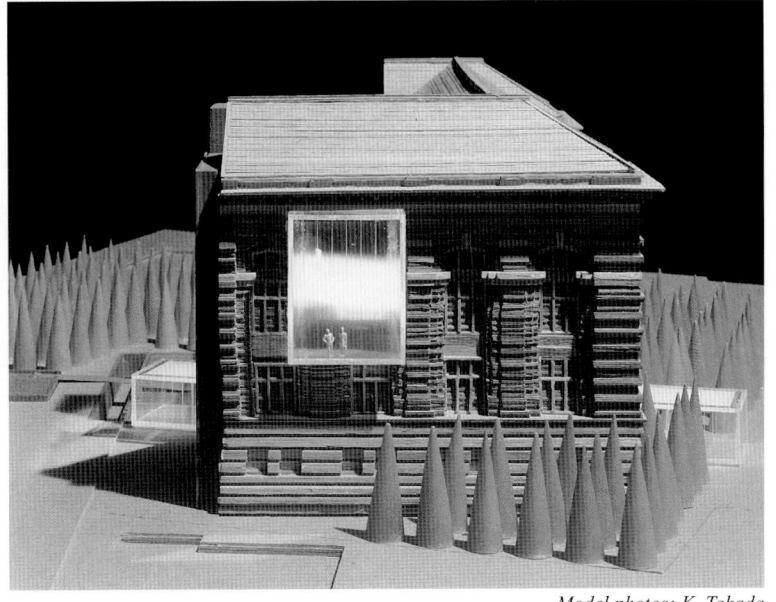

Model photos: K. Takada

MECANOO

R.C. CHAPEL ST. MARY OF THE ANGELS
Rotterdam, The Netherlands Design: 1998–99 Construction: 2000–01

St. Mary of the Angels
November 1998. I am about to leave for Venice. The telephone rings. It is father Joost de Lange asking if I would like to design a chapel for a cemetery. It has to be ready for use in the year 2000. He does not want to tell me the location yet. We make an appointment for after my return. I cannot shake off the request in Venice: a chapel for the year 2000! I am there with art historian Jan van Adrichem. He takes me to the many chapels and churches of Venice for three days. He tells me about Byzantine Gothic, Early and High Renaissance, Baroque and Rococo, the paintings of Titian with their dramatic light effects, the fourteen stations, and the Chapel of Mary. I study the ground plans. I sit and dream in every chapel. What atmosphere do I want to create? What is the specific element of a funeral for me?

Venetian dream
Three days later, Jan van Adrichem laughs as he asks me what my chapel will look like. I reply cautiously but very firmly. 'I have a dream that is not complete yet, because the location is missing, but I know the ingredients. It must be a jewel casket, with a big expressive roof, a golden canopy and a beam of light. I am thinking of a blue, continuous, narrative wall. And the chapel will be a part of a route, which in turn is a part of a ceremony: a ceremony of standing still, reflecting, and then going on again, as a symbol of the life that goes on. I don't want a dead end chapel. And it must be intimate, whether it is for ten or a hundred people.' Immediately upon my return I have my first meeting with the pastor and his board at the Rotterdam episcopacy. I blurt out my Venetian dream. They show me the location and invite me to imagine the chapel of my dreams.

Transience
I am walking in the Roman Catholic cemetery of St. Lawrence in Rotterdam. I go through the porch in a wall and enter an atmosphere of transience, of old trees and graves. In the middle a chapel is on the point of collapse, beside a dilapidated arcade. Faded photographs of a very different chapel, a kind of small church, hang in the porch. I am curious about the history.

The cemetery replaced the St. Lawrence cemetery around St. Lawrence church in the centre of Rotterdam. That cemetery had to make way for the vegetable market in 1680. Catholics were buried in the church itself until 1830, when it was no longer allowed for reasons of hygiene. The Catholics urgently needed a new cemetery. The donation of the former estate of Groenendaal facilitated the construction of a Roman Catholic cemetery. It was opened on 13 March 1865.

Campo Santo
The architect H.J. van den Brink designed the cemetery as an Italian field of the dead, a *campo santo*. He was a disciple of the architect P.J.H. Cuypers and had a reputation as an architect of churches in Neo-Classical style. This was also the style in which he designed the porches and a chapel situated in the centre, which were connected with one another by a straight lane. The chapel was surrounded by a circular path with main paths radiating from it. A Neo-Romanesque arcade on top of double burial chambers was built around the perimeter of the cemetery.

Unstable ground
The roof of the original arcade was removed thirty years ago because of its poor condition. The Neo-Classical chapel, which was opened in 1869, had subsided because of the bad quality of the subsoil. Given the risk of its collapsing, it was decided to demolish it. A new chapel was constructed on the vaults of the old one in 1963: a building shaped like a large Indian tent, covered with copper, with a clock at the top. It is incredible, but this chapel was affected by foundation problems as well. Once again there was a risk of collapse and the chapel had to be demolished. So we are designing the third chapel for the Roman Catholic cemetery of St. Lawrence in Rotterdam; this time with a new foundation.

Golden ceiling
The routing of the chapel is based on trust in the continuation of life. You carry the deceased into the chapel, have a moment of reflection in a quiet, meditative building, and then leave the chapel in a single, continuous movement. The space has an organic form: a continuous, curving wall, raised seventy centimetres above the ground. The wall has an intense colour, with texts from the Requiem in many languages; the cemetery is a place for the multicultural population of Rotterdam. The roof floats like a folded sheet of paper above the space. The golden ceiling is artificially lit from below. An opening in the ceiling allows daylight to enter the chapel in a bundle of light that is further accentuated at the moment when incense is used. The chapel stands on a plateau of gravel within the contours of the previous Neo-Classical chapel. Two heated, wooden decks indicate the place of the priest and the congregation. The clock from the 1963 chapel hangs in the tower. The chapel of St. Mary of the Angels is like a precious jewel and a beautiful example of palimpsest: a roll of parchment that has been reused after the previous text has been erased or covered up.

天使聖母マリア教会
1998年10月，私はヴェネツィアに向かおうとしている。電話が鳴る。ヨースト・デ・ランヘ神父からで，墓地の礼拝堂を設計してくれないか，と言う。2000年には使えなければならない。彼はまだ場所については話したがらない。旅から帰ってから会う約束をする。ヴェネツィア行きを止めることはできない。2000年紀の礼拝堂！ヴェネツィアでは美術史家のヤン・ファン・アドリヘムと一緒だ。彼は3日間，私をたくさんの聖堂や教会に連れて回る。彼はビザンチン・ゴシック，初期及び盛期ルネサンス，バロックやロココ，ティツィアーノの絵画とその劇的な光の効果，14のステーション，聖母マリア教会の礼拝堂について話してくれる。私は1階平面をスタディしてみる。礼拝堂のなかに座り，夢見る。私がつくりたいのはどのような雰囲気だろうか？私にとって葬儀に相応しいエレメントとは何だろうか？

ヴェネツィアの夢
3日後，ヤン・ファン・アドリヘムは，君の礼拝堂はどんなものになるんだろうと訊ねながら笑う。私は慎重に，しかしきっぱりと答える。「夢はあるが，まだ完全じゃない。場所が欠けているからね。だが，材料は分かっている。それは宝石箱でなければならないんだ。大きな表情豊かな屋根と金色のキャノピーが付いていて，一条の光線が入る。青い色をして，切れ目なく続く，物語風の壁を考えている。この礼拝堂は道筋の一部，一転して儀式の一部になるだろう。静かに立ち，深く思い，そして再び進んで行く。絶えず動いて行く生命の象徴としての儀式だ。デッド・エンドな礼拝堂にはしたくない。そして親密な雰囲気を持たせなければならない。10人の場合だろうと，100人の場合だろうとね」。帰国するとすぐ，ロッテルダム主教団の，司教とその理事たちと最初の会合を持った。私はヴェネツィアでの夢についてうっかり口をすべらした。彼らは敷地を見て，私の夢の礼拝堂をイメージするように招いてくれる。

無常
ロッテルダムの聖ローレンス教会。私はそのローマカトリック教会の墓地を歩いている。壁のなかのポーチを抜けて，無常感の漂う，老木や墓の立ち並ぶなかに踏み入る。中央に，荒廃したアーケードの傍ら，礼拝堂が今にも崩れそうに建っている。目の前のものとは似ても似つかない礼拝堂，一種の小さな教会の褪せた写真がポーチにかかっている。私はその歴史について興味が湧いた。

この墓地は，ロッテルダムの中心，聖ローレンス教会の周りにある聖ローレンス墓地に取り代わったものである。以前の墓地は1680年に野菜市場に場所を譲らなければならなかった。カトリック教徒は1830年，衛生上の理由から不許可となるまで，教会のなかに埋葬された。カトリック教徒たちは大至急新しい墓地を必要とし，フローネンダールが以前所有していた広大な地所が寄贈されたことで，ローマカトリック教徒の墓地の建設が促進された。墓地は1865年3月13日に完成した。

カンポ・サント
建築家，H・J・ファン・デン・ブリンクはこの墓地を，イタリア式の埋葬地，カンポ・サントとしてデザインした。彼は建築家P・J・H・カイパースの弟子で，新古典様式の教会建築家としての評判を得ていた。この墓地も同じ様式を用いて，ポーチと中央に位置する礼拝堂をデザインし，2つは1本の真っ直ぐな道で互いに結ばれている。礼拝堂は円形の道で囲まれ，そこから主要な道が放射状に延びている。墓地の周縁を囲んで，2層の埋葬室の上に，ネオ・ロマネスクのアーケードがつくられた。

不安定な地盤
元のアーケードの屋根は，状態が悪いため30年前に撤去された。1869年に完成した新古典の礼拝堂は，下層土の状態が悪いため沈下してしまった。倒壊の危険から，それは取り壊されることに決まった。1963年，元のヴォールトの上に新しい礼拝堂が建設された。インディアンの大テントのような形をした建物は銅で覆われ，頂部に時計が付いていた。素晴らしいものだが，この礼拝堂も，同じように，基礎の問題からの悪影響を受けた。再び倒壊の危険が生まれ，取り壊さなければならなかった。そんなわけで，私たちは，ロッテルダムの聖ローレンス教会ローマカトリック墓地の3番目の礼拝堂を設計している。今回は新しい基礎をつくることになる。

金色の天井
この礼拝堂の道筋は生命の連続性に対する確信に基づいている。死者を礼拝堂に運び，静かな，黙想のなかにある建物で，思いにふける。そして，一つの，連続的な動きのなかで礼拝堂を去る。その空間は有機的な形である。地上から70センチ持ち上げられた，連続し，湾曲する壁。壁は濃い色に塗られ，様々な言語でレクイエムからとった文章が書かれている。この墓地は多様な文化的背景をもつロッテルダムの人々のための場所なのだ。屋根は紙を折り畳んだように空間の上方に浮かんでいる。金色の天井は下からの照明を受けている。天井に取られた開口から，昼の光が束となって礼拝堂のなかに差し込み，香がたかれるとき，その瞬間をさらに引き立てる。礼拝堂は，前の新古典の礼拝堂の外郭内につくられた小石の台地の上に建つ。暖められた2つの木造デッキが司祭と会衆の位置を暗示する。1963年の礼拝堂に付いていた時計が，塔のなかに吊られている。天使聖母マリア教会の礼拝堂は，貴重な宝石やパリンプセストの美しい見本に似ている。前に書かれていた文字が消され，あるいは覆い隠されたあと再び使われてきた一巻の羊皮紙のような。

First chapel (1880)

Situation with first chapel

Foundations of the first chapel

West elevation of the Mecanoo's chapel

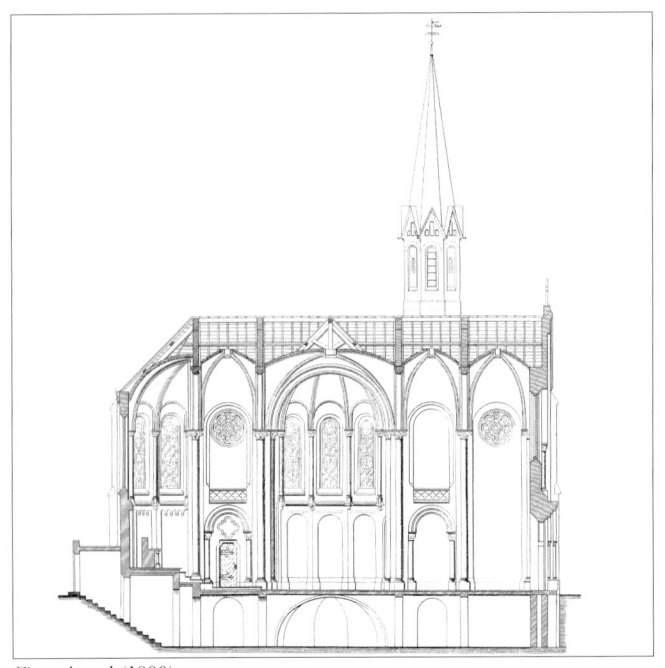

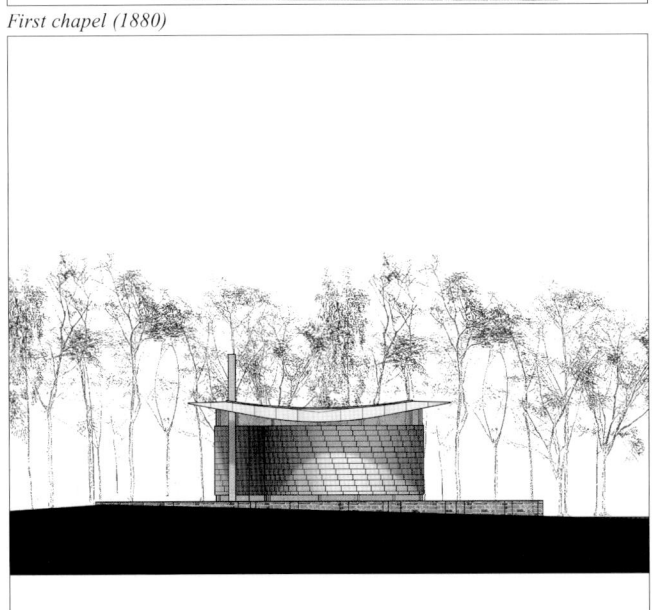

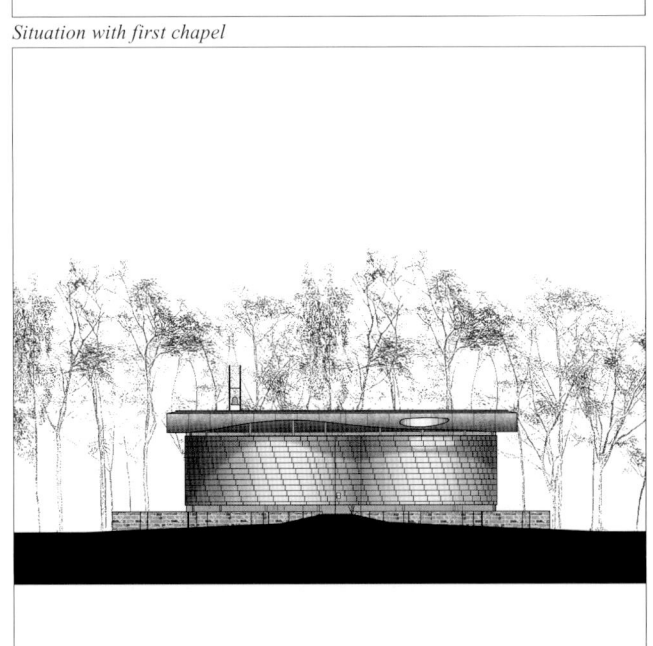

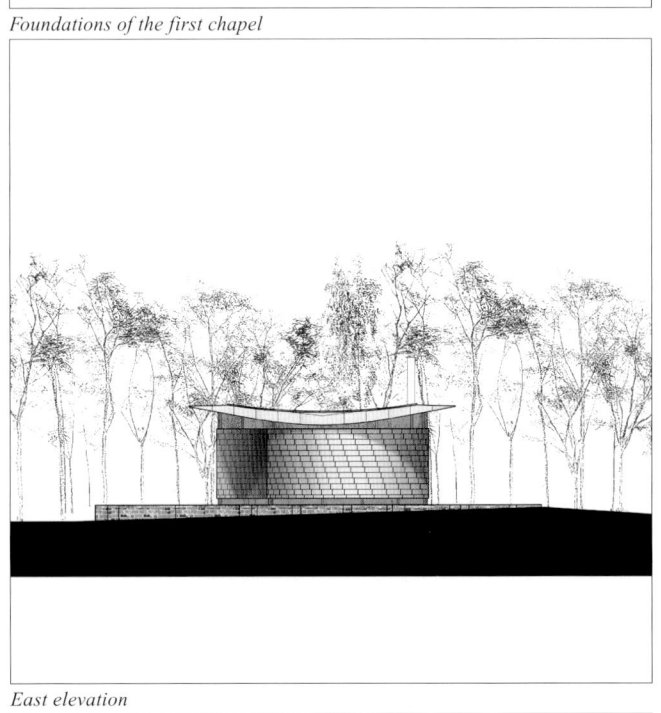

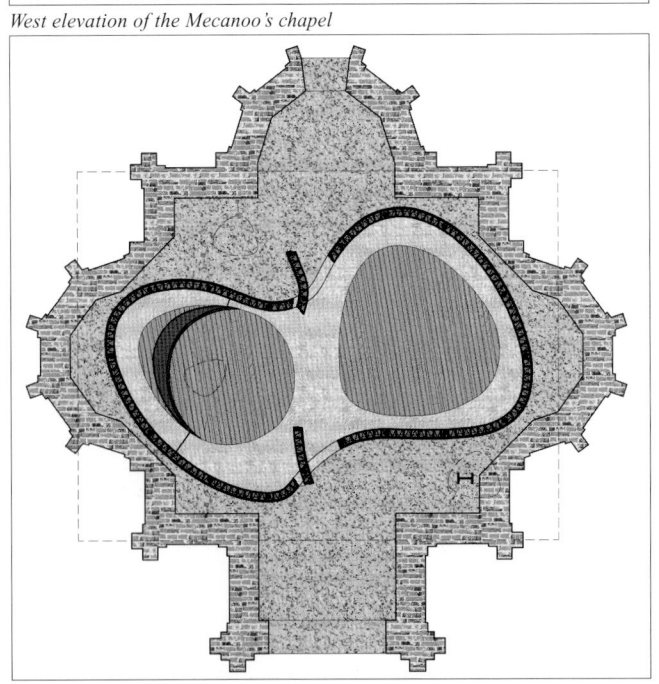

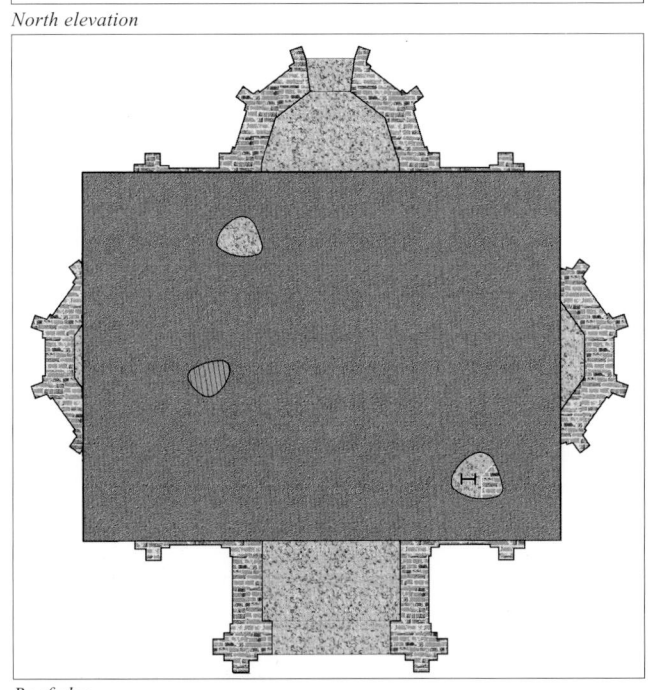

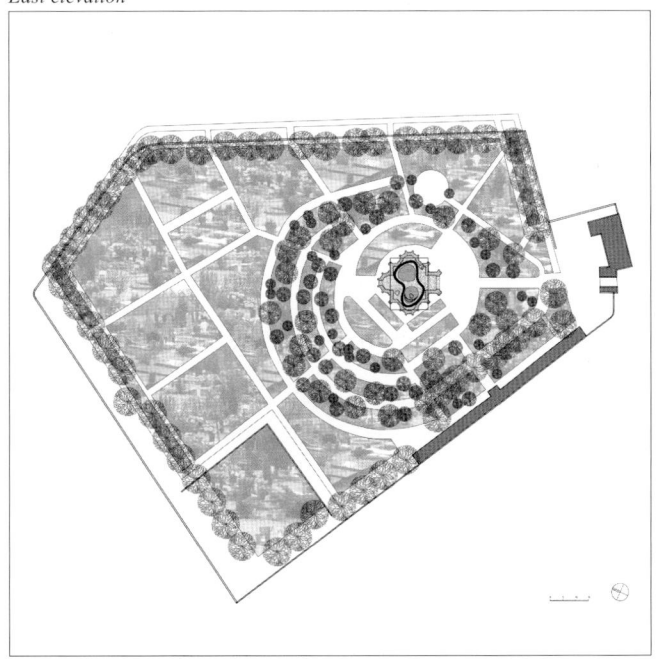

North elevation

East elevation

Plan of the Mecanoo's chapel

Roof plan

Site plan

Foundations of the first chapel

Second chapel

Sketches of the Mecanoo's third chapel

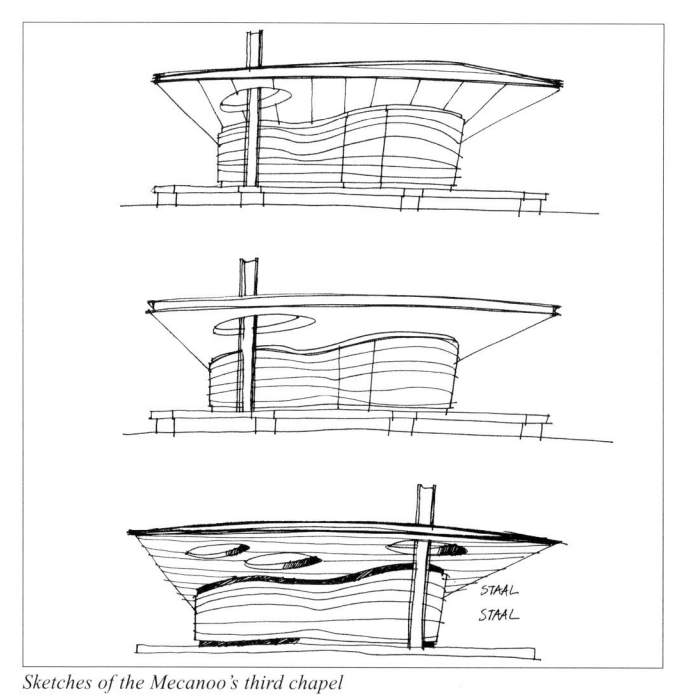

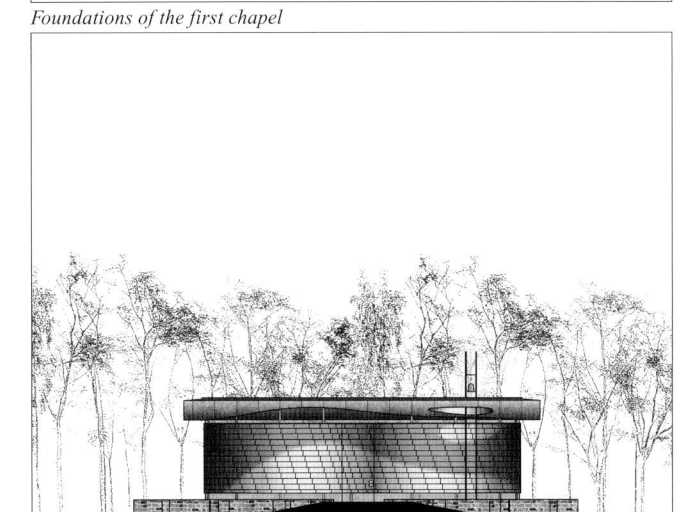

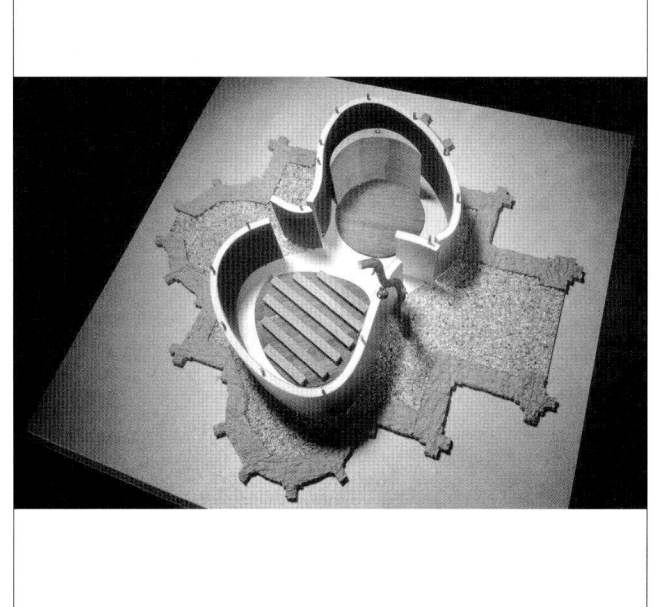

South elevation

Model

Model

Architects: Mecanoo architecten b.v., Delft—Francine Houben, Francesco Veenstra, Ana Rocha, Huib de Jong, Martin Stoop, Natascha Arala Chaves, Judith Egberink, Henk Bouwer, project team
Client: R.C. St. Lawrence Cemetry, Rotterdam
Consultants: ABT adviesbureau voor bouwtechniek b.v., Delft, structural
Model: Pieter Vandermeer

PETER EISENMAN

MUSÉE DES CONFLUENCES
Lyon, France Design: 2001(competition)

In ancient cities, gates always marked a symbolic point of arrival. In the Industrial Age, these gates took on functional as well as symbolic significance with the great glass and iron railroad termini that announced one's arrival in the cities of Europe. Today the car and the airplane are the primary means of arrival, but the autoroute and the airport are not the gates we knew in the 19th and early 20th centuries. Now that these termini have been largely replaced by virtual terminals, by the computer and the Internet, there is more than ever a need to mark places of arrival and departure: to mark moments that signal experience in real space and time. Our project therefore is more than a functional museum. It is also a symbol of entry and departure for Lyon; a virtual gate, a water terminus, an object responding to the natural flows of the particular landscape in which it finds itself.

As one arrives in Lyon from the south, on the A7 from Marseilles, one is greeted by the building at the confluence of the Rhone and the Soane rivers. It stands like the prow of a ship plying between the two waters, or from another view, as being driven apart by the current of each river. From every bridge spanning the Rhone and from every direction, the building moves differently in space and time, shadowed and lit in an ever-changing pattern.

Our project is not a simple tower with ground elements (required to cover a certain site area by the rules of the competition) but rather a girded zone that lifts off the ground, bifurcating and enfolding as it moves upward, generating in its warped forms an object that is neither figure nor ground, tower nor slab, but a melding of the two, like the confluence of the Rhone and Soane rivers with a new symbol, the illuminated towergate. The forms of the building begin in a horizontal orthogonal girded mat that is distorted by the flows of the rivers, as they merge, forcing the mat upward, like a waterspout. The detail of the towers is reminiscent of the muscular and ligaments of Leonardo Da Vinci's anatomic drawings. The east tower has an exoskeleton of structure on the outside, which warps to the veining of glass and solid that allow for illumination at night. The west tower appears more sinuous and opaque on the exterior with its structural exoskeleton.

The Musée des Confluences is a museum of two parts, "science and society." It is intended to simultaneously examine and signify the locus of these two discourses. As such, the museum must function as both vessel and text. In this role it is a multilayered signifier, housing the thematic and programmatic elements in a manner consistent with the idea of "confluence," and physically representing it at a scale consistent with its role as a symbolic gateway to Lyon.

At the heart of the design challenge are the dual requirements of situating the complementary foci of the reference and variation galleries and giving them access to each other in a flexible series of options. Given the site coverage requirement, one might expect a horizontal stacking of the program—one that lies close to the ground and follows the course of the river. But this is the "expected." It lacks the capacity to surprise, to confront, to challenge. Without the capacity to act critically, the building itself will not have the vitality to become a civic monument on one of the most unique and prominent sites of any city. The program requirements which specify three reference exhibitions as the core of the MDC experience integrates and related to the seven variation spaces, suggests that a vertical interconnection is as viable as a horizontal one i.e. that a horizontal plan diagram is little different from a vertical one. Thus this project design chooses to organize the key elements of the program vertically in paired towers that reflect the dual nature of the museum at the same time creating a significant marker in the city.

Vehicular access to the museum from the boulevard quickly sorts auto, bus, and service traffic. Visitors arriving by foot or by bus enter the building, and join the principal flow in the urban lobby at the north end of the complex, which is parallel to and overlooks the riverside park. Groups are received in the adjacent group area, which contains the programmatic elements necessary to support the group experiences, including offices and an orientation room. Directly accessible from the urban lobby are the self-service restaurant, coat check, and storage lockers. Tickets and information are placed at the central point of the lobby.

At this point a public passage begins that bends with the form of the building and at times reveals the towers rising above along this public way flanking the inwards are the boutique, reading room, and bookstore. Along the inside arc of the passage is the auditorium and, beyond it, adjacent to the base of the east tower, the VIP room. Visitors to the museum as well as the general public are welcome to use this space, which allows for, through public access from the north and south providing access to important programmatic and retail elements without requiring museum admission. This plan provides a structure for the organization of the other functions both above and below. The garage is placed along the western face below the lobby connected by several points of direct access for visitors and staff. On the outside of the arc on the second level are the museum offices. At the extreme southern end of the public way is a second lobby, which provides an entrance to the museum to the south from the Soane riverbank walkway and to the brasserie and its terrace.

The key to the functionality of the vertical arrangement is the way in which it is conceived and executed, with the towers sharing the void space between them as a virtual lobby. The visitor is made aware of this organization through the transparency of the undulating and faceted roof along the public way that allow for views of the towers. This roofscape recalls the abattoir of Tony Garnier located just across the river. The quadrants of the towers that face each other are transparent and interconnected by bridges and escalators. This transparency reveals the lobby spaces and activity on each level. Thus from any vantage point, the range of options in the reference and variation galleries is visible. On each of the principal reference levels a bridge crosses to a corresponding variation level in the other tower, and escalator ramps connect to the intermediate variation levels. Visitors can traverse the space as easily and clearly, and with as many route options, as they would if the galleries were arranged on horizontal levels surrounding a public lobby. Here, the vertical arrangement is flexible, functional, and adaptable. It establishes an extensive series of possible interactions between the reference exhibitions and the variations as they change over time.

While the defined reference and variation spaces meet the goals for space, format, and accessibility established by the program, they are also flexibly organized, anticipating a much broader range of commentary and response. This is especially important as the program components evolve in the future. All the galleries are supported by the technical and fabrication spaces that are organized below in the base of the building. This provides a controllable service zone that is secure, accessible to the loading docks, and able to support and supply any of the programmatic spaces via simple vertical cores that rise directly to the exhibition spaces. Thus one is able to take a single gallery off line without disrupting the functioning of the building as a whole.

The resulting Musée des Confluences provides a clear, rational organization of space and functions that is manageable and controllable by the staff, yet easily accessible and open in its public spaces. But more importantly, the project captures the energy manifest in the site and the confluence of the rivers with a dynamic harnessing of today's technology. It is a threshold building, a zone between ground and figure, abstraction and figuration, the virtual and the real. It will be the landmark of the computer age, of the confluence of science and society.

古代都市では，ゲートは常に到着地点を象徴する存在だった。産業社会においてそれは，ヨーロパの諸都市への到着を知らせる，ガラスと鉄でつくられた壮大な終着駅というかたちで，象徴的であると同時に機能的な重要性を持つに至った。今日，車と飛行機が主要な交通手段であるなかで，高速道も空港も，19世紀や20世紀初頭にわれわれが知っていたようなゲートではなくなっている。これらの終着地は，ヴァーチャル・ターミナルやコンピュータやインターネットに大きく取って代わられている。だからこそ到着と出発の場所における空間と時間のリアルな体験の瞬間を告知することがかつてなく必要になっている。それゆえこの計画案は機能的なミュージアム以上のものである。それはまたリヨン市への到着出発の象徴である。ヴァーチャル・ゲート，水の終点，場所固有の風景に見いだされる自然の流れに応答するオブジェクトなのだ。

南から，マルセーユを起点とする高速道A7に乗ってリヨンに着くと，ローヌ川とソーヌ川の合流点に建つこの建物に迎えられる。建物は，2つの川を往来する，あるいは視点を変えれば，それぞれの川の流れに押し離されている船の舳先のように屹立する。ローヌ川に架かるそれぞれの橋から，それぞれの方角から，建物は，光と影が絶えず変化する模様を描き，空間と時間のなかを多彩に揺れ動く。

われわれのプロジェクトは，地上階を持つ（設計競技概要は，一定の敷地領域を覆うことを求めていた）単純なタワーではなく，地上から引き上げられた囲まれたゾーンであり，上昇するに従って分岐し，襞をつくり，そのワープする形態のなかに，図でもなく地でもなく，タワーでもスラブでもない，ローヌとソーヌが合流するように，その2つが混合した新しいシンボル，照明されたタワー＝ゲートが生まれてくる。建物の形態は，水平に広がる直角で囲まれたマットから始まる。そこから，2本の川の流れによって歪みを与えられ，川が混合するにつれて水面に生まれる竜巻のように押し上げられて行く。2つのタワーのディテールはレオナルド・ダ・ヴィンチの解剖学的なドローイングに見られる筋肉や靱帯を連想させる。東のタワーは外側に構造体の外骨格を持ち，それは，夜間には照明されるガラスとソリッドな壁がつくる脈状の縞模様へとねじれて行く。西のタワーはその構造的外骨格によって，その外観はさらに曲がりくねり，不透明なものとして現れる。

ミュゼ・デ・コンフリュアンスは，"科学と社会"という2つの部分からなるミュージアムである。それは，これら2つの論考の中心を検証すると同時に提示することを意図している。そのようなものとして，このミュージアムは器でありテクストでなければならない。この役割のなかで，それは，多層のシニフィアンであり，いわば"合流"という考えと一

致する，主題にかなった計画要素を収め，リヨンの象徴的な門としての役割に相応しいスケールをもって，それをフィジカルに表現する。

デザイン上の挑戦の中心には，参照のギャラリーと変化のギャラリーという補足し合う焦点を設定し，フレキシブルな選択肢のなかで互いに行き交わせるという二重の要求がある。敷地建蔽率に対する条件から，計画要素を水平に積層し，地面に近接して広がり，川の流れに沿った建物を予測するかもしれない。しかし，これは"予測"にすぎない。それには，驚きを与え，正面から対峙し，挑戦する能力が欠けている。批評的に働く能力無しには，この建物自体，あらゆる都市のなかで，最もユニークで目立つ敷地の一つに建つ都市のモニュメントになる活力を持ち得ないだろう。7つのヴァリエーション・スペースを統合し関係づけるMDC体験のコアとして3つのレファレンス展示を指定しているプログラムの要求項目は，垂直方向での相互連結は水平方向によるものと同様に実行可能であることを示唆する。つまり水平プランによるダイアグラムは垂直なプランのそれと大差ないのだ。こうして，このデザインは，プログラムの鍵となる要素を対のタワーというかたちで垂直方向に構成することを選択する。対のタワーはミュージアムの二元的性格を反映すると同時に，魅力的な都市標識をつくり出す。

大通りからミュージアムへの車輛アクセスは，自動車，バス，サービス関係車輛を迅速に振り分ける。徒歩またはバスで来た来館者は，建物内に入ると，コンプレックスの北端に位置し，川岸の公園に並行し，そこを見晴らすアーバン・ロビー内の主要な流れに加わる。人々の一団は隣接するグループ・エリアに迎えられる。ここには団体での見学を補助するのに必要な計画要素をはじめオフィス，オリエンテーション室が置かれている。アーバン・ロビーからは，セルフサービスのレストラン，クローク，ロッカーへ直接入れる。切符売り場と案内はロビーの中央に配置される。

この地点から一般の人の通路が始まる。通路は建物形態に合わせて曲がり，上に聳えるタワーが時々見える。通路の両側にブティック，読書室，書店が並ぶ。通路内部の弧に沿ってオーディトリアムがあり，その先，東タワーの基部に隣接してVIP室がある。ミュージアムへの入場者同様，一般の人もこのスペースを自由に使えるので，入館料を払わずに，プログラムに盛り込まれている重要な場所や店舗に，北と南から入ることができる。その他の機能空間は通路の上や下の階に構成される。ガレージは来館者や職員が直接入るいくつかの地点で連結されたロビーの下側，西面に沿って配置される。3階にある弧の外側はミュゼのオフィスである。一般通路の最南端には2つ目のロビーがあり，南にあるソーヌ河岸の歩行路からミュージアムやブラッスリーとそのテラスへの入り口となる。

垂直構成に機能性を持たせる鍵は，ヴァーチャル・ロビーとしてのヴォイドをその間に共有する2つのタワーをどう構成するかその方法にある。来館者はこの構成に，タワーが垣間見える一般通路に沿った，小面に刻まれた波形屋根の透明性を通して気付かされる。この屋根構成は川の対岸にあるトニー・ガルニエの設計した食肉処理場を連想させる。互いに向き合う2つのタワーの描く四分円は透明で，ブリッジとエスカレータで連結される。この透明性を通してロビーと各階の動きが見える。この結果，見通しの利く地点からはどこからでも，レファレンス及びヴァリエーション・ギャラリーが備えている広範な選択肢を簡単に理解できる。主要なレファレンス・レベルには，ブリッジがもう一方のタワーの対応するヴァリエーション・レベルに架け渡され，エスカレータ・ランプが中間にあるヴァリエーション・レベルに通じている。来館者はこのスペースを簡単明瞭な場所として行き来できるし，ギャラリーが中央のロビーを囲んで水平に重なるプランの場合と同じように，様々なルートを選べる。ここでは垂直構成は柔軟で，機能的で，調整可能である。それは，レファレンス・ギャラリーとヴァリエーション・ギャラリーの間に可能な交流の広範な系を，変化に合わせながら確立する。

レファレンス及びヴァリエーション・スペースは，プログラムが設定する空間，フォーマット，アクセスの簡単さという目的をかなえる一方，より広範な注解や応答を予知しながら，柔軟に編成されている。このことは，将来，プログラムの構成要素が徐々に進展するので特に重要である。すべてのギャラリーは，建物の基部にあるテクニカル・スペース，製作スペースによって支援されている。ここは，制御可能なサービス・ゾーンを提供する。このゾーンは安全で，積み荷ドックに簡単に入れ，展示空間に向けて直接立ち上がる単純な垂直コアを経由して，プログラム空間のどこへでも支援供給が可能である。これによって，建物全体としての機能を損わずに，一つのギャラリーを切り離すことができる。

ミュゼ・デ・コンフリュアンスは，スタッフが管理制御でき，しかもそのパブリック・スペースが開放的で入りやすい，明快で合理的に編成された空間を提供する。しかしさらに重要なのは，このプロジェクトが，敷地に明白なエネルギー，そして2つの川の合流を現代技術のダイナミックな利用によってとらえることである。これは敷居としての建物，図と地，抽象化と形象化，ヴァーチャルとリアルの間に存在する領域である。それはコンピュータ・エイジの，科学と社会が合流する時代のランドマークとなるだろう。

Night view

Site

Architects: Eisenman Architects and Felice Fanuele Architecte et Museographe
Eisenman Architects: Peter Eisenman, design principal-in-charge; Hernan Dias Alonso, Guido Zuliani, project architect; Matteo Cainer, Andri Gerber, Lukas Kueng, Matias Musacchio, Selim Vural, project team; Bobby Fogel, Christian Guttack, Kylene Tan, Raphael Niogret, Martina Zurmuehle, Wulf Walter Bottger, Sophie Lamort de Gail, project assistants
Felice Fanuele Architecte et Museographe: Felice Fanuele, principal-in-charge; Vanessa Fanuele, Suh Sang Ha, project architect; J.Loup Baldacci, Rebecca Herschkovitch, project assistants
Associated Architects: C.R.B.
Client: SERL. Société d'équipement du Rhône de Lyon
Consultants: Technip, B.E.T, structural; Peutz &Associés, aqusttical; Voutay S.A, economic; S'PACE environnement, landscape

Section

Section

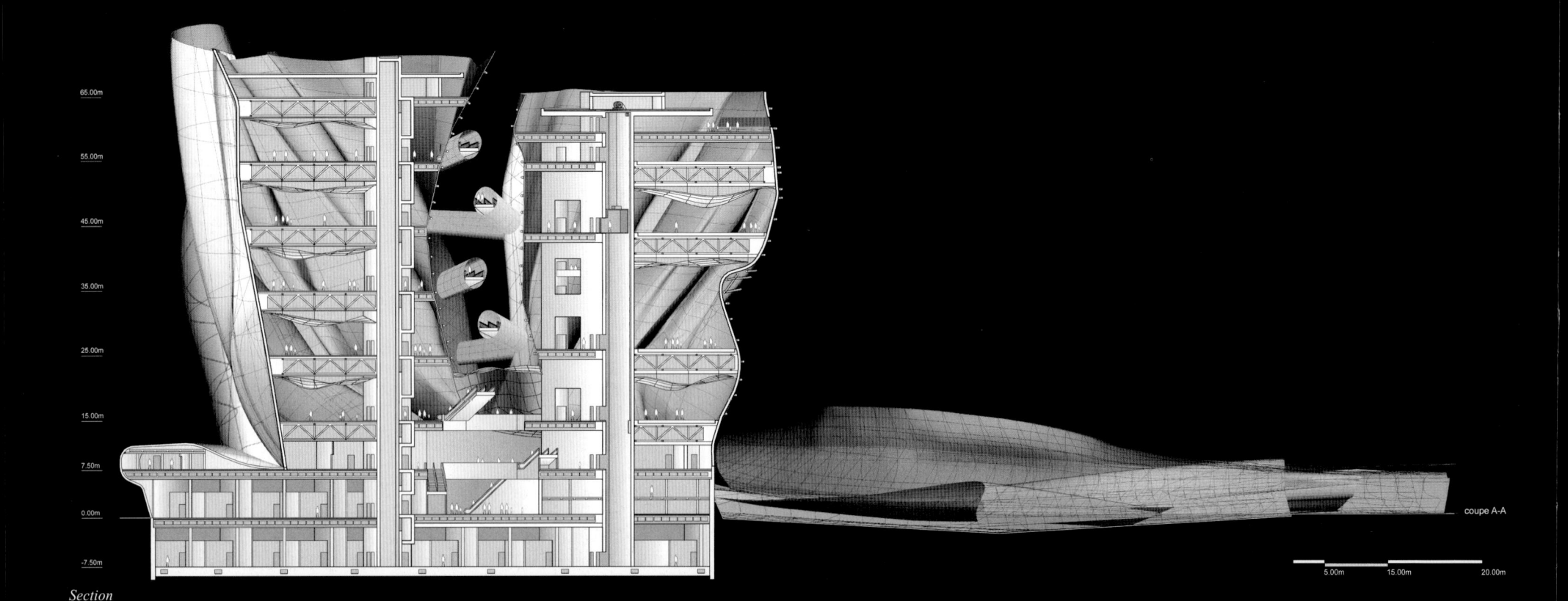

Level +7.5

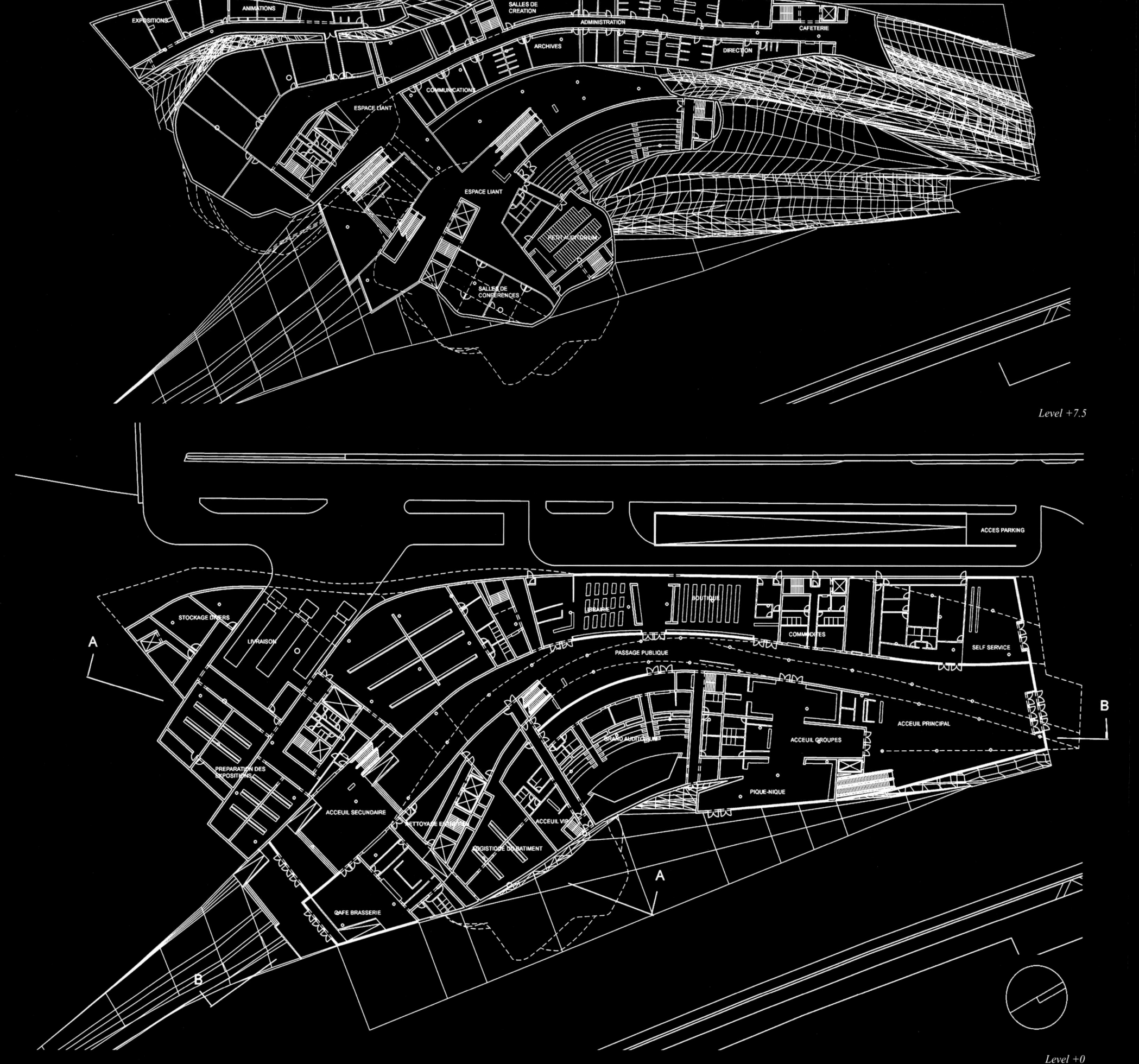

Level +0

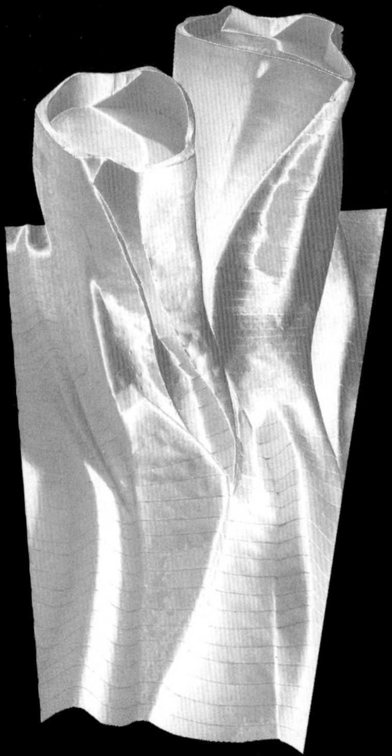
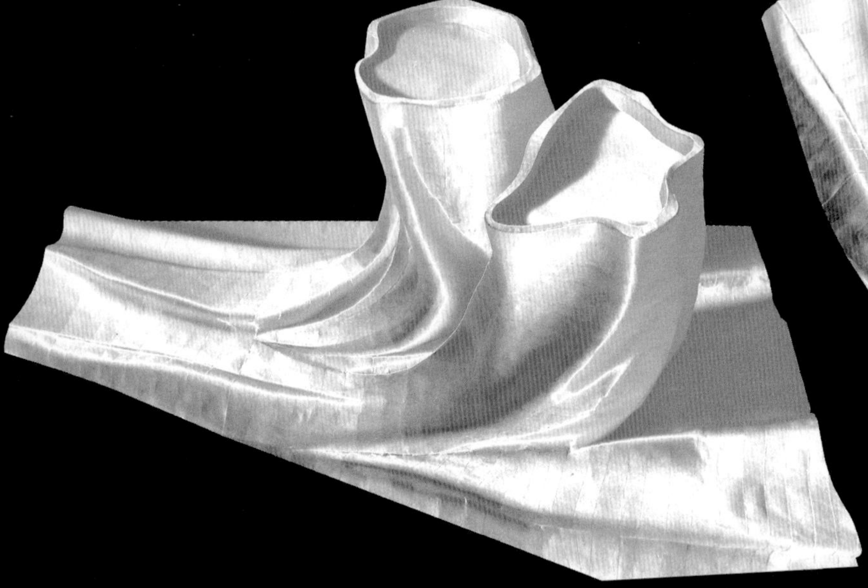
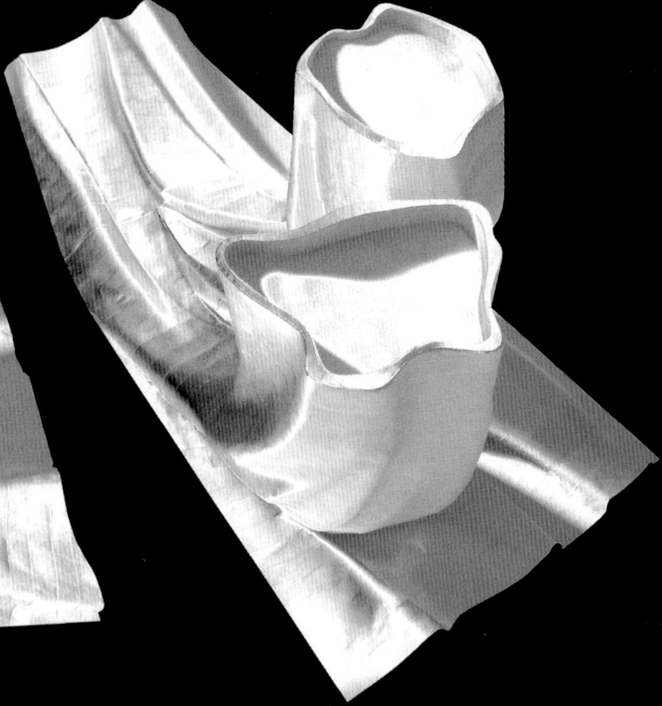
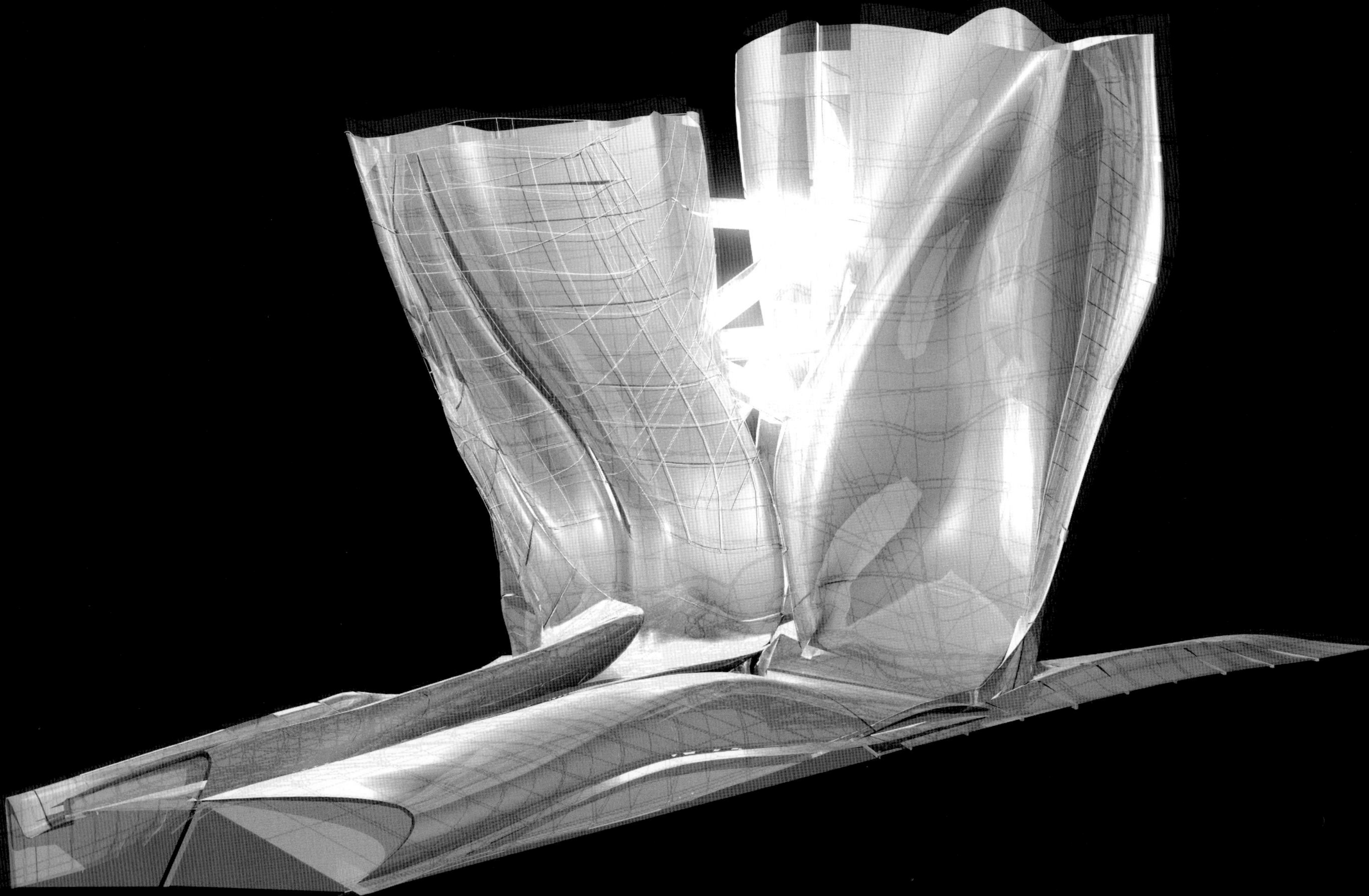

45

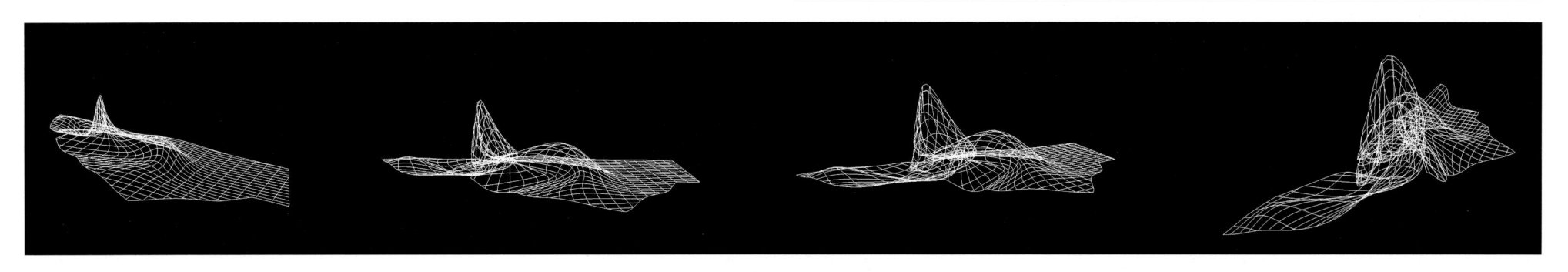

GA PROJECT

RICHARD MEIER

173/176 PERRY STREET
New York, New York, U.S.A. Design: 1999–2000 Construction: 2000–02

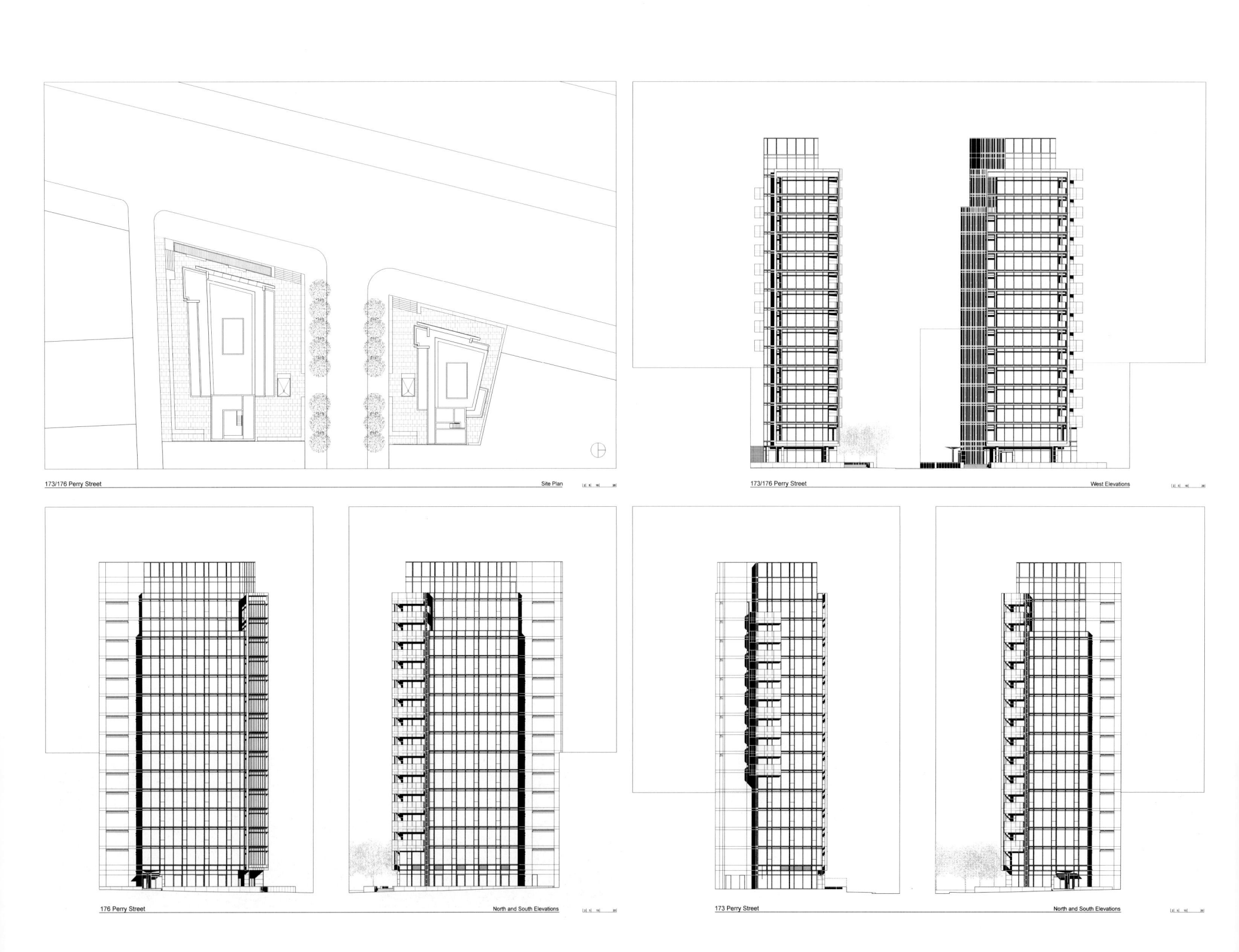

GA PROJECT

These two residential towers located in Greenwich Village mark the first construction in Manhattan by Richard Meier. The 15-story towers stand at the north and south corners of Perry and West Street in the West Village overlooking the Hudson River. Their transparent minimal form makes a striking addition to the New York City skyline.

Each building is clad in insulating laminated glass with white metal-clad framing expressing the individual floor plates. The apartments are afforded with unobstructed panoramic views of Manhattan, the Hudson River and the New Jersey riverfront. Entering from Perry Street, residents pass beneath a covered canopy to their independent lobbies. Each floor houses individual apartments of approximately 1,800 g.sf. in 173 Perry Street (the North Tower) and 3,750 g.sf. in 176 Perry Street (the South Tower). The mechanical cores are located to the east so as to maximize the striking river views. Operable windows are provided in a modulated, syncopated pattern with perimeter radiant heat allowing for an expansive floor to ceiling glass curtain wall.

176 Perry Street will have a cafe on ground level that will be entered from West Street via a bridge spanning a reflecting pool. This cafe will be open to the public along with an adjacent non-profit art gallery. These public amenities serve to tie the buildings into the vibrant pedestrian life of the neighborhood. The buildings embrace the newly renovated Hudson River Park, a network of green and paved open spaces providing a promenade for walkers, joggers, bicyclists and rollerbladers all the way from Battery Park City to 59th Street.

グリニッチ・ヴィレッジに計画されている，2棟のタワーから成る高層アパートは，リチャード・マイヤーにとって，マンハッタンに実現する最初の建物となる。15階建てのタワーは，ハドソン川を見晴らすウエスト・ヴィレッジの，ペリー・ストリートとウエスト・ストリートの角に建てられる。その透明で，ミニマルな姿はニューヨークのスカイラインに印象的な存在として加わるだろう。

2棟の外壁仕上げは白の金属製枠組みと断熱処理された合わせガラスで構成され，ガラスを通して各階の床が外からも見える。各戸からは，マンハッタン，ハドソン川，ニュージャージー側の川岸の景色が一望に見晴らせる。ペリー・ストリートからキャノピーの下を抜け，各戸専用のロビーに出る。一戸の床面積は，173ペリー・ストリート（ノース・タワー）で約1,800平方フィート，176ペリー・ストリート（サウス・タワー）で約3,750平方フィートである。川の素晴らしい眺めを最大限生かすため，機械設備を収めたコアは東側に配置する。周縁部の幅射熱に備えて，開閉できる窓を，位置をずらしながらリズミカルに配置し，床から天井の高さまでを広く覆うガラス・カーテン・ウォールを可能とした。

サウス・タワーの1階にはカフェがあり，ウエスト・ストリートからリフレクティング・プールに渡されたブリッジを通って入る。カフェは，隣接する非営利のアート・ギャラリーと共に，一般の人にも開放される。こうした公共的なアメニティは，この建物を近隣の活気に満ちた歩行者の動きに結びつける役割を果たす。建物はまた，新しく補修されたハドソン・リバー・パークも取り込んでいる。緑と舗装されたオープン・スペースのネットワークが，歩く人，ジョギングする人，自転車の人，ローラーブレードで行く人たちに，バッテリー・パーク・シティーから59番街まで続く遊歩道を提供する。

Architect: Richard Meier & Partners, Architects—Richard Meier, Don Cox, principal-in-charge; Carlos Tan, project architect; Chris Ford, Kevin Hamlett, Kevin Lee, Hans Put, Adrian Ulrich, project team
Client: West Perry, LLC
Consultants: Robert Silman & Associates, structural; Ambrosino, DePinto & Schmieder, mechanical; Fisher Marantz Stone, lighting; Ove Arup & Partners, energy & acoustics; Vignelli Associates, building graphics
General contractor: Gotham Construction Corp.
Structural system: reinforced cast in place concrete with flat plate system
Major materials: architectural concrete, metal panel, glass curtainwall
Site area: 14,429 sq.ft.
Total floor area: 100,459 sq.ft. (15 stories each building)
Costs: $30 million of construction

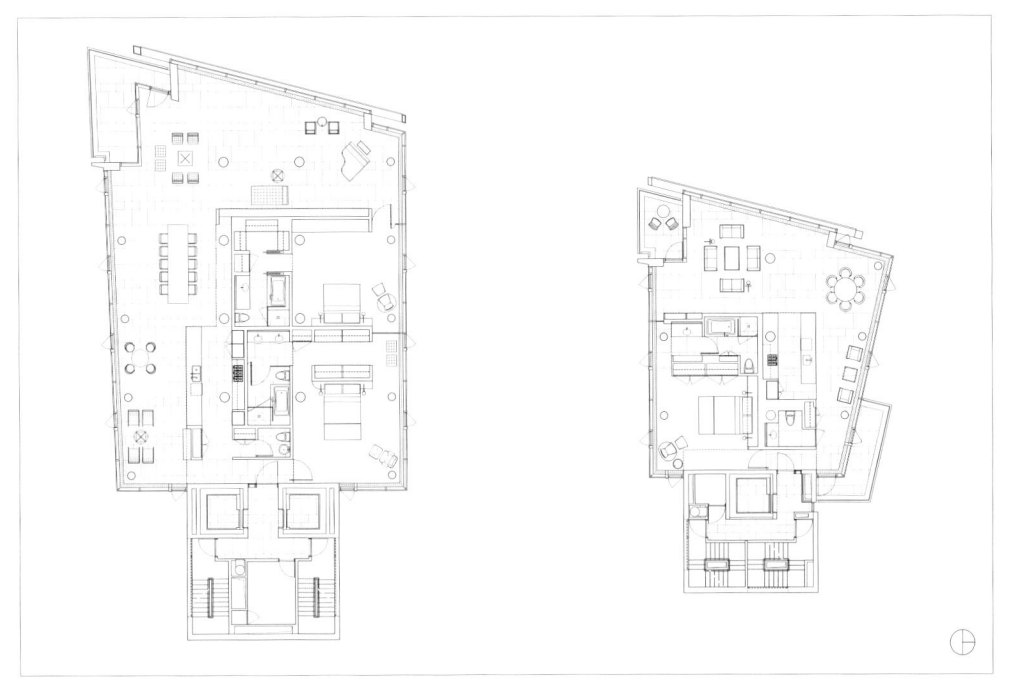

Model photo: Jock Pottle/©Esto

173/176 Perry Street — Typical Plans

Interior view

BERNARD TSCHUMI

SCHOOL OF ARCHITECTURE, FLORIDA INTERNATIONAL UNIVERSITY
Miami, Florida, U.S.A. Design: 1999–2001 Construction: 2001–02

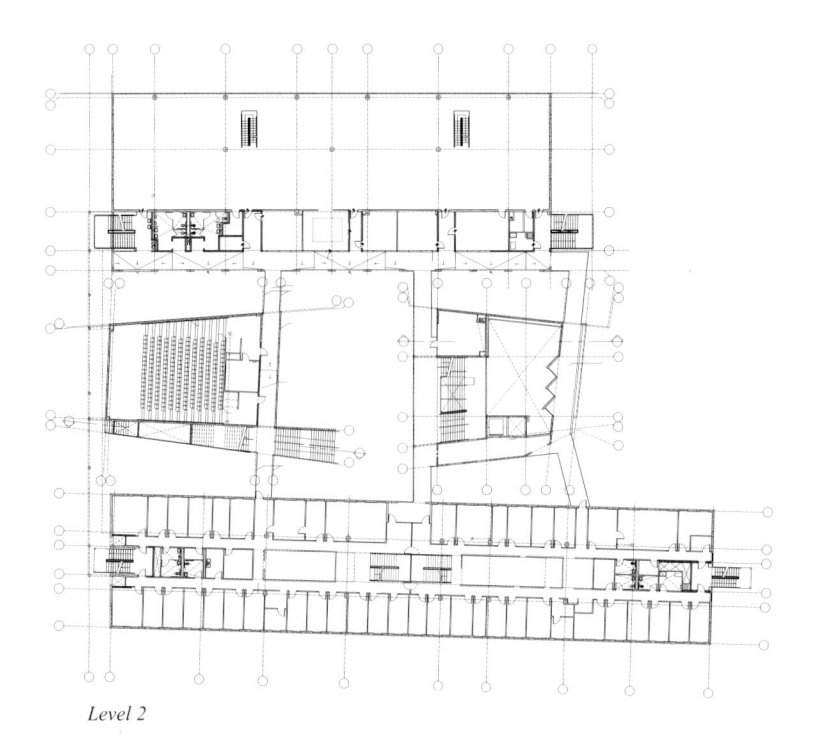

Key for a school of architecture is the ability to set a stage, a scene, a culture and to become identified with it. What a building does is of equal importance to what it looks like; it activates spaces as well as defines them.

The project starts from the thesis that there are buildings that are generators of events and interaction. Two sober wings, made of precise yet user-friendly pre-cast concrete, define a space activated by the exuberance of three colorful "generators," formed of, respectively, varied yellow ceramic tiles, varied red ceramic tiles, and nature (Royal palm trees).

The requested programmed activities of the school are arranged around a 60 by 90 foot central courtyard, animated by the two tiled generators on either side, one containing a lecture hall, the other, an art gallery and reading room. Review rooms and a demonstration room overlook the courtyard so that it becomes a space for encounters and debates, celebrations and balls, end-of-year exhibitions, serious symposia, and avant-garde exhibitions. Gathering together the school circulation and major social and cultural spaces, the central generators shade the courtyard during the morning and late afternoon hours. Studios, classrooms, faculty offices and administration arranged in the two wings open onto the large communal, multi-purpose courtyard, lending dynamism to the whole.

In contrast to the linear rigor of the wings, the three volumes challenge the poetry of the right angle. Here, the movement of bodies in space and deflected wind has informed form, defining the geometry of the envelopes of the red and yellow generators with warped surfaces and fluid irregularities. The materials chosen for construction reflect both the required economy of the project budget and specific climate conditions, e.g. concrete for high heat temperatures and broad expanses of glass with southern light for the studios.

Architects: Bernard Tschumi Architects (New York)—Bernard Tschumi, principal-in-charge; Anne Save de Beaurecueil, Johanne Riegels Oestergaard, Valentin Bontjes van Beek, Robert Holton, Joel Rutten, Kim Starr, Roderick Villanova, project team
Associated architect: Bruno-Elias Associates (Miami)—Brunc-Elias Ramos, Gustavo Berenblum, Susan Lauredo, Andrew Sribyatta, J.P. Alvarez, project team
Client: Dean William McMinn, dean of School of Architecture of Florida International University
Consultants: Bruno-Elias Associates, structural; Tilden Lobnitz Cooper Engineers, mechanical; Charles Alden, landscape; David Harvey, audiovisual/acoustic
Structural systems: precast concrete
Major materials: concrete, ceramic tiles, glazing
Total Floor Area: 92,000 sq.ft.
Costs: $12,570,000

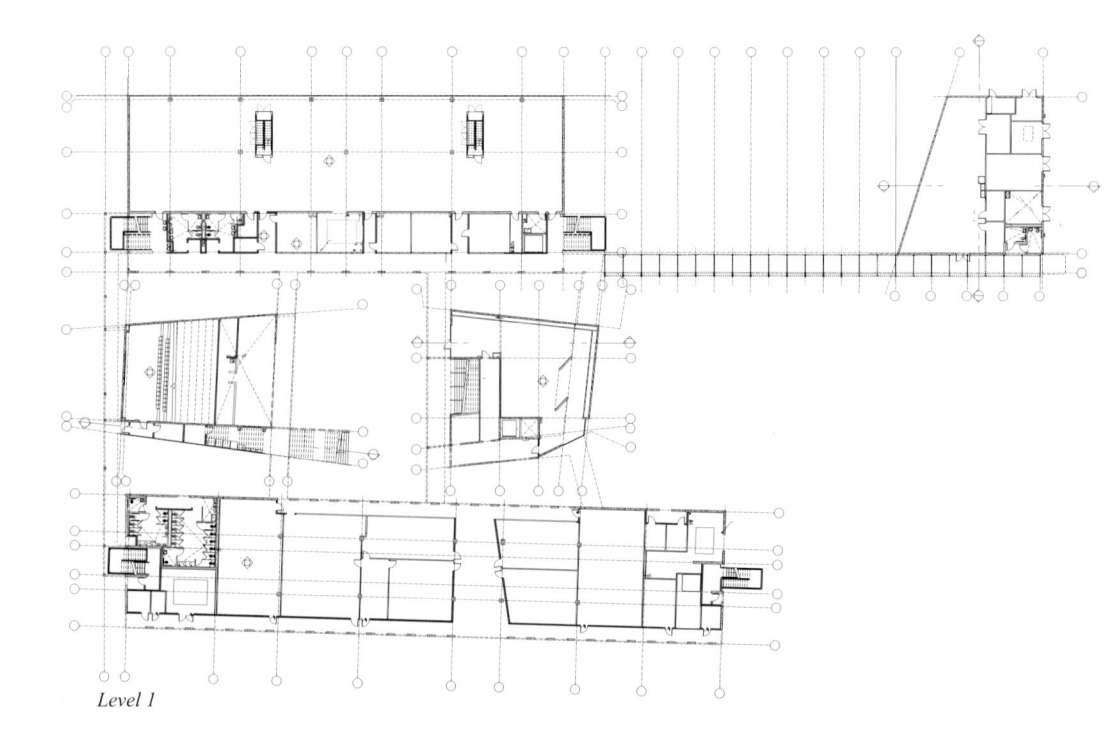

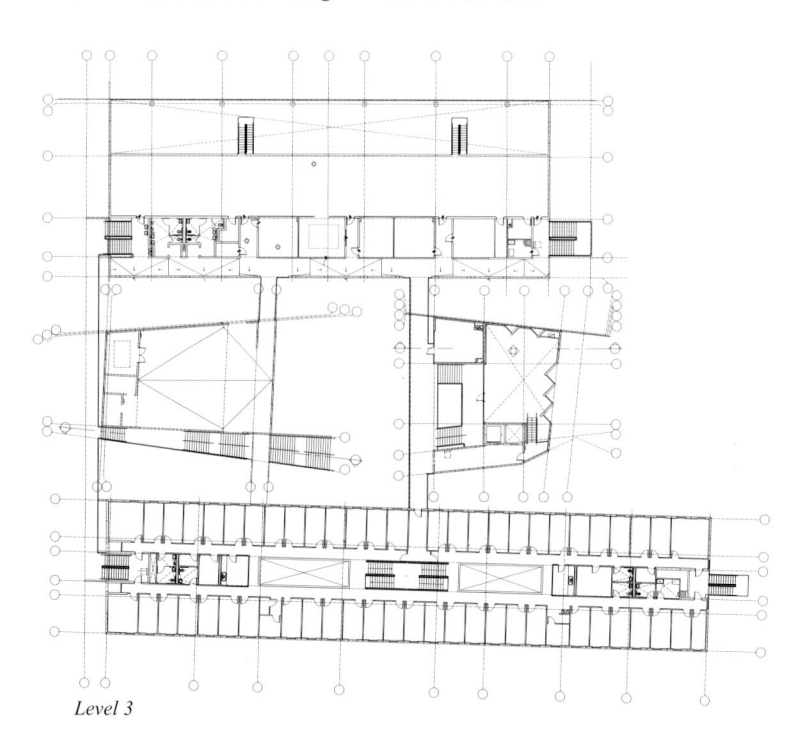

Level 2

Level 1

Level 3

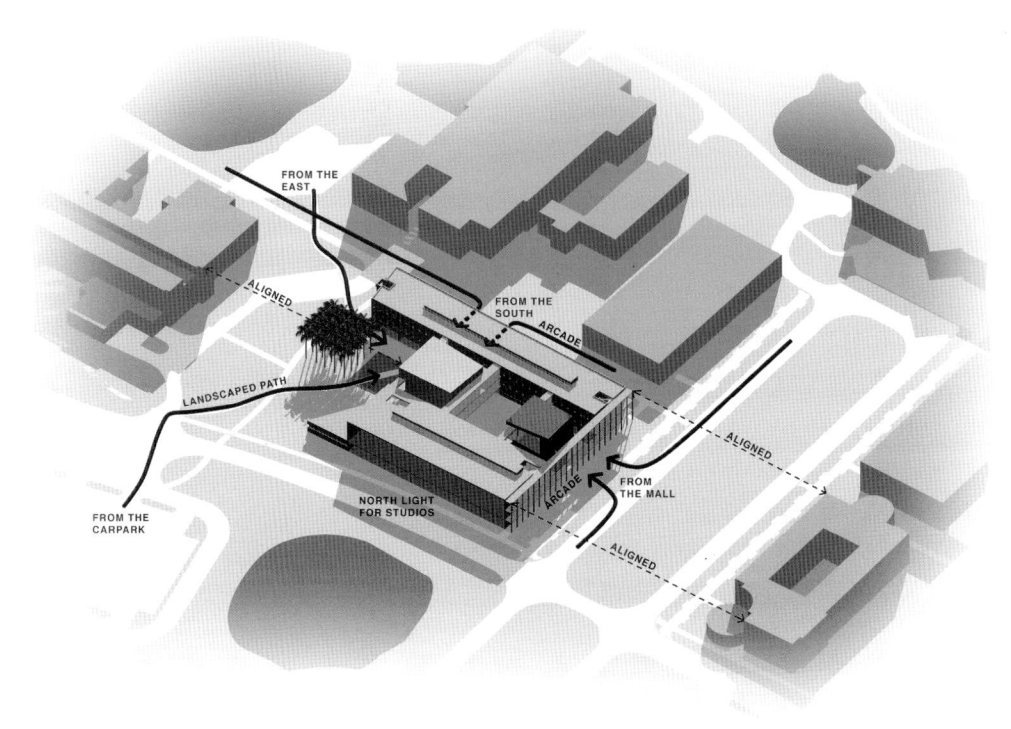

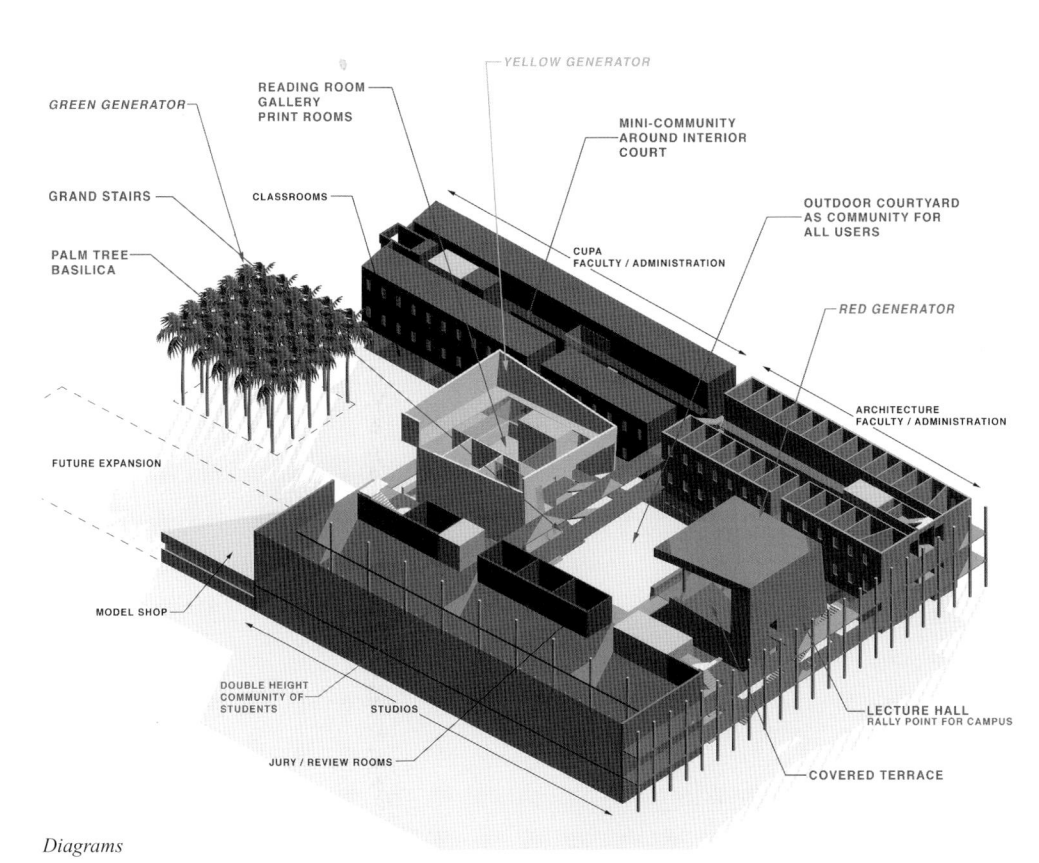

学校建築の鍵は、ある舞台、ある情景、ある文化を設定し、それと結びつける能力にある。建物が何をするかは、建物が何のように見えるかと同様に重要なのだ。それは空間を定義すると同時に活気づけてくれる。

このプロジェクトは、様々なイベントや交流の発生装置（ジェネレイター）である建物が存在するという命題から出発する。厳格な構成だが使いやすい、プレキャスト・コンクリート造の、地味な2つの翼棟が規定する空間を、3つの鮮やかな色調を持つ"ジェネレイター"が活気づける。"ジェネレイター"は、それぞれ、変化に富む黄色のセラミック・タイル、変化に富む赤いセラミック・タイル、自然（ダイオウヤシ）でかたちづくられている。

学校側が要求している活動プログラムは、60×90フィートの中央コートヤードの周囲に配置される。その両側に位置するタイル貼りの2つの"ジェネレイター"が中央コートを生き生きとさせる。ジェネレイターの一方にはレクチャー・ホール、一方にはアート・ギャラリーと読書室が置かれている。いくつかの講評室、公開授業室はコートヤードを見下ろせる位置にある。こうして、中央コートは出会いや論争、祝祭や舞踏会、学年末の展覧会、堅いテーマのシンポジウム、前衛的な展覧会などが生まれ、行われる空間となる。校内のサーキュレーション、そして交流や文化的活動が集中する主要空間にあって、中央の"ジェネレイター"はコートに差し込む朝日や夕日を遮る。共有され、全体にダイナミズムを添加するこの広い多目的コートに面した2つの翼棟は、スタジオ、教室、教員室、事務室である。

翼棟を構成する厳格な線形とは対比的に、3つのジェネレイターはこの"直角の詩"に挑戦する。ここで、空間内の人の動きと、屈折して流れる風は特徴のある形を描き、赤と黄色の"ジェネレイター"を包む被膜のジオメトリーに、表面の歪みと流動的な不規則性を付与する。選択された建築材料は、要求された工事予算の経済性と固有の気候条件を反映したものである。たとえば、非常に高い温度に対してはコンクリートを、スタジオに南の光を採り入れるためには広いガラス面を用いている。

Diagrams

PROGRAMMATIC CARVING: ELEVATOR LOBBY

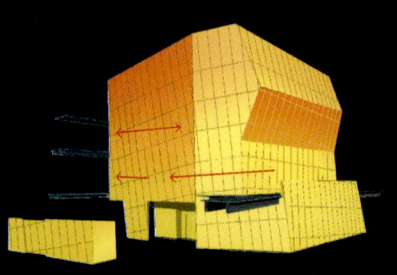

PROGRAMMATIC CARVING: VIEW-LIGHT PENETRATIONS

PROGRAMMATIC MOVEMENT VECTORS: CARVINGS
→ WALKWAY-ELEVATOR LOBBY ACCESS

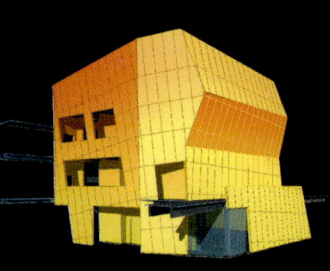

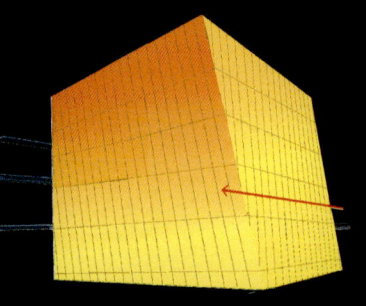

PROGRAMMATIC MOVEMENT VECTORS-CARVINGS
→ WALKWAY-MOVEMENT BETWEEN WINGS
→ SHORT-CUT PATH

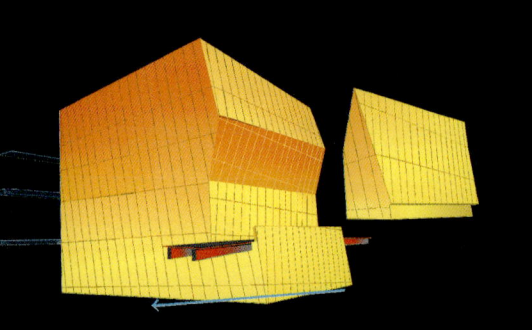

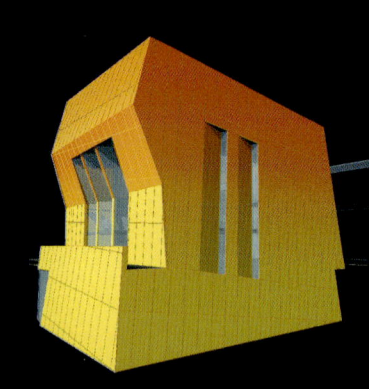

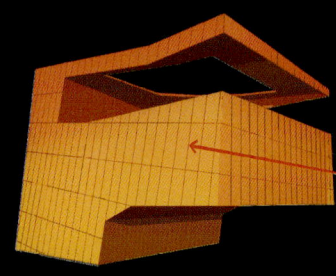

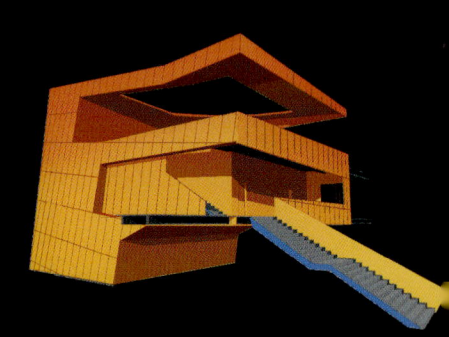

PROGRAMMATIC MOVEMENT VECTORS
→ WALKWAY -MOVEMENT BETWEEN WINGS
→ STAIRWAY-MOVEMENT BETWEEN COURTYARD & TERRACE

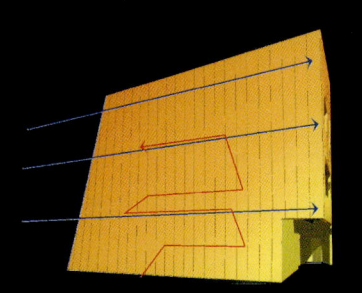

PROGRAMMATIC MOVEMENT VECTORS: CARVINGS
→ WALKWAY-MOVEMENT BETWEEN WINGS
→ MOVEMENT OF SPIRAL STAIRS

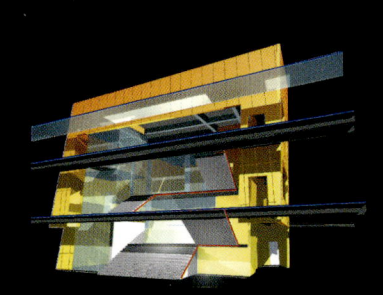

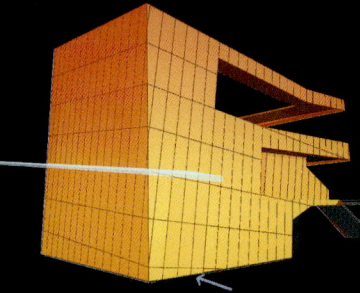

PROGRAMMATIC MOVEMENT VECTORS
→ STAIRWAY-MOVEMENT BETWEEN ARCADE AND TERRACE
→ ENTRANCE PENETRATION

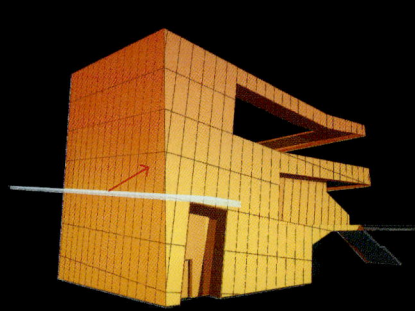

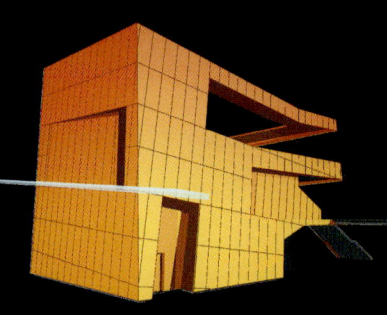

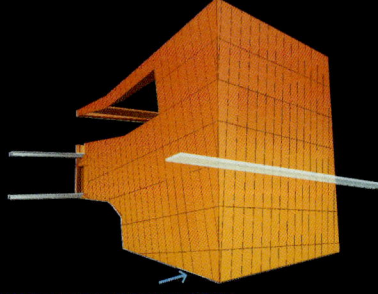

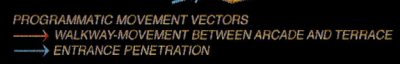

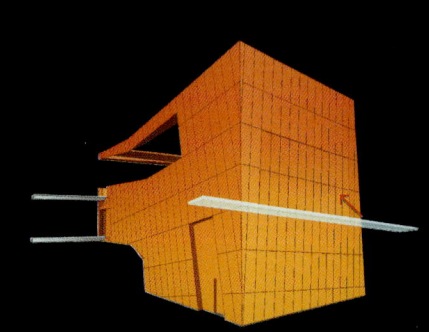

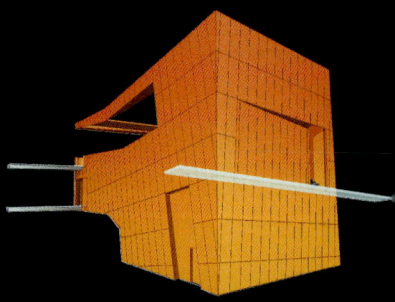

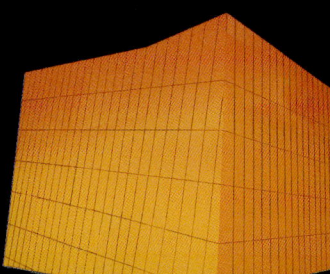

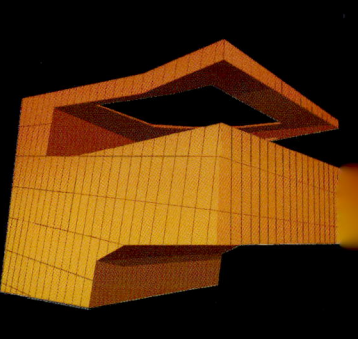

PROGRAMMATIC MOVEMENT VECTORS
→ WALKWAY-MOVEMENT BETWEEN ARCADE AND TERRACE
→ ENTRANCE PENETRATION

PROGRAMMATIC CARVINGS   COURTYARD-TERRACE ANIMATION

GA PROJECT

TRANSFORMATION SEQUENCE

Flows inform form... The digitally simulated flows of the movement of people from the south campus, the north parking lot, and the Mall have informed and shaped the envelope of the "generator" volumes. Likewise, simulated prevailing wind flows have molded wind tunnels into these volumes, creating channels of air flow, cooling and ventilating the courtyard and buildings.

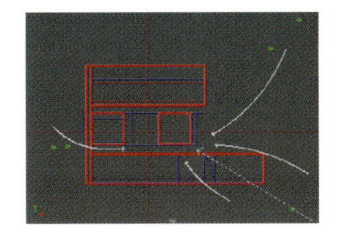

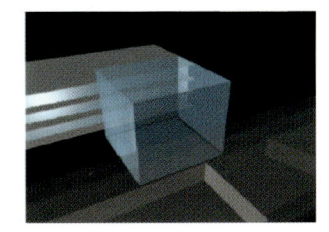

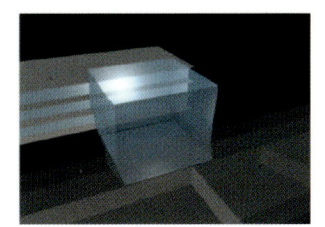

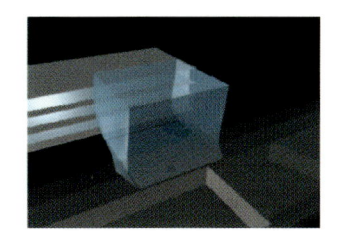

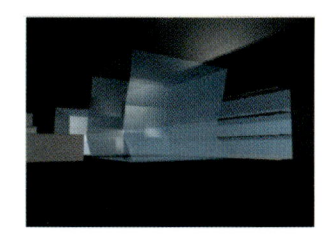

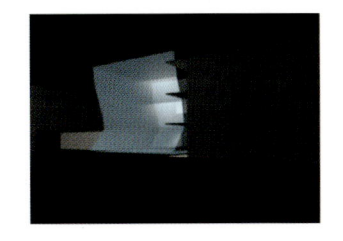

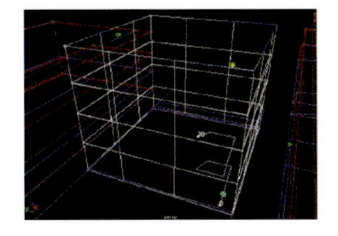

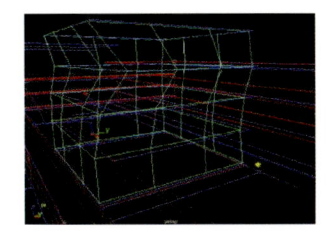

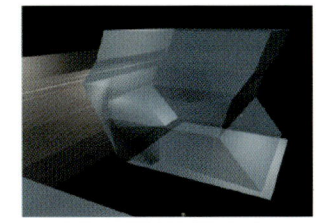

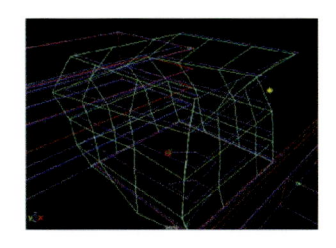

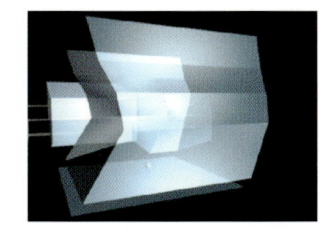

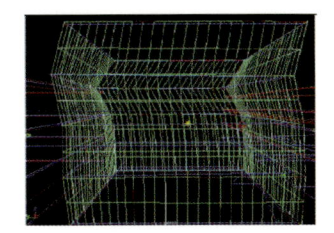

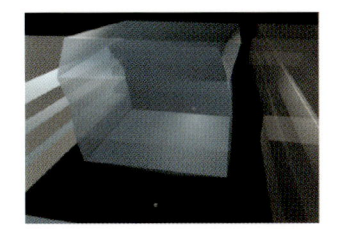

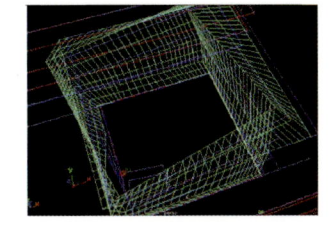

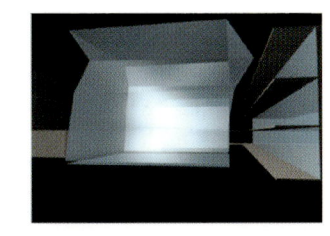

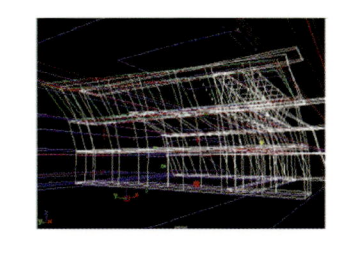

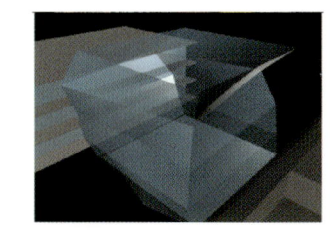

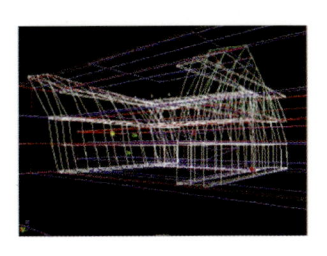

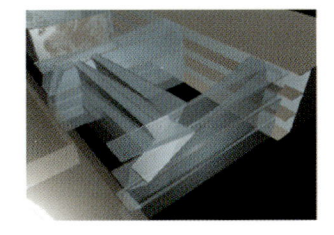

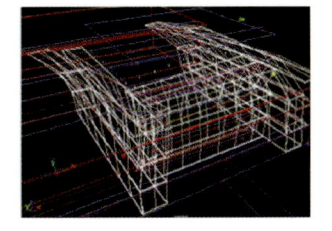

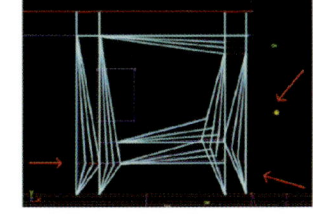

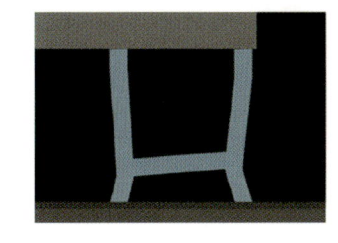

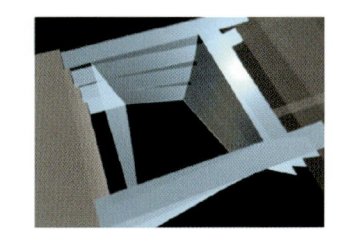

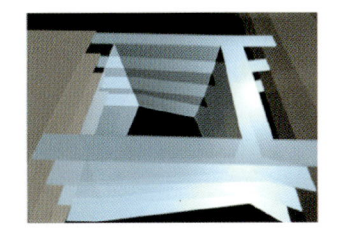

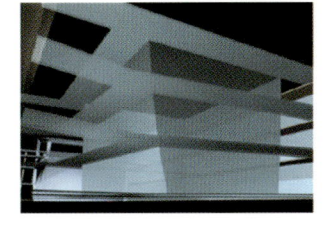

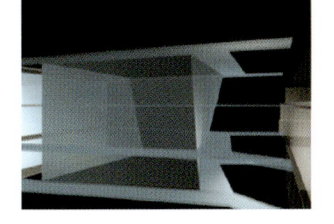

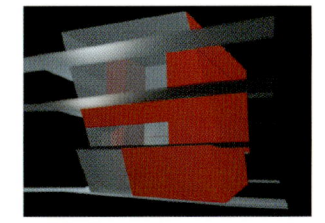

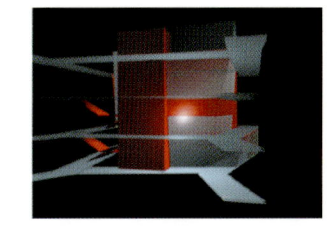

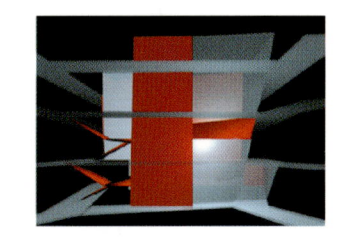

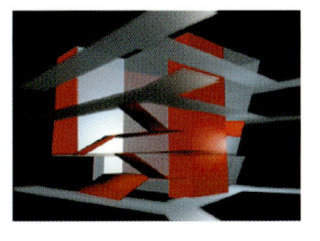

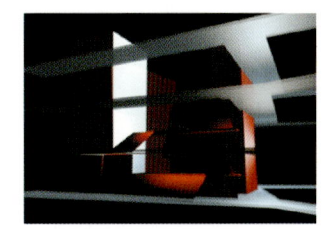

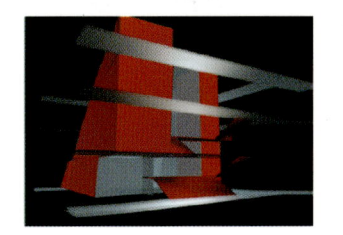

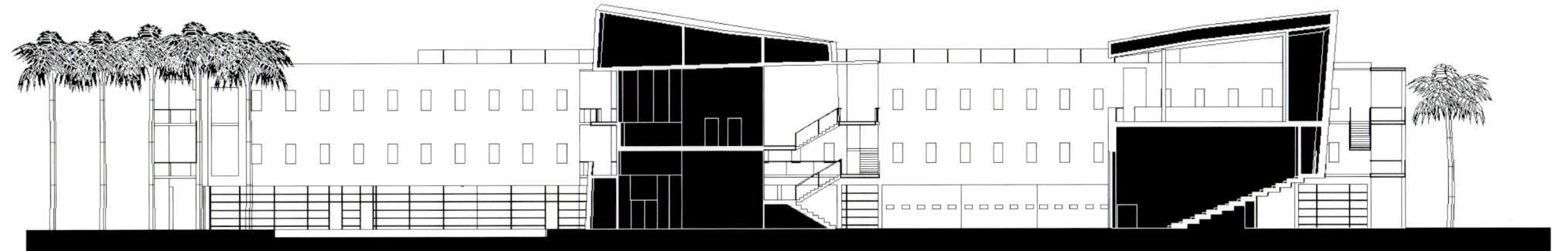

Section

MOVEMENT SEQUENCE

From the University gate to Lecture Hall [frames 1 to 4]; through the Exterior Courtyard [frames 5 to 7]; to the car park [frames 7 to 9]; to the Main Entrance of SOA and CUPA [frames 10 to 12]; through the Exterior Courtyard [frames 13 to 16]; through the Office wing [frames 17 to 19]; through the Studio wing [frames 20 to 23]; towards the sky [frames 24 to 26].

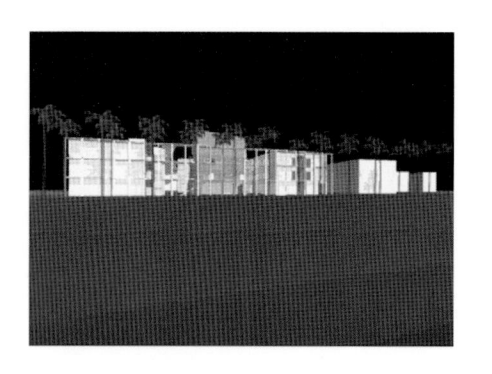

GA PROJECT

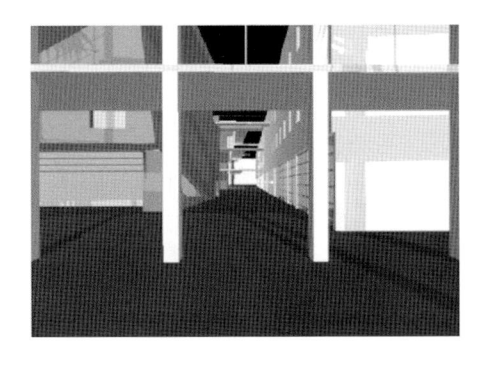

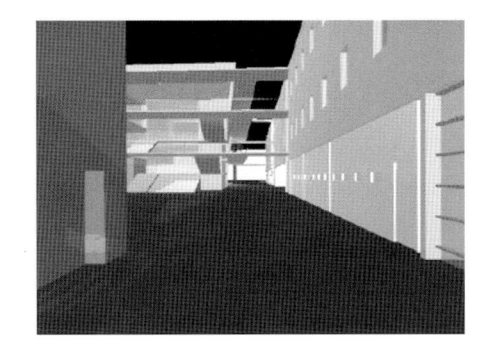

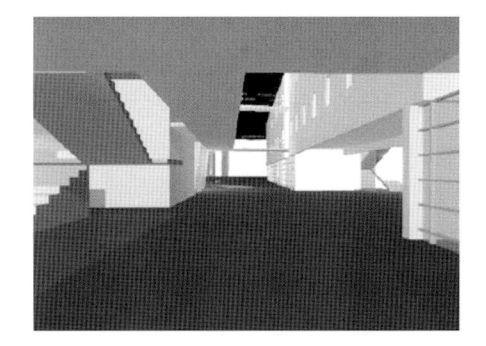

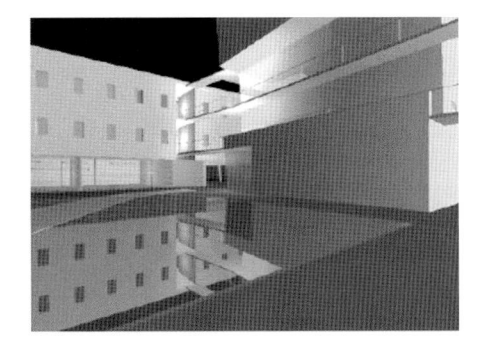

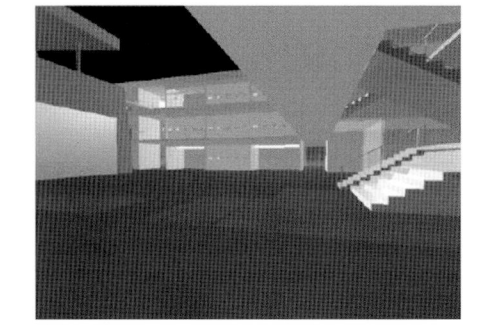

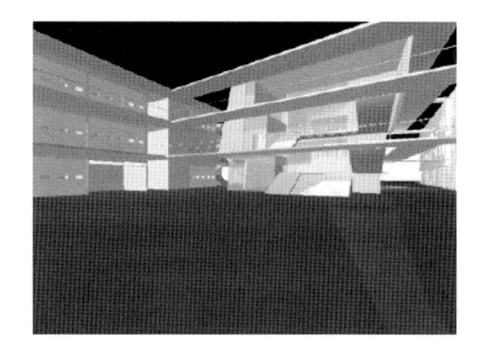

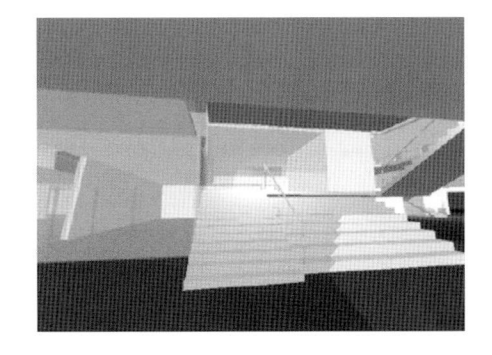

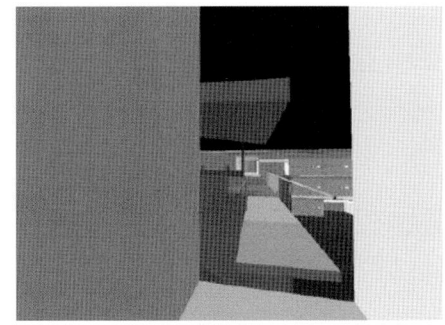

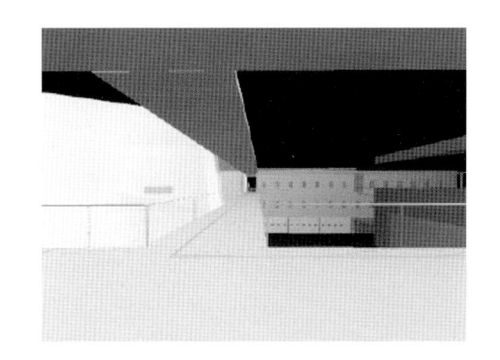

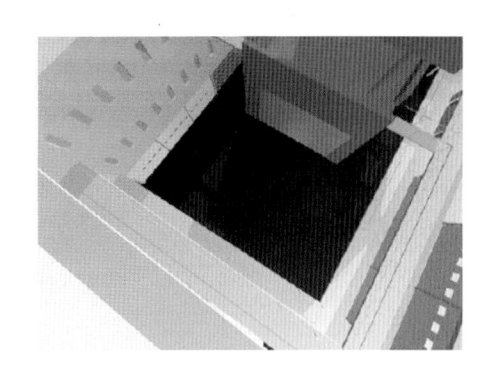

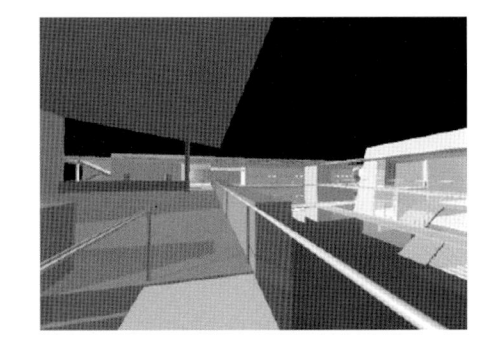

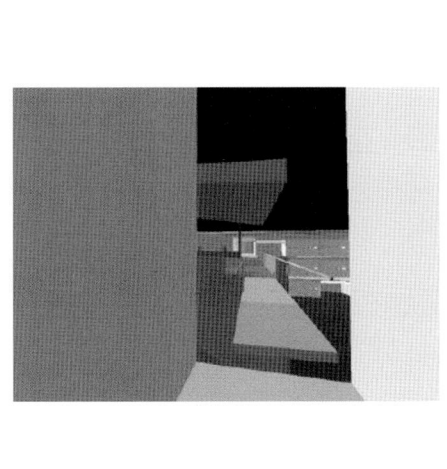

HIROSHI HARA

NEW PALACE OF THE REGION IN TORINO
Turin, Italy Design: 2000–01

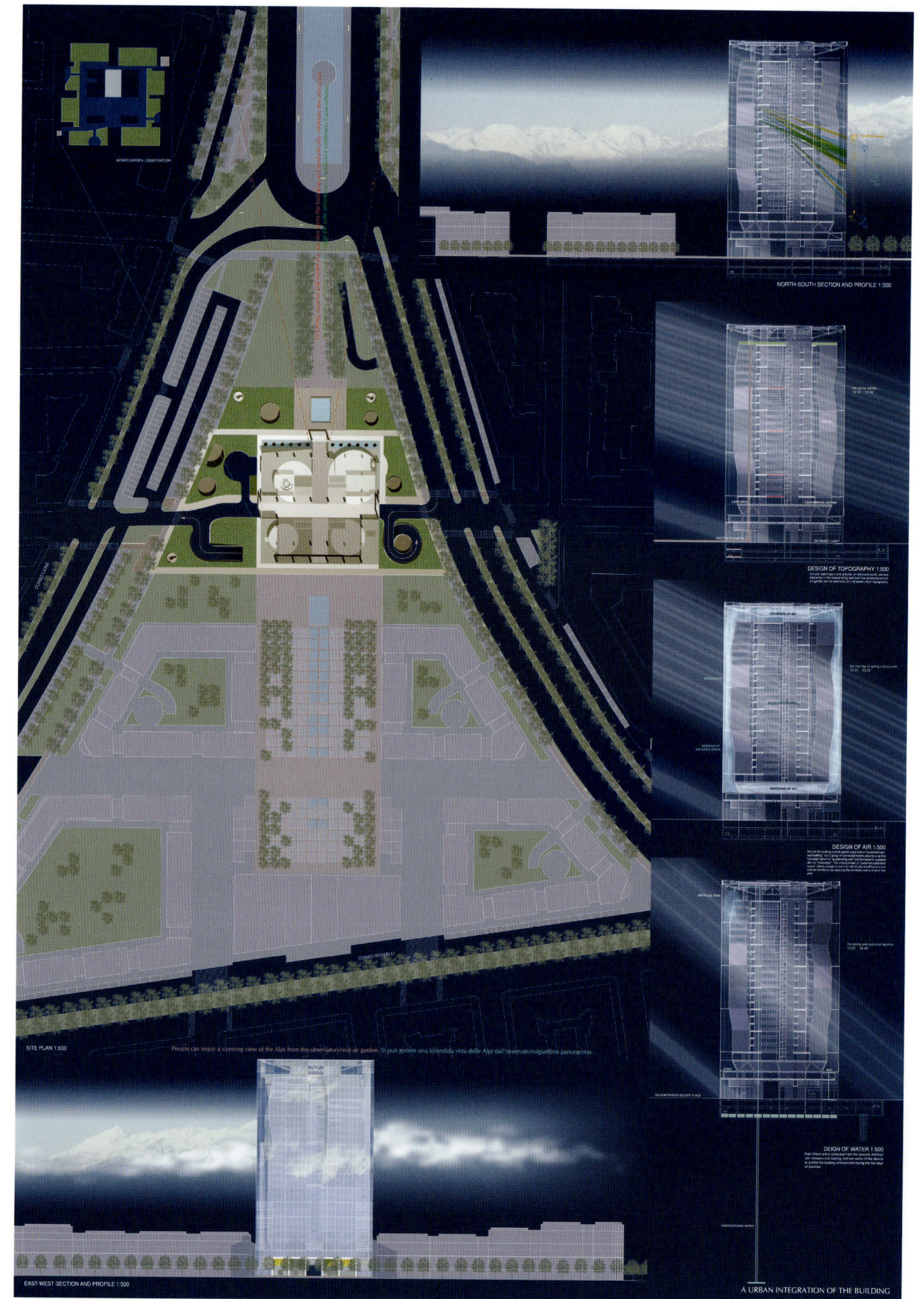

Urban integration of the building

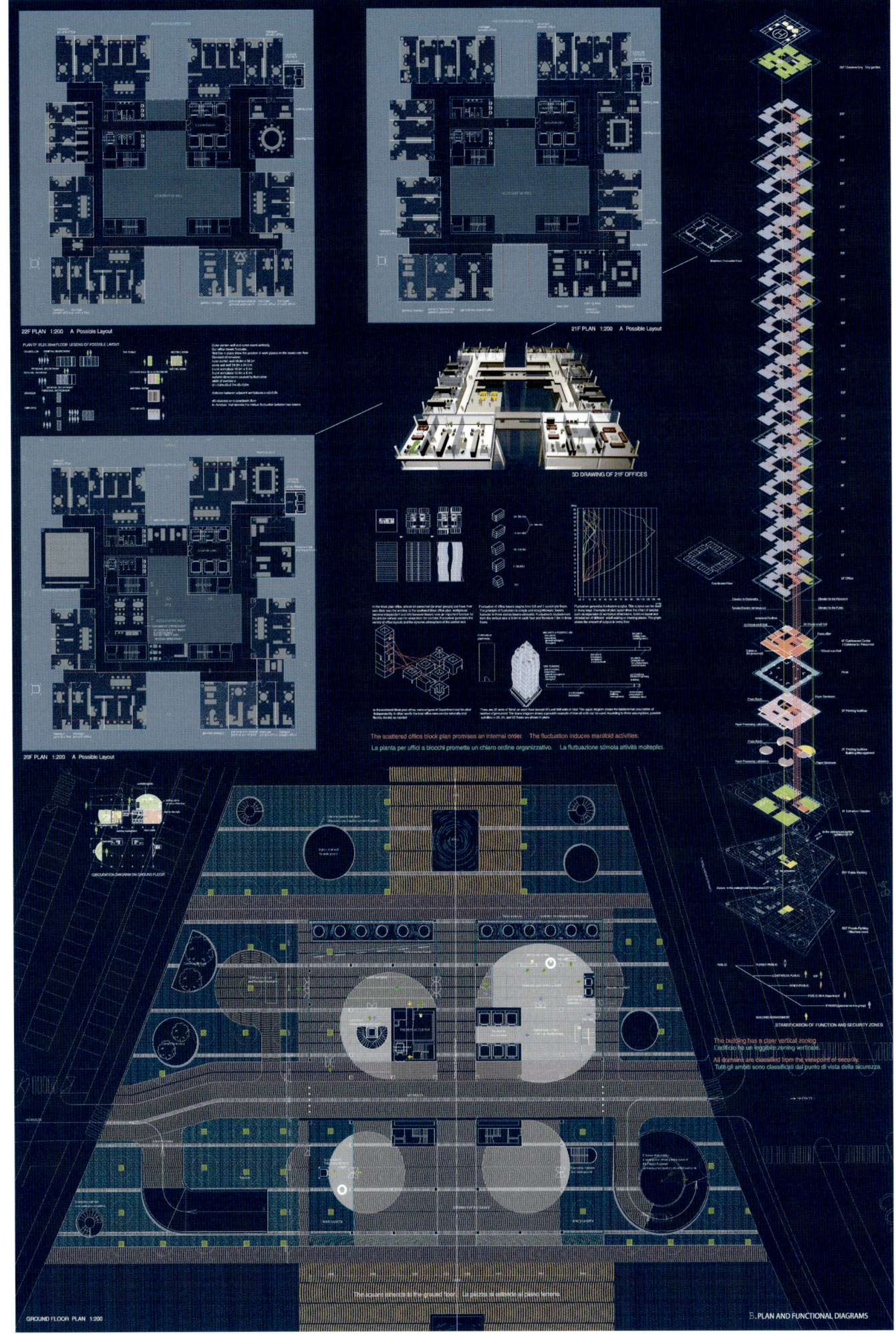

Plan and functional diagrams

The project was originally an entry for a competition for the public office building of the region of Piemonte in Italy. The competition took place in February 2001, where the first prize was given to Fuksas' proposal, the second to mine, and the third to Jean Nouvel's.

This proposal features a group of high-rise office towers arranged dispersively within a glass curtain wall (Moderator). Between the office towers and the Moderator is the 'Moderated Space' that makes use of natural forces. Whereas conventional high-rise buildings' space makeup may be characterized as
exterior / interior
this plan may be described as
exterior / *moderated space / interior
with /* representing the Moderator.

The Moderator is composed of fixed glass sheets and movable glass louvers. Louvers and air-conditioning facilities are controlled automatically by the 'sensor group' that detects various values from external and internal climates. The entire mechanism is called 'climatological device'. Windows may be opened and shut at the office user's will. 'Moderated Space' contains two paths of airflow, 'Underpath' and 'Overpath', that basically involve vertical motion. In winter time, air is heated in the south side, circulates through the 'Overpath' and comes back to the original position in the south. Such circulatory airflow has already been confirmed by simulated experiments using data from hourly weather observation of Turin during the year 2000. The plan proposed features an 'accelerating well' as part of the climatological device, accounting for effective circulation of various airflow. In the proximity of the 'Underpath' is placed a 'pond' which would cool the air down in summer. At times of extreme high temperatures, rain can be sprayed over this 'pond' from the 'Overpath'. The 'Moderated Space' is thus a newly-created 'micro climate'.

The series of slender, high-rise buildings provide change to the wellhole with 'fluctuation', all the while promoting infiltration of natural light through the buildings. They permeate light according to the seasons with respect to urban axes.

This climatological architecture can be seen as a model variation of Mies van der Rohe's universal space, modified along Buckminster Fuller's idea of urban dome.
Hiroshi Hara

Architects: Hiroshi Hara+Atelier Φ—Hiroshi Hara, Wakana Hara, Tomoaki Ogawa, Koichiro Ishigurro, Francesco Montagnana, Yoshihito Iwasaki, Aya Yamagishi, Satoko Hiraoka, Yoshihiko Yoshihara, Kotoaki Asano
Client: The Region in Torino
Consultant: Sasaki Structure Consultants—Mustsuro Sasaki, Hiroki Kume, structural
Collaborators: Kunitoshihiko Tanahashi, Kazuhiro Tomita, Bruno Zan, Valeria Tatano, Priscilla Giaccone
Structural system: steel frame
Site area: 8,863 m²
Built area: 3,136 m²
Total floor area: 40,026 m²
Stories: 26 floors above grade, 2 floors below grade, maximum height 100m

GA DOCUMENT

このプロジェクトは，2001年2月に審査がなされたイタリアのピエモンテ州庁舎のコンペティションに向けた応募案である。結果はフクサス案が1位，この案が2位，ジャン・ヌヴェル案が3位であった。

この案は，ガラスのカーテンウォール（Moderator）のなかに，離散的に配置された高層のオフィス塔が連立している形式をもっている。オフィス塔群とモデレイターの間には，自然力を活用して「調整された空間（Moderated Space）」がある。従来の高層建築の

　　exterior ｜ interior

という形式に対して

　　exterior ｜ *moderated space ｜ interior

と表記できる形式である。｜*がモデレイターである。

モデレイターは，固定されたガラスと可動ガラスルーバーからなっている。ルーバーと空調設備は，外部の気候と，室内気候の状態を感知する「センサー群」からの情報で，コンピューターによって自動的に動く。この機構の総体は「気候学的装置（climatological device）」と呼ばれる。手許のオフィスの窓は住み手の意志によって，自由に開閉することができる。「調整された空間」には，空気の「アンダーパス」と「オーバーパス」をもっており，主として空気は，鉛直方向に動く。冬期には，南側で暖められた空気は，「オーバーパス」を経て再び南へ戻る巡環が発生する。これらの空気の動きは，シミュレーションによって確認されている。シミュレーションは，トリノの2000年における1時間毎の気候観測データによってなされた。計画案には，「気候学的装置」の一部として，「中央吹き抜け部分（accelerating well）」があり，様々な空気の動きを効果的に促進している。また，「アンダーパス」の周辺には，「池」があり，夏期の空気を冷やす。高温の瞬間には，「オーバーパス」から「池」に向けて霧状の雨を降らせることもできる。つまり，「調整された空間」は，新たに作られた「微気候（micro climate）」である。

細い連立高層建築群は「ゆらぎ（fluctuation）」をもって，吹き抜けに変化を与えると同時に，建物の自然光の透過をうながす。つまり，都市軸に対して，季節に応じた光を透過する。

この気候学的建築は，ミース・ファン・デル・ローエの均質空間を，バックミンスター・フラーの都市ドームの考えに従って，改変したモデルであると考えられる。
　　　　　　　　　　　　　　　　　　（原広司）

Sections

GA PROJECT

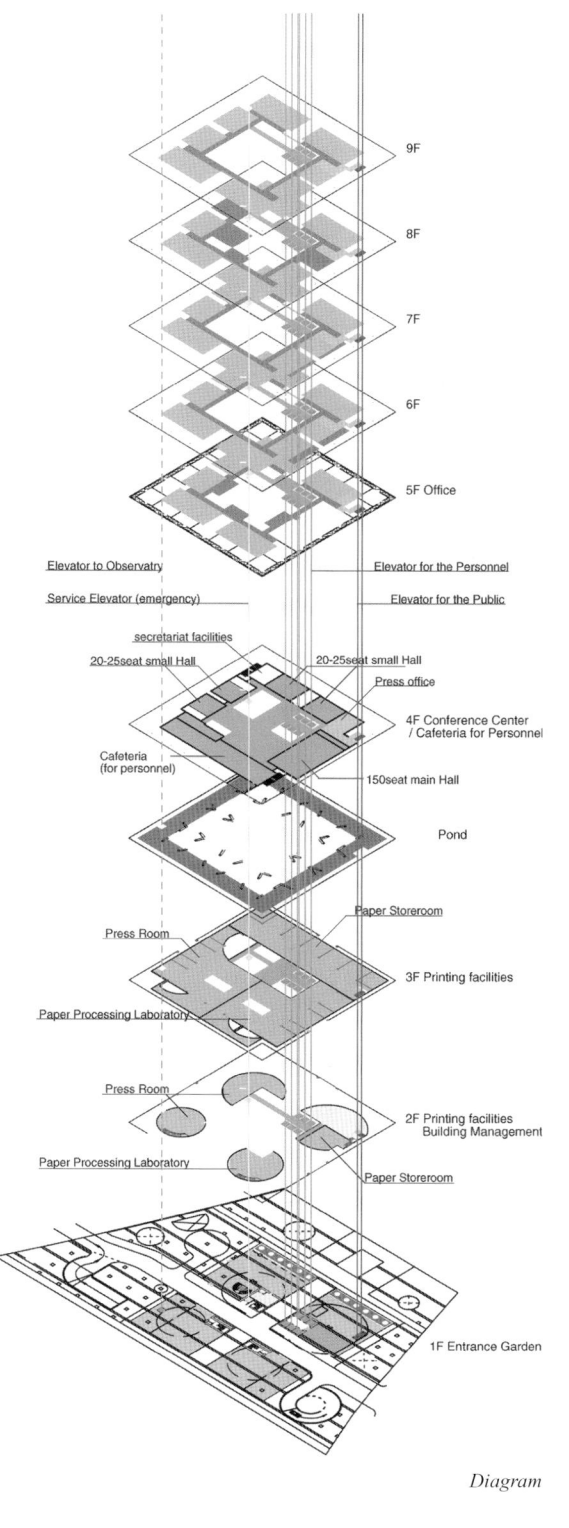

Model photo: H. Ueda

Diagram

- Elevator to Observatry
- Service Elevator (emergency)
- Elevator for the Personnel
- Elevator for the Public

9F

8F

7F

6F

5F Office

secretariat facilities
20-25seat small Hall — 20-25seat small Hall
Press office
4F Conference Center / Cafeteria for Personnel
Cafeteria (for personnel)
150seat main Hall

Pond

Press Room — Paper Storeroom
3F Printing facilities
Paper Processing Laboratory

Press Room
2F Printing facilities / Building Management
Paper Processing Laboratory — Paper Storeroom

1F Entrance Garden

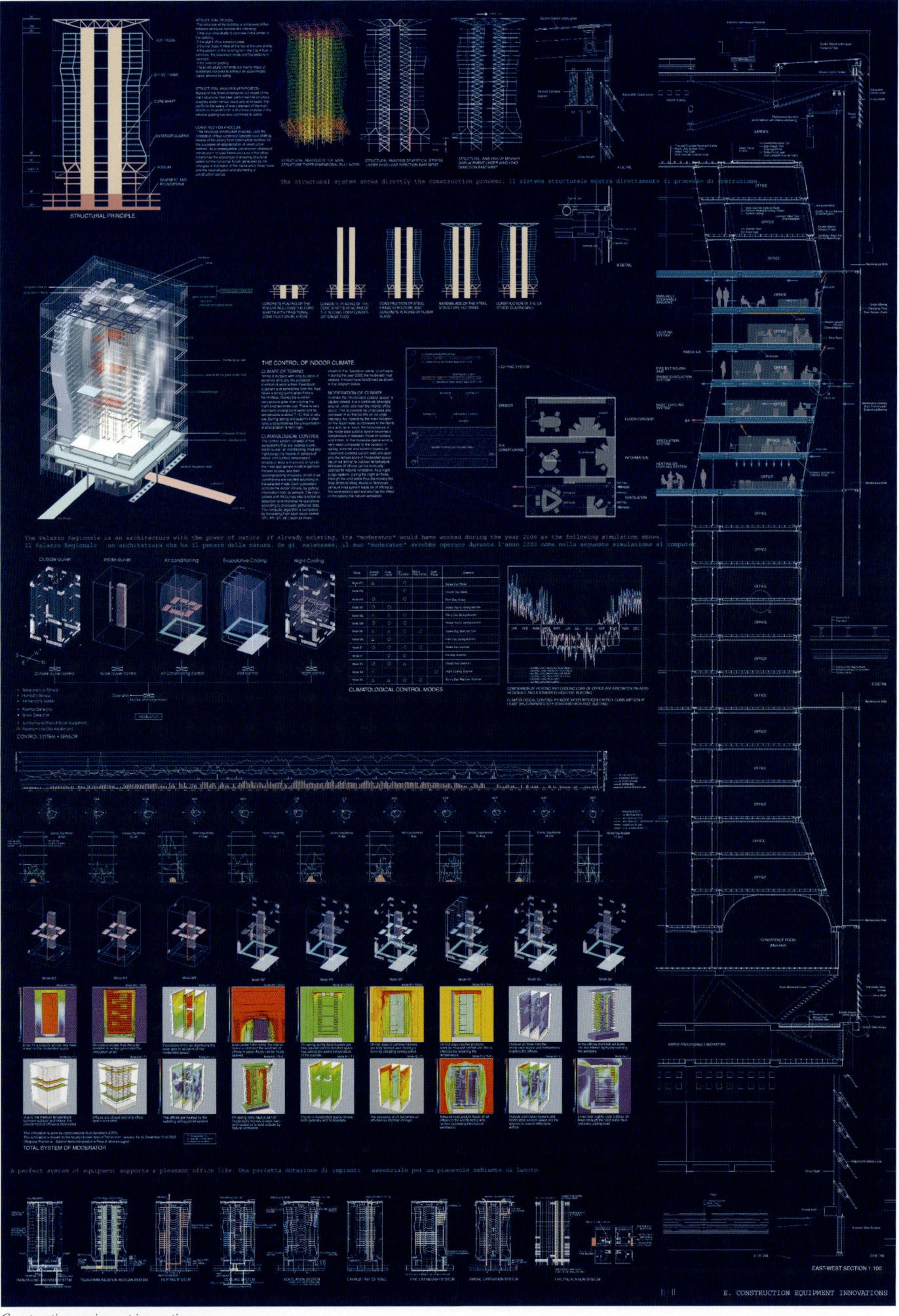

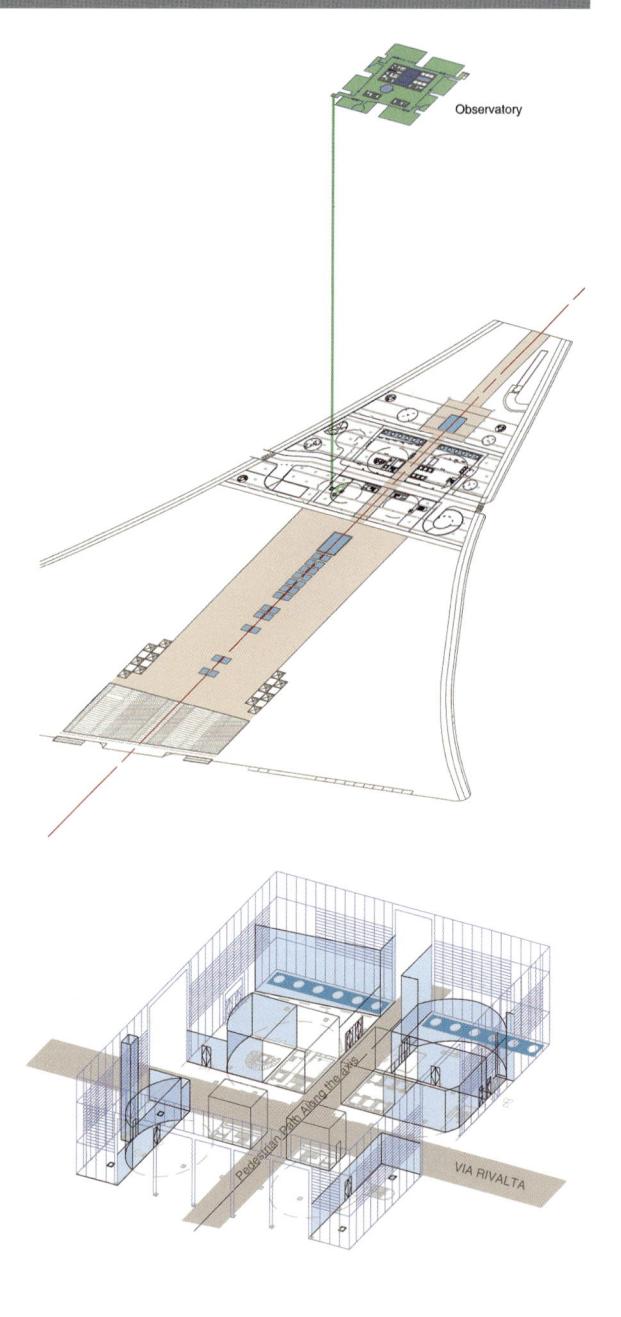

Construction equipment innovations

SHIN TAKAMATSU+MAMORU KAWAGUCHI

TIANJIN GREAT MUSEUM
Tianjin, China Design: 2000

West elevation

North elevation

The city of Tianjin is situated approximately 140km southeast of Peking. Like most cities in China, it is now experiencing an unprecedented construction boom. The structural engineer Mamoru Kawaguchi has invited me to join him in entering for the 'International Design Competition for the Museum of Tianjin' hosted by the city of Tianjin. Our collaboration was a success and hit the bull's-eye.

The city's request for this building was clear and simple to the extreme: 'an architecture as a symbol of a new city'. The heaviness of this assignment has lead us through a series of trial and error until we have come up with a proposal for an architectural form with a sufficiently overwhelming power. Finally, a highly primitive solution was derived, in which a large-space structural system would determine the architecture's overall form.

Structure was fully determined by geometry based on spherical surfaces, which made it possible to design all of the details within a single system. A shell with a diameter of 200m and height of 34m is sliced off by a glass surface which narrows itself as it falls down into water with a diameter of 130m. It was only at the last moment before deadline that the image of a 'SWAN' has suddenly struck me. The swan-like shell would then be finished with snow-white ceramic tiles, and be named 'SWANIUM'.

We were given notice at the end of February that our proposal has won the competition, and that actual construction works would begin in three month's time, in May. The news has stirred an upheaval among us. But it is more likely that such upheaval is the very energy of this city and of China today. Our mission is now clear and evident—to synchronize ourselves with this dynamism without a moment's delay.
Shin Takamatsu

Museum exterior

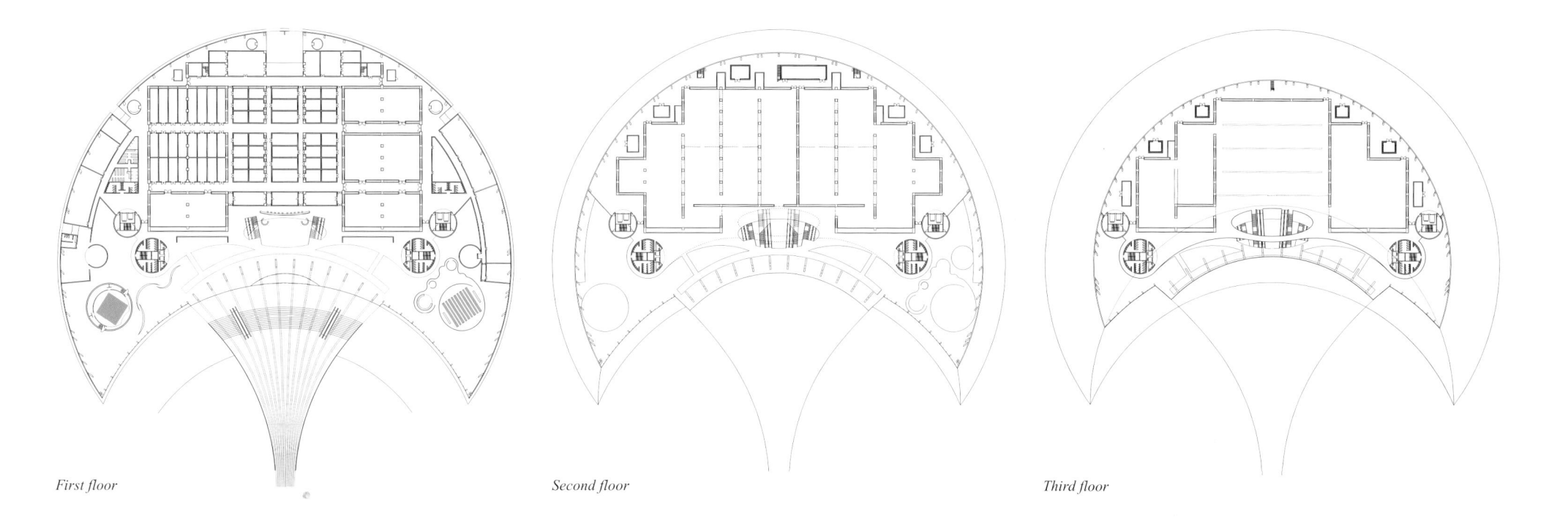

First floor

Second floor

Third floor

West elevation

北京市の南東約140キロメートルに位置する天津市は，中国の他の都市の例に漏れず，現在史上空前の建設ラッシュのただ中にある。その天津市が主催する「天津博物館国際指名設計競技」に，構造家・川口衛氏のお誘いを受け共同で参加し，金的を射止めた。

この建築に対する市の要請は，過激なまでに明解かつ簡潔である。即ち「新たな都市の象徴としての建築」。この重い課題に圧倒的な力強さで応答するに足る建築の形態を提案するべく，試行錯誤を繰り返した。結果的に，大空間を架構する構造システムが全面的に建築のフォルムを決定する，極めてプリミティブな回答を得た。

構造は全て球面に基づく幾何学によって決定され，これによってあらゆる細部の全てを単一のシステムで意匠することが可能となる。直径200メートル，高さ34メートルのシェルを削ぎ落とすようになだれ打つガラス面が，細く狭まりながら直径130メートルの水中をくぐるフォルムに，唐突に「SWAN」をイメージしたのは提出も間近になってからである。その白鳥の似姿のままに，シェルを純白のセラミックタイルで仕上げることにし，その名も「SWANIUM」とした。

コンペ当選の通知を受けたのが2月末。同時に着工が3ヵ月後の5月であることを知った。震天動地である。が，この震天動地こそおそらく現在の中国の，そしてこの都市のエネルギーなのだ。我々の使命は明白である。即ちこのダイナミズムと一刻も早くシンクロナイズすることである。　　　（高松伸）

Entrance

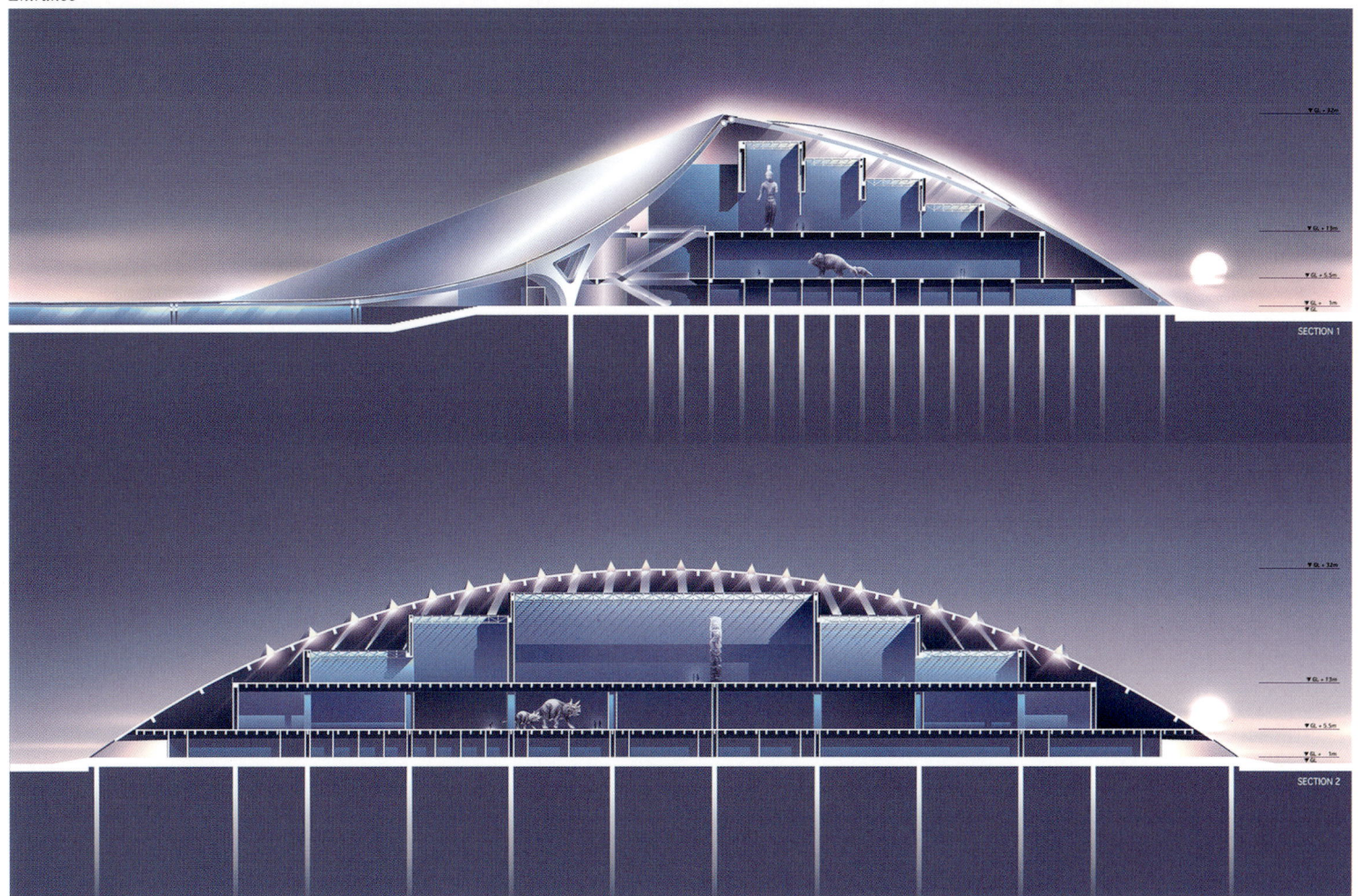

Architects: Shin Takamatsu+Mamoru Kawaguchi—Shin Takamatsu, Mamoru Kawaguchi, principals-in-charge; Taiyo Jinno, Anna Nakamura, Yuushi Aso, Xiaodun Wang, Zhihua Chen, project team
Client: Tianjin city

Sections

MORPHOSIS

UNIVERSITY OF CINCINNATI STUDENT RECREATION CENTER
Cincinnati, Ohio, U.S.A. Design: 1999

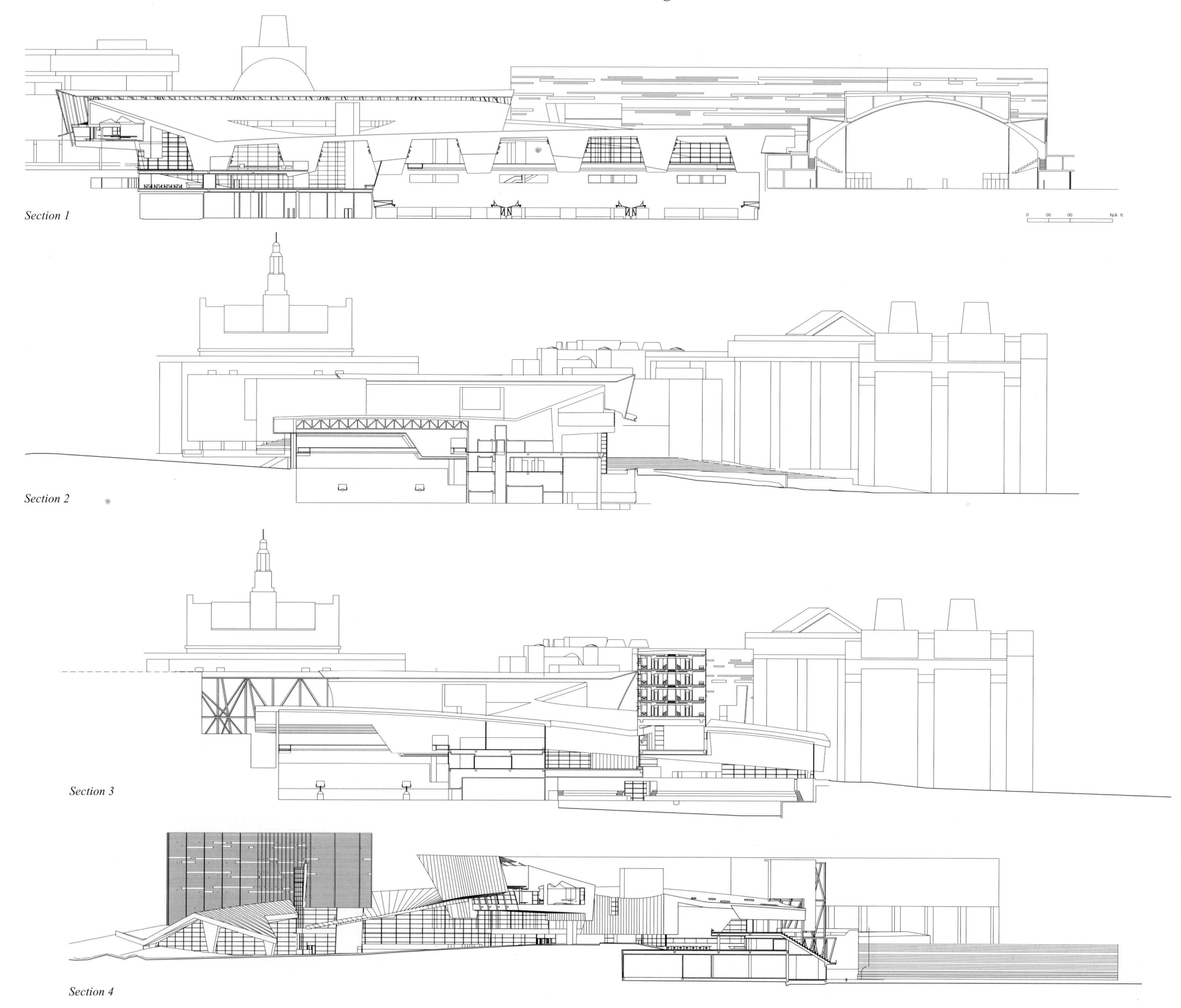

Section 1

Section 2

Section 3

Section 4

Site
University of Cincinnati Campus, Cincinnati, Ohio

Program
350,000 sq.ft. includes a recreation center (2 pools, basketball gymnasium, racquetball courts, multipurpose rooms, fitness and weightlifting areas, a food court, student housing (224 beds), a convenience store and varsity gymnasium facilities.

Resolution
This building occupies a central location on the university campus and has, as it's primary task, the goal of integrating contrasting existing buildings and site conditions. Surrounding the site is the football stadium, the main pedestrian thoroughfare, and a large campus green. The project extends the unresolved open edges and weaves them together across the facility. A folded roof-scape picks up the artificial green of the stadium and establishes the main spaces of the recreation facility. The edge of the stadium is repeated in the undulated shape of the housing component. This element forms the urban edge of the complex along the main street of the campus leading toward the campus green. Continuing the line of one of the main axes on campus, the existing field house is given a new facade, which encompasses the cooling towers and the convenience store at grade.

On the ground level three public pedestrian walkways through the facility allow access and insight to the various programmatic elements on the levels below and above. Main street develops into a passage through the building's main entrance lobby, passing a climbing wall and juice bar and inviting views up to the open fitness areas or down over the pools and the basketball gymnasium. Along the east, a "Walk of Fame" establishes a new access to the existing varsity basketball arena to the south. The covered exterior path overlooks the new basketball gymnasium on the west and the remodeled multipurpose courts in the field house to the east. To the north side of the stadium a bridge passes a set of new bleachers which create outside seating space at the entrance to the food court overlooking the field.

Three levels of student housing, organized in four-bedroom apartments, are lifted off the ground on pilotis and look out over the folded roofscape, the stadium, campus green and the activities along main street.

敷地
オハイオ州シンシナティ，シンシナティ大学構内。

プログラム
延べ35万平方フィートの施設。レクリエーション・センター（プール 2，バスケットボール専用ジム，ラケットボール・コート，多目的室，フィットネス／ウェイトリフティング・エリア），フード・コート，学生寮（224室），コンビニエンス・ストア，代表チーム専用体育施設が含まれる。

解
建物は大学構内の中央を占め，その主要任務は，既存建物や敷地状況と対比を描きながら全体を統合することである。フットボール・スタジアム，メインの歩行路，広い芝生が敷地を囲んでいる。プロジェクトは境界があいまいな周辺端部を拡張し，センター全体と一緒に織り合わせることになる。折り畳まれた屋根の光景はスタジアムの人工芝を取り込み，レクリエーション施設のメイン・スペースを確立する。スタジアムの端部は学生寮の波のようにうねる形態に反復される。学生寮は芝生に通じるメイン・ストリートに沿ったコンプレックスの都市的な端部を形成する。構内の主軸線の一つを延長した先にある，既存のフィールド・ハウスには新しいファサードが構成され，冷却塔と地上階のコンビニエンス・ストアを取り囲む。

地上階には，建物全体を貫いて3本の歩行路が延び，通行する者に様々なプログラム領域が上下の階に配置されていることを知らせ，そこへ至るアクセスを提示する。メイン・ストリートは建物のメイン・エントランス・ロビーを抜ける通路に流れ込み，クライミング・ウォールやジュース・バーを過ぎ，さらに行くと上方には開放的なフィットネス・エリア，下方にはプールやバスケットボール・ジムが見えてくる。東側に沿って"ウォーク・オブ・フェイム"（有名スターの名を入れた星形メダルを埋め込んだハリウッド大通りの歩道の名）が，南側に位置する既存の代表チーム専用バスケットボール競技場への新しいアクセスを構成する。覆い付きの外部通路が，西側の新しいバスケットボール場と東側のフィールド・ハウス内の改修された多目的コートを見下ろしている。スタジアムの北側に向けて，新設された青空スタンドを横断してブリッジが渡される。このスタンドはフィールドを見下ろすフード・コートへのエントランス部に屋外席をつくりだす。

4寝室ユニット構成，3階建ての学生寮は，ピロティに乗って地上から持ち上がり，そこからは折り重なる屋根の光景，スタジアム，芝生，そしてメイン・ストリート沿いの動きが見渡せる。

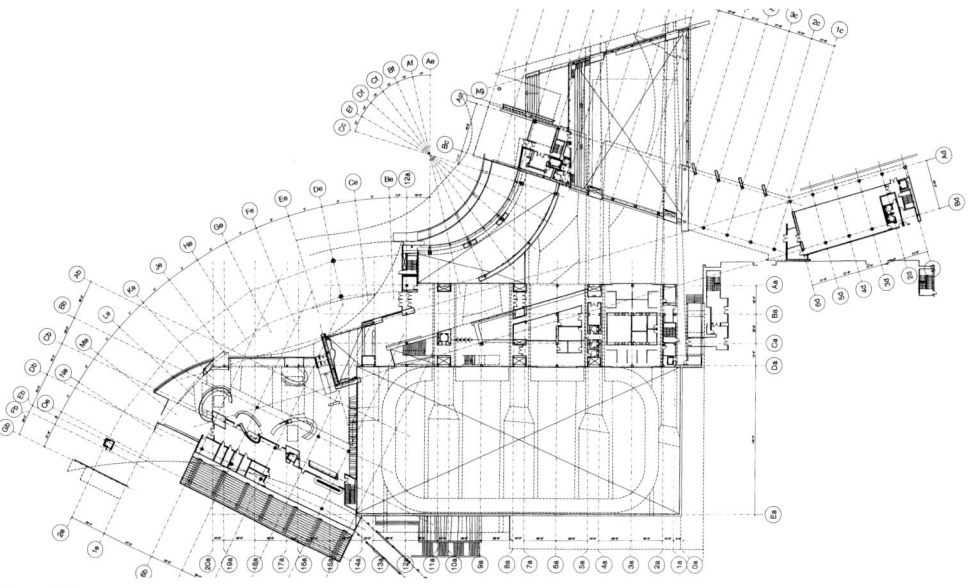

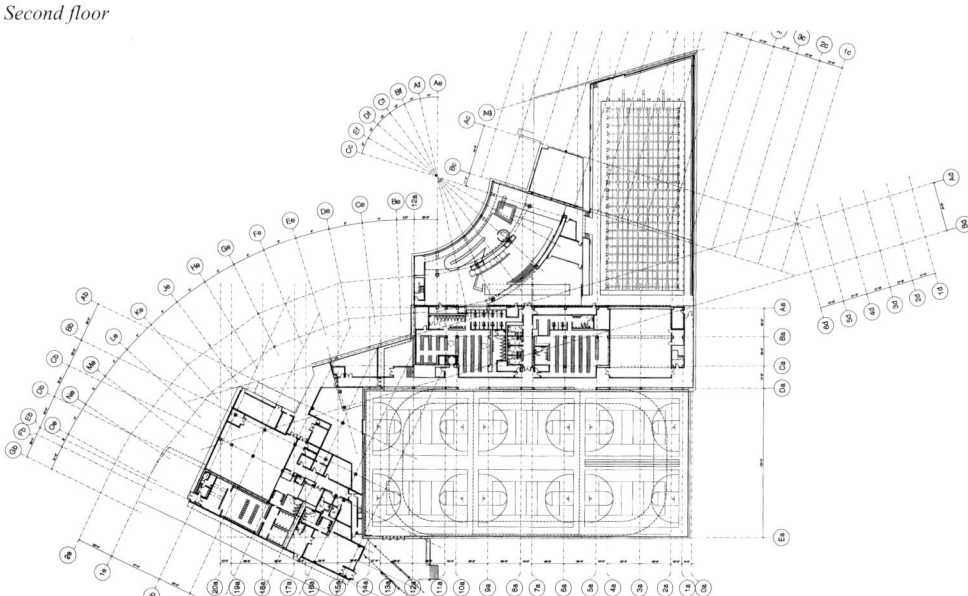

Second floor

Fourth floor

First floor

Third floor

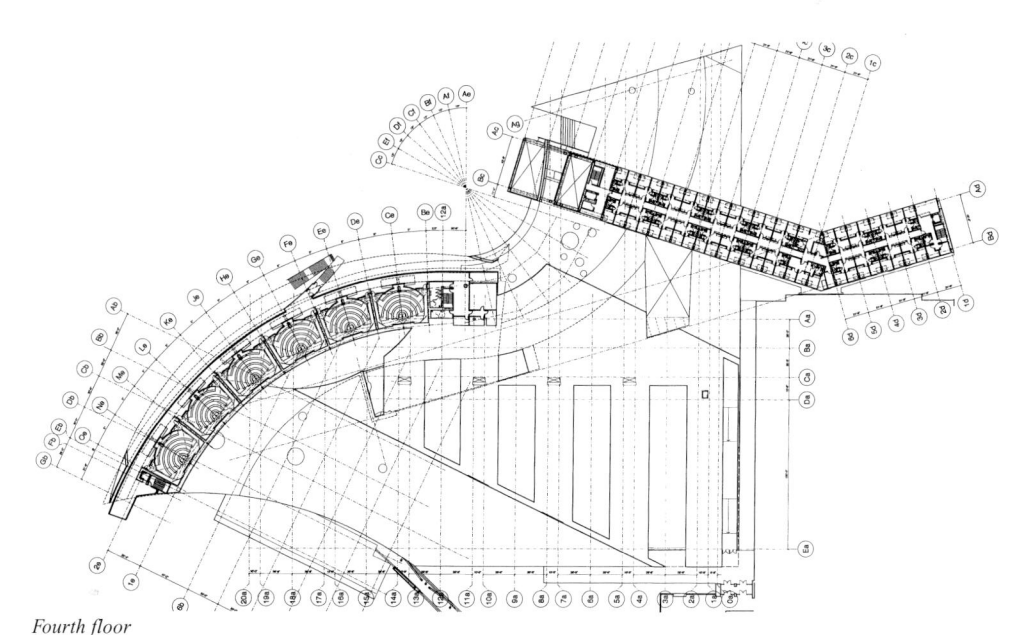

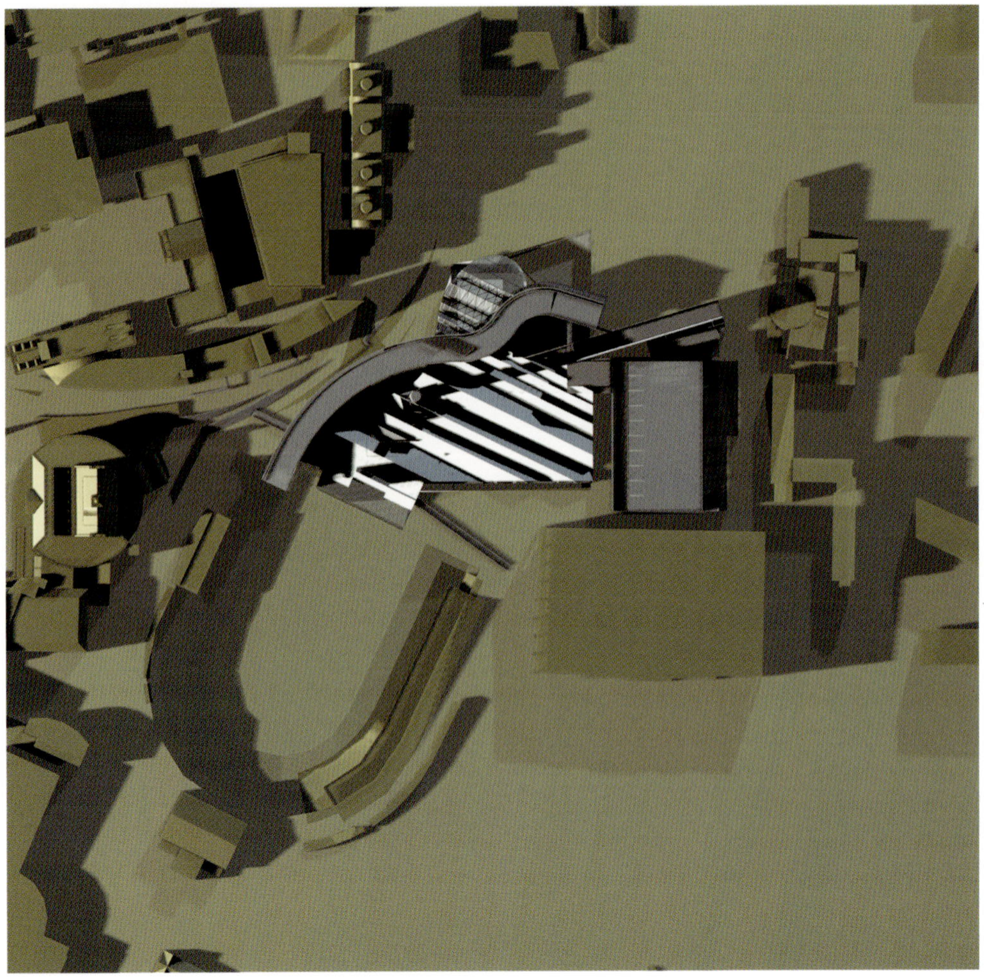

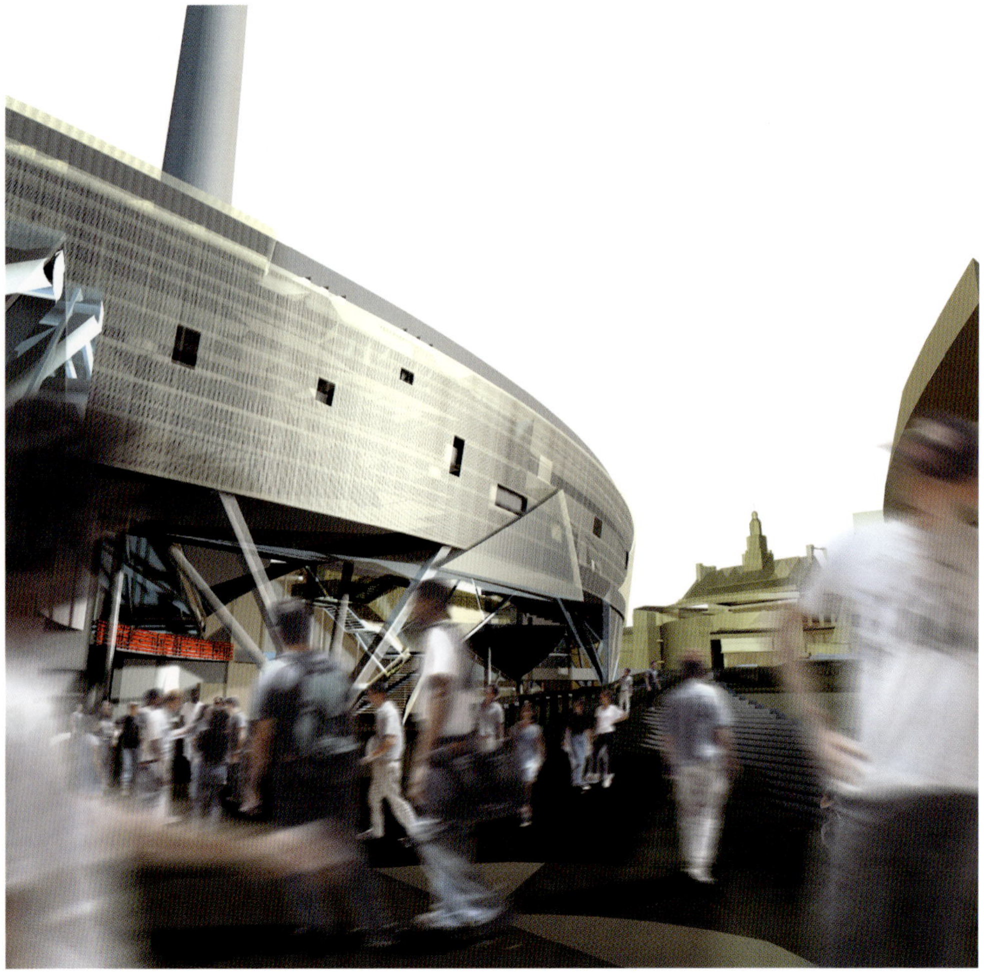

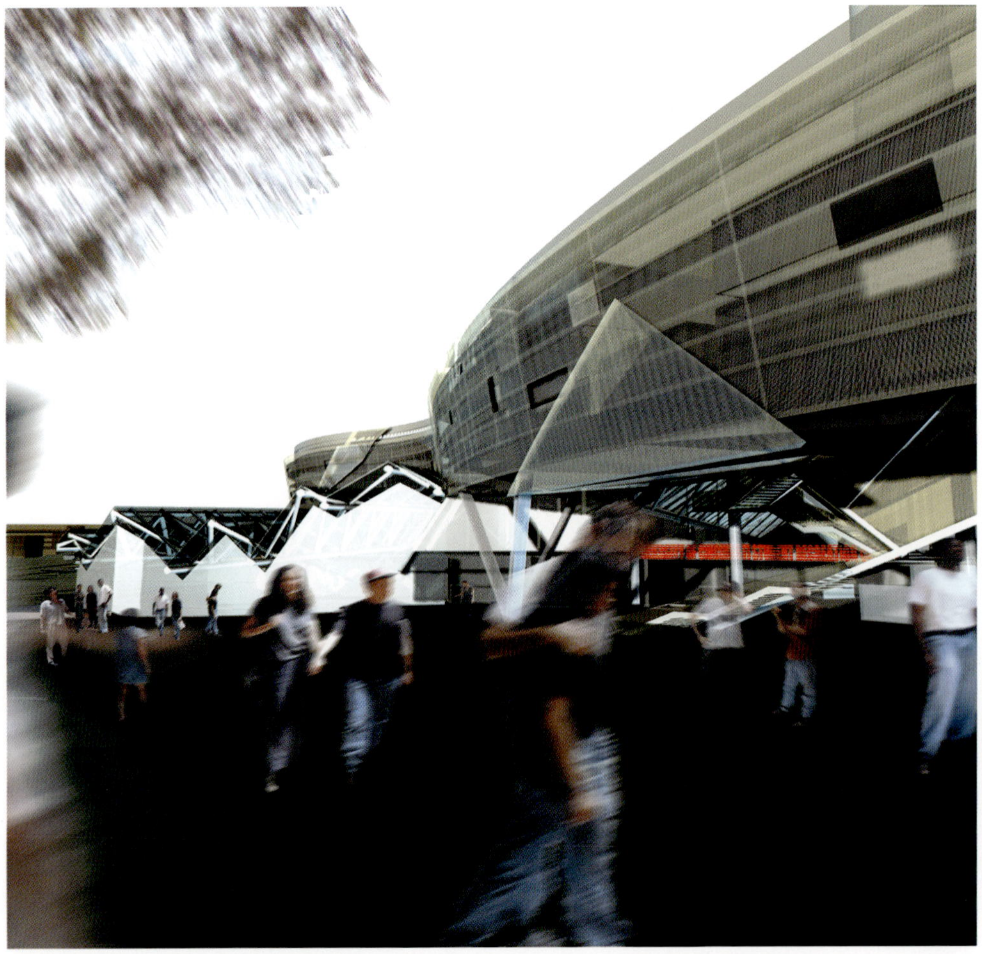

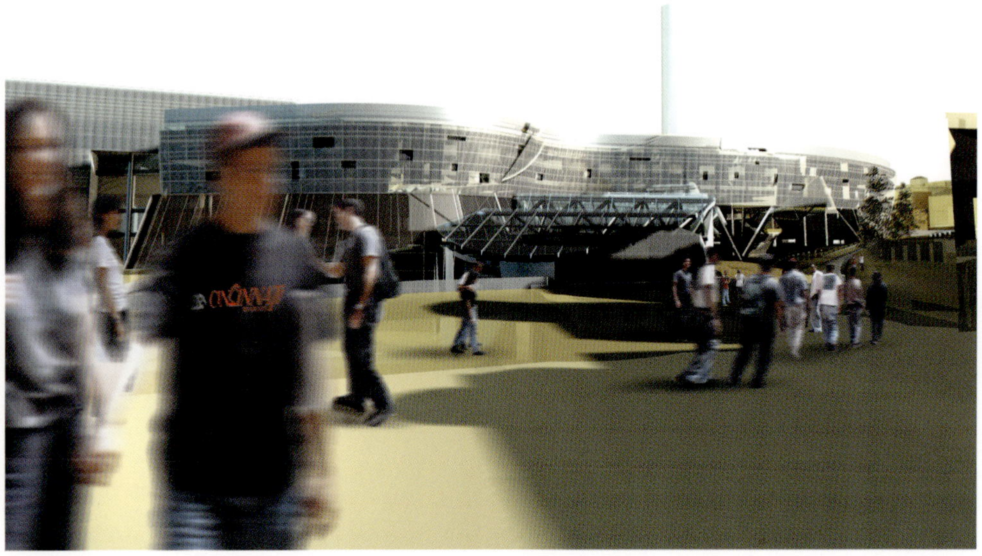

GA PROJECT

Section 1: north

Section 2: northwest

Section 3: west

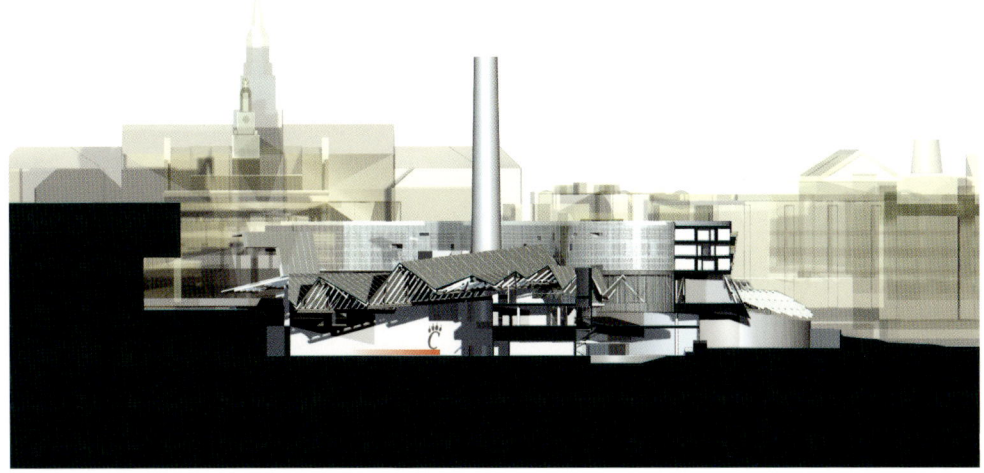

Section 4: west

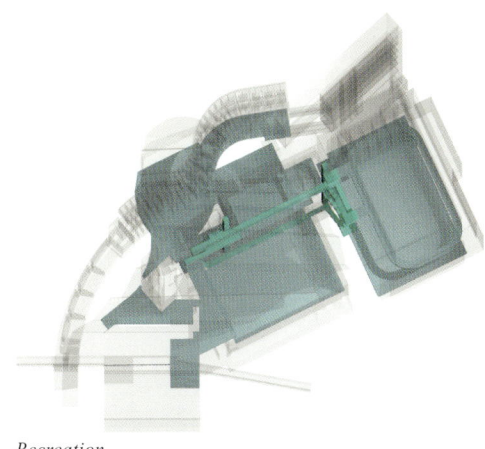

Recreation

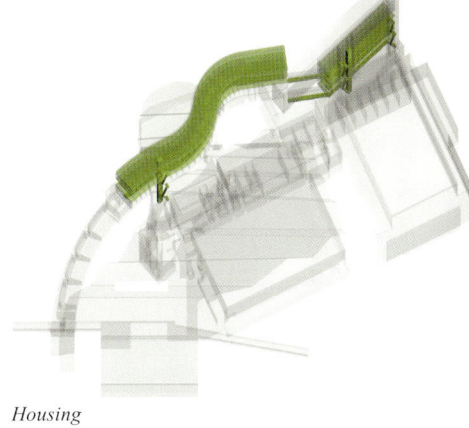

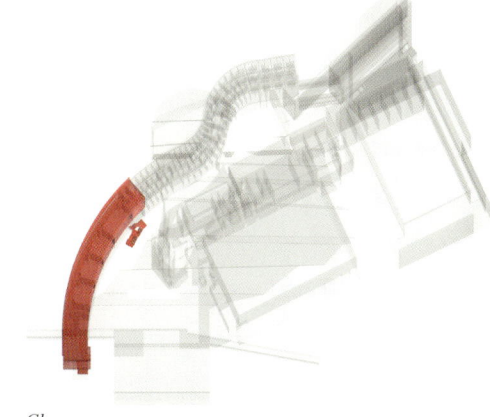

Housing

Classrooms

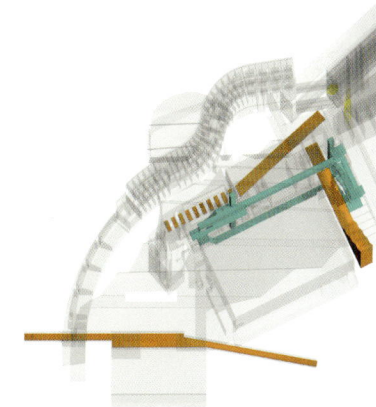

Circuration

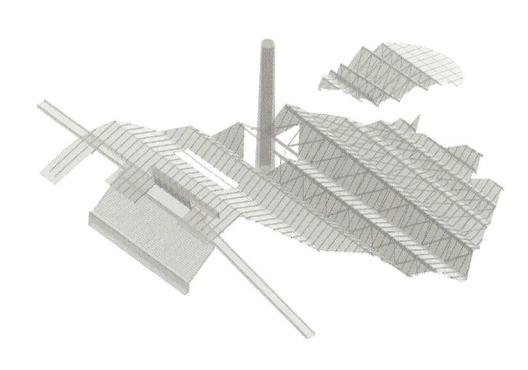

Landscape

Free form

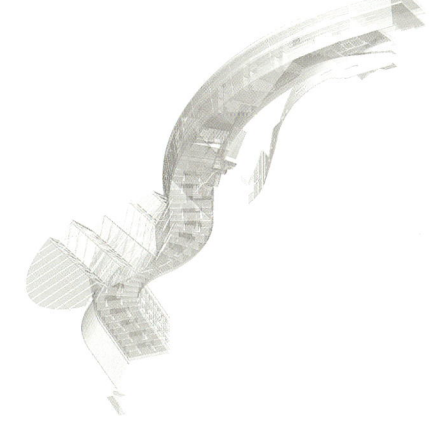

Classroom

Orthogonal

Screen/class study   *Screen study*

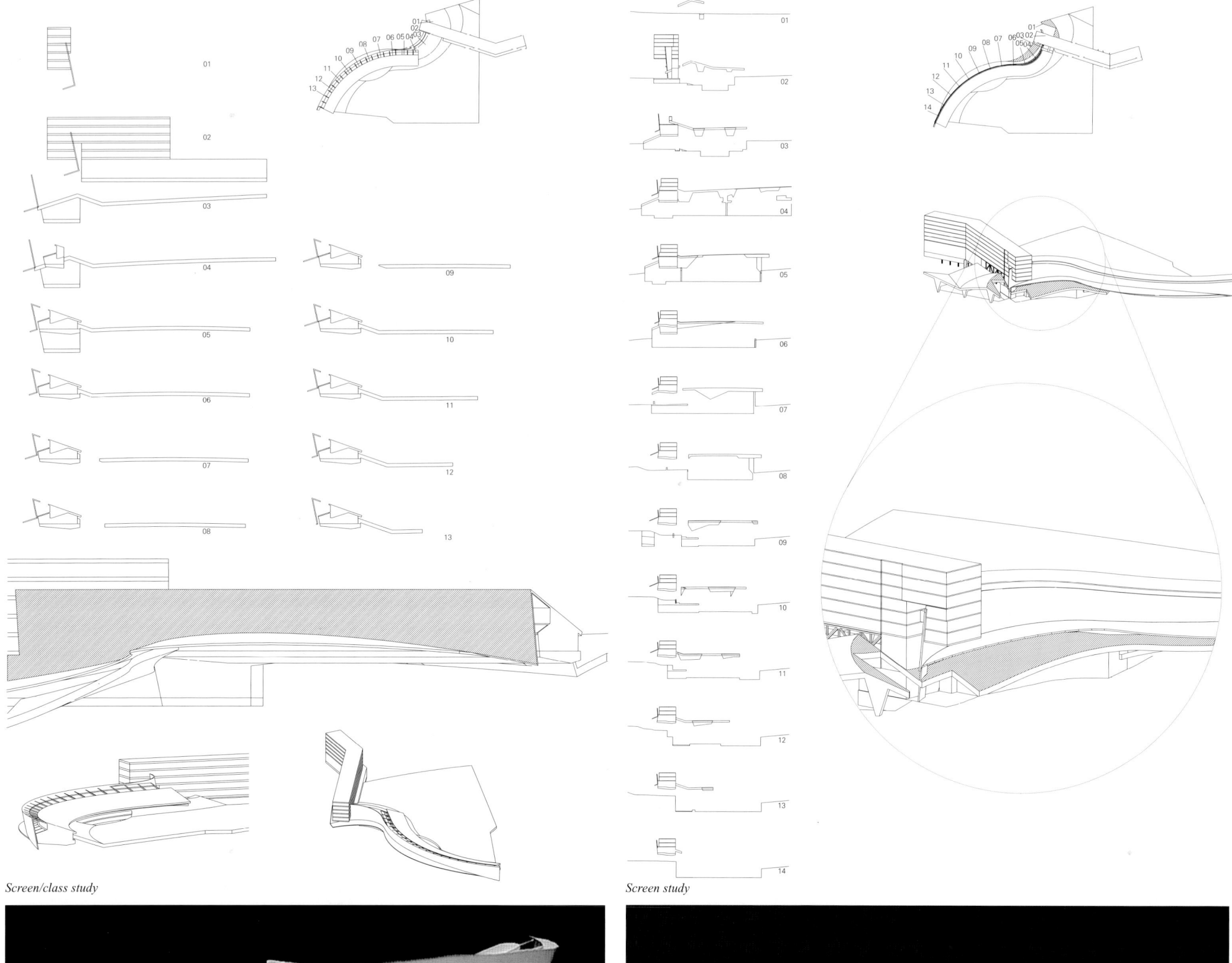

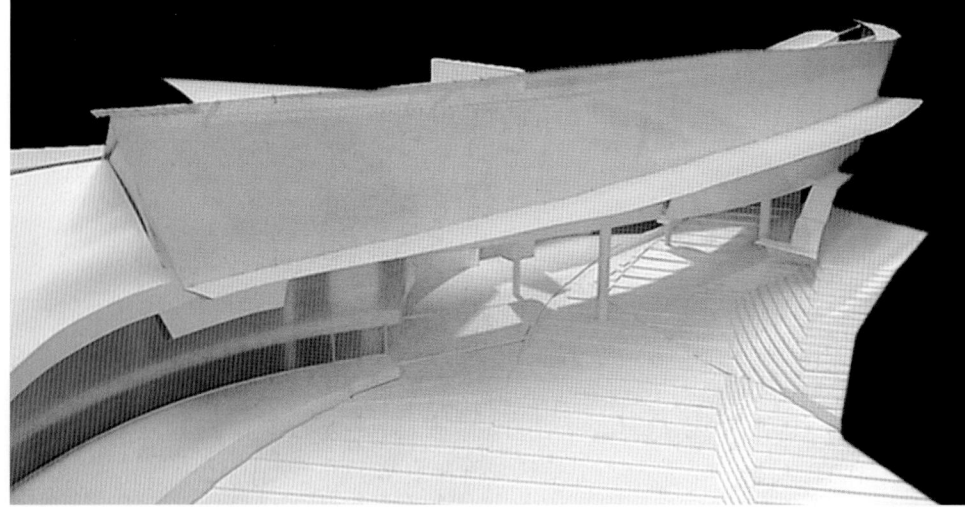

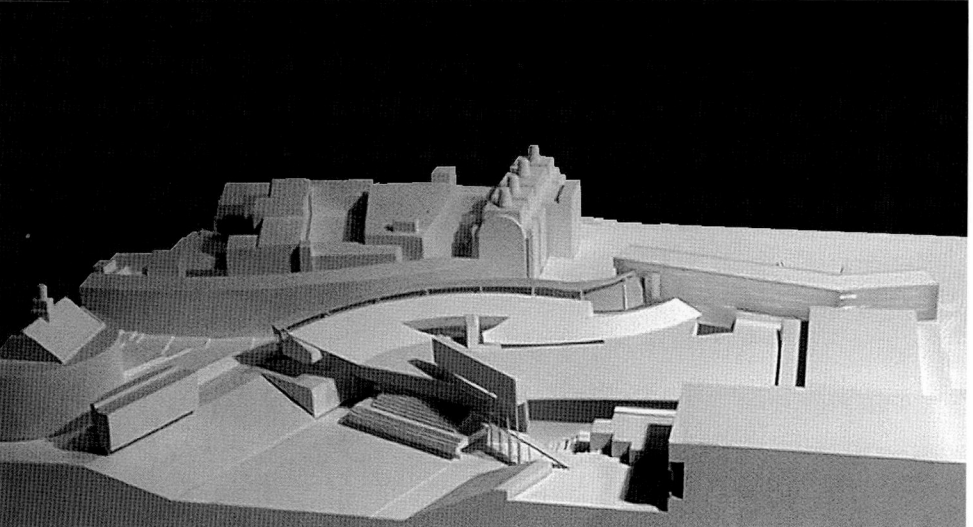

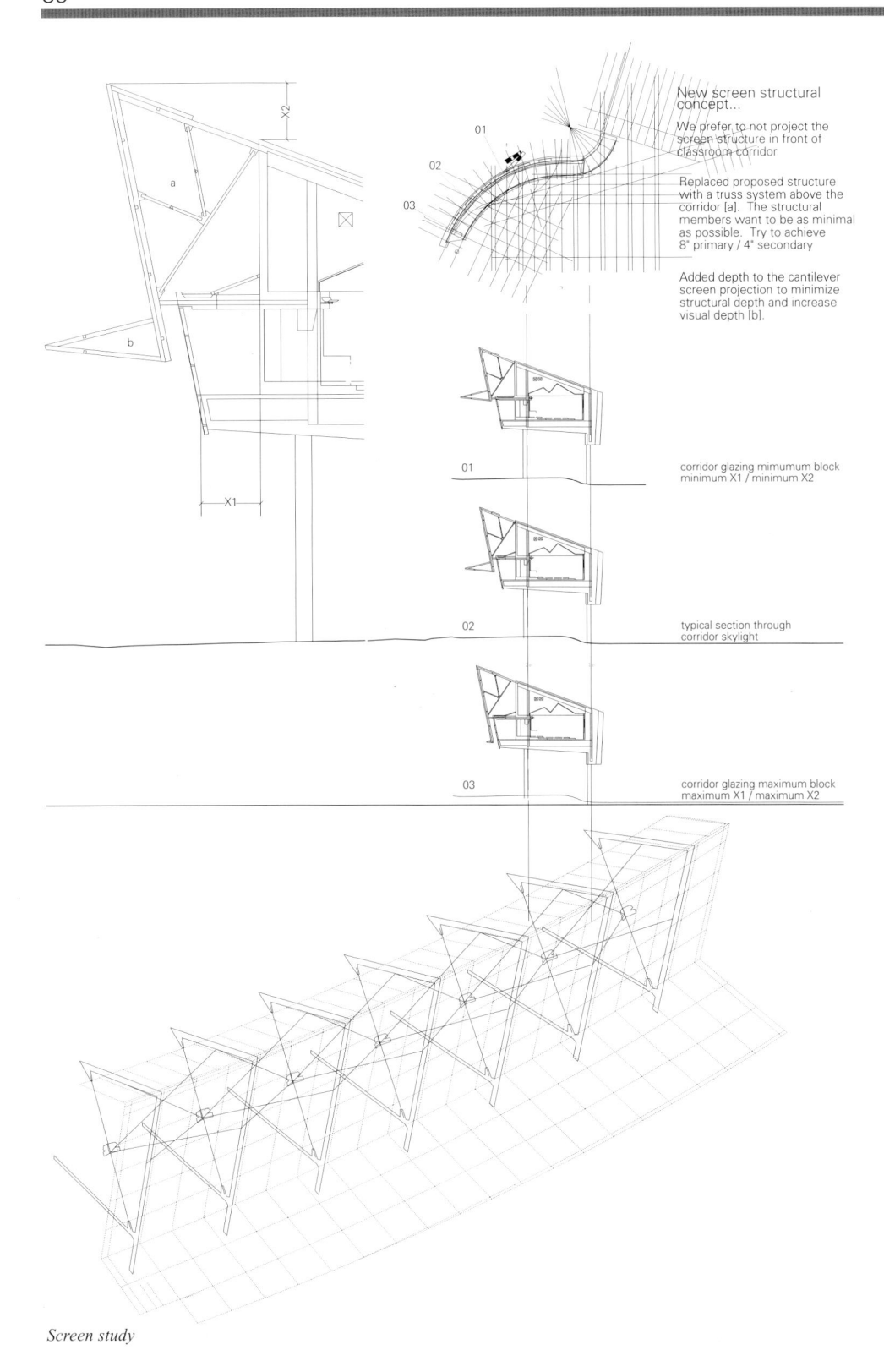

New screen structural concept...

We prefer to not project the screen structure in front of classroom corridor

Replaced proposed structure with a truss system above the corridor [a]. The structural members want to be as minimal as possible. Try to achieve 8" primary / 4" secondary

Added depth to the cantilever screen projection to minimize structural depth and increase visual depth [b].

01 corridor glazing minimum block minimum X1 / minimum X2

02 typical section through corridor skylight

03 corridor glazing maximum block maximum X1 / maximum X2

Screen study

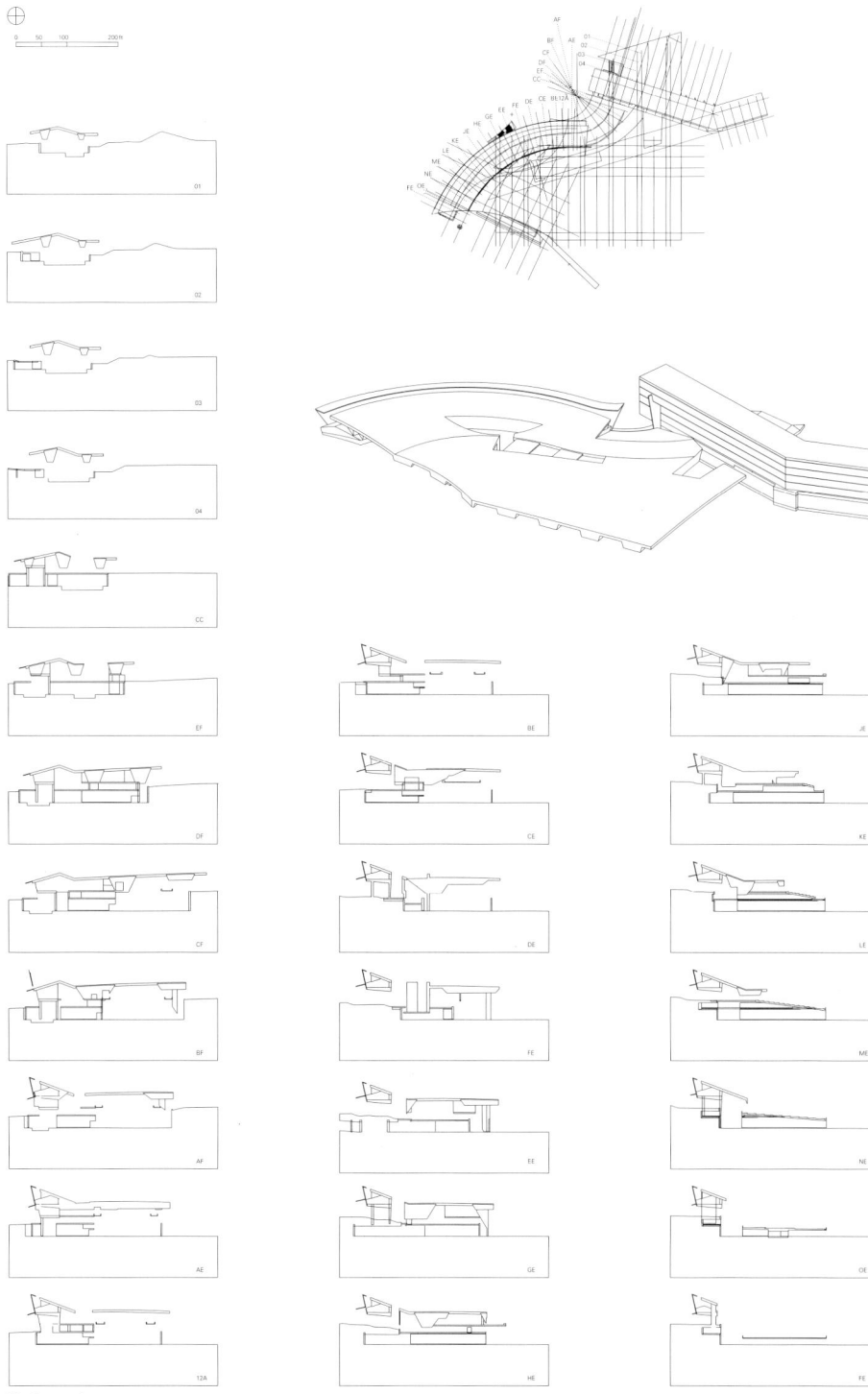

Vault section

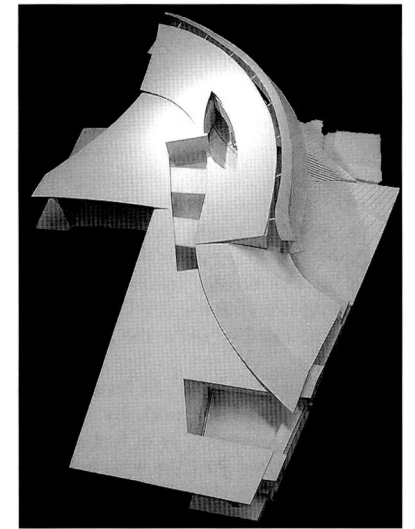

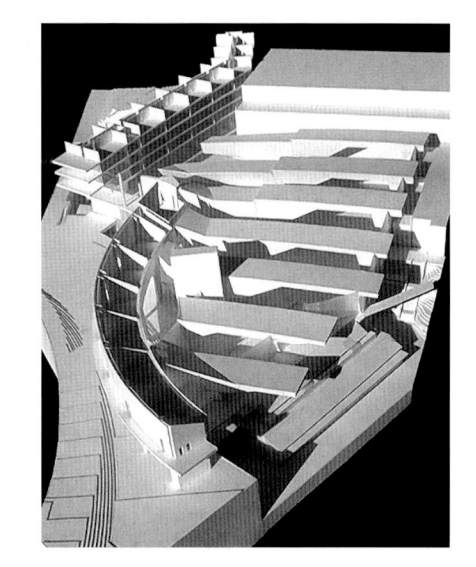

Architects: Morphosis—Thom Mayne, principal-in-charge; Kim Groves, project manager; Kristina Loock, Brandon Welling, project architect; Ben Damron, Silvia Kuhle, Henriette Bier, Eric Nulman, Martin Summers, project team; Jason Anthony, Crister Cantrell, Delphine Clemenson, Simon Demeuse, Manish Dessai, Hanjo Gellink, Lisa Hseih, Dwoyne Keith, Patricia Schneider, Scott Severson, Paxton Sheldahl, John Skllern, Christian Taubert, Chris Warren, Petar Vrcibradic, Eui Sung Yi, project assistants
Executive Architect: KZF Inc.—Don Cornett, principal-in-charge; Bill Wilson, project architect
Costs: $71 million

ARATA ISOZAKI

ISOZAKI ATEA
Bilbao, Spain Design: 1999–2001 Construction: 2001–04

©PANORAMICAS—Julio San Sebastian

Bilbao River's left bank is now undergoing redevelopment with architects summoned by the city of Bilbao. F. O. Gehry's Guggenheim Museum and Federico Soriano & Dolores Palacios' Palacio de Congresos y de la Musica have already been completed, with C. Peli's office building that is yet to be constructed standing in between.

The site of this project is located 500 m upstream from the Guggenheim Museum. Early in the last century a 5-storied bonded warehouse was planned, but its construction came to an end when the third floor, roof terrace and balustrade were finished. The building went through a dismantling of its interior in the 1990s, leaving only the facade intact. This time, the plan featured a commercial office building with 5 floors overground and 5 floors underground, but its construction was abandoned when the structure frame has reached the third floor overground. The current project involves dismantling of the existing structure with the exception of the old bonded warehouse's facade and basement structure, putting together the site, the public road and its adjoining plots of land, and through alteration of the urban planning, redeveloping the area as a public plaza, business facilities, and housing complex.

A plaza in the shape of stairs is arranged along the axis extending from Plaza Moyua in the center of Bilbao, in such manner that the downtown area would be connected to S. Calatrava's pedestrian bridge and to the riverside promenade. Both sides of this stepped plaza border a pair of high-rise apartment buildings. Inside the existing facade are the low-rise apartment buildings arranged in the shape of a folding screen. The facade, facing the river, would be dismantled leaving the central part intact, and a patio is planned to draw the promenade into the premises.

'Atea' stands for 'gate' in Basque language. This project, named unexpectedly 'Isozaki Atea' by the local participants, is in fact one manifestation of the Gate Project which Isozaki has been planning in various places in the world.
Yasumi Taketomi/Arata Isozaki and Associates

ビルバオ川左岸ではビルバオ市主導により建築家を起用した再開発が進行中であり、既にF・ゲーリーによるグッゲンハイム美術館、F・ソリアーノとD・パラシオスによるコンベンションセンターが完成、その中間にはC・ペリによるオフィスビルが計画されている。

本計画の敷地はグッゲンハイム美術館より500メートル程上流にある。20世紀前半に地上5階建の保税倉庫が計画されたが、3階とルーフテラス、バラストレイドをもって工事は終了、完成となった。1990年代に入りファサードのみを保存して内部は解体され、地下5階・地上5階建ての商業オフィスビルが着工されたものの、地上3階の躯体ができたところで放棄されたままになっていた。本計画では旧保税倉庫のファサードと地下構造体を残して解体し、公道とそれをはさんで隣接する敷地とを併せ、都市計画変更を経て公共広場、商業施設、集合住宅として整備・再開発を行う。

ビルバオの中心であるモユア広場から延びる軸に沿って階段状に広場を設け、中心街とS・カラトラバによる歩行者専用橋および川沿いのプロムナードとの連続を図る。階段広場の両側には2本の高層住居棟、既存ファサードの内側には低層住居棟を屏風状に連ねて配置する。川に面した既存ファサードは中央部を残して解体され、プロムナードを引き込むようにパティオを計画している。

計画名称のAteaはバスク語でゲートを意味する。図らずも地元によってIsozaki Ateaと命名された本計画は、磯崎が世界各地で計画しているゲート・プロジェクトを示顕している。
（武富恭美／磯崎新アトリエ）

GA PROJECT

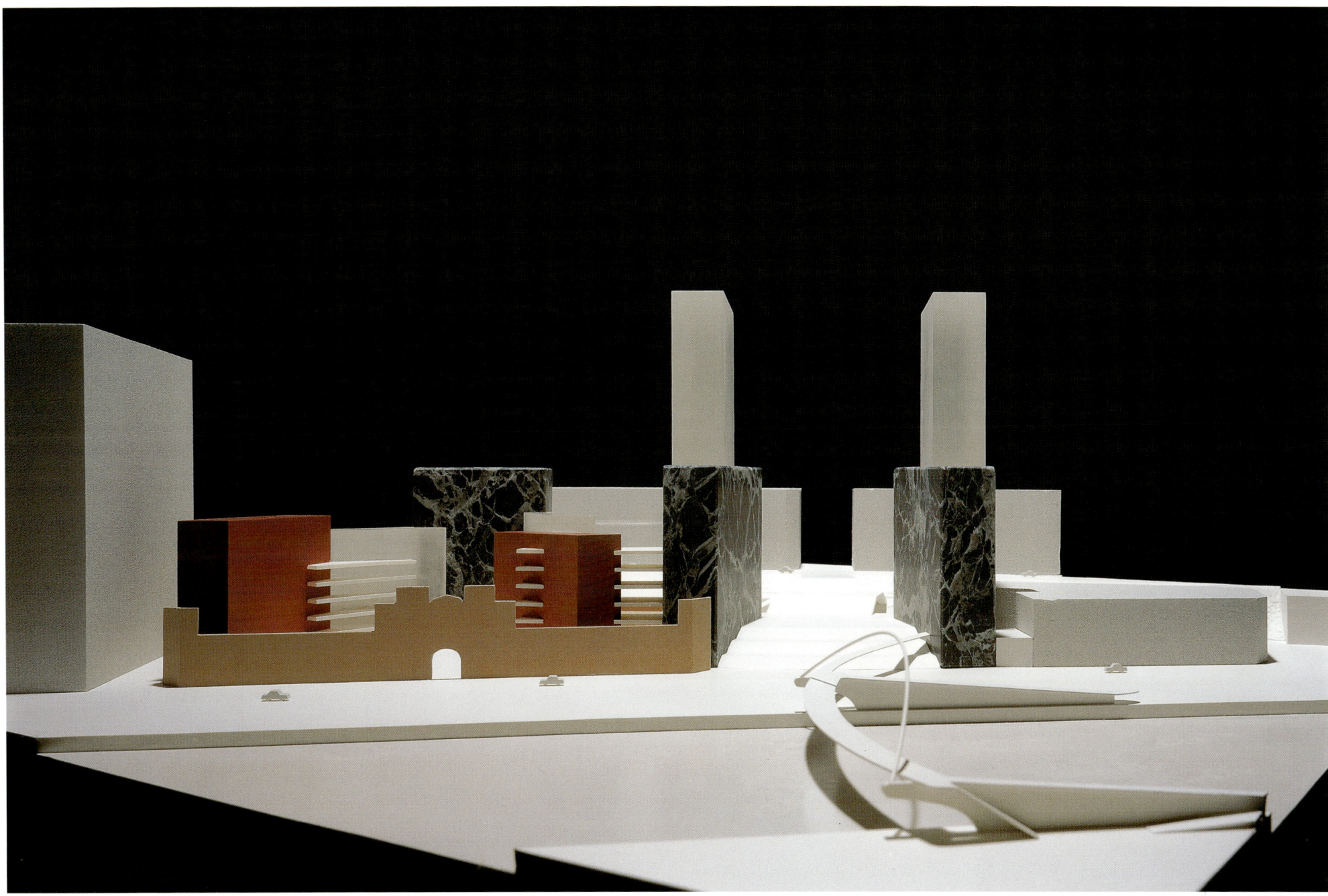

Model photo: Y. Takase

Architects: Arata Isozaki and Associates—Arata Isozaki, principal-in-charge; Yasuyori Yada*, Toshiaki Tange, Naoki Ogawa*, Yasumi Taketomi, project team (*: ex-staff)
Collaborating architects: Integrated Design Associates, Japan
Local associated architects: I Aurrekoetxea & Bazkideak, S.L., Spain
Consultants: Robert Brufau i Associats, S.A., Spain, structural; Estudi Francesc Labastida, Spain, mechanical and electrical; IFFT, Germany, facade technical consultant
Structural system: steel, partially reinforced concrete structure
Major materials: stone, brick, glass curtain wall, exterior; stone, brick, wood flooring, stucco, interior
Site area: 11,500 m²
Total floor area: 80,800 m² (54,000 m², new construction area; 26,800 m², renovation area)
Stories: 23 floors above grade, 5 floors below grade, Maximum height 82 m

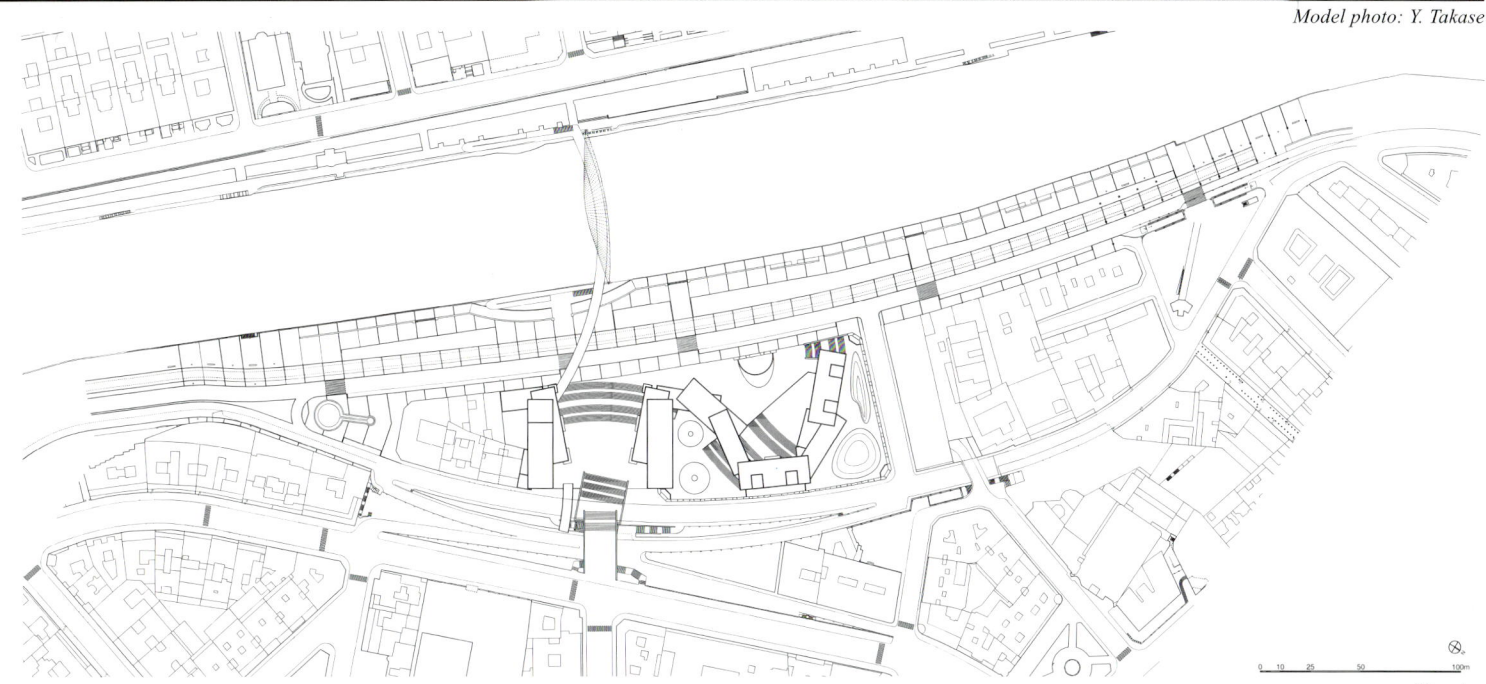

Site plan

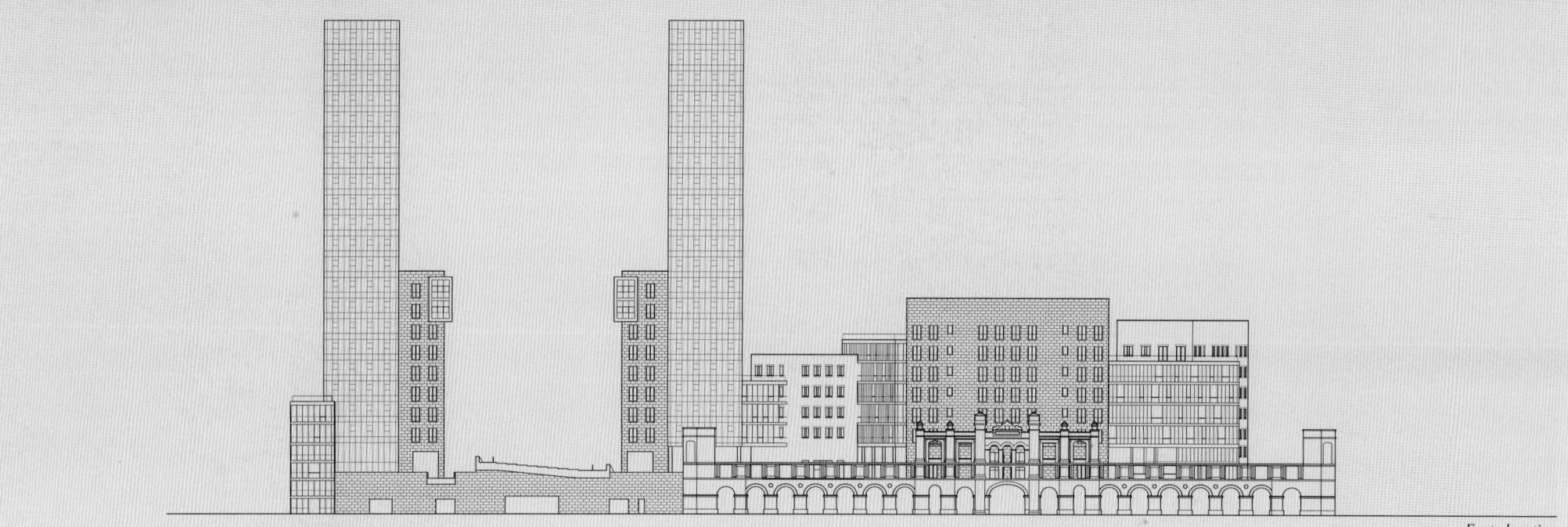

East elevation

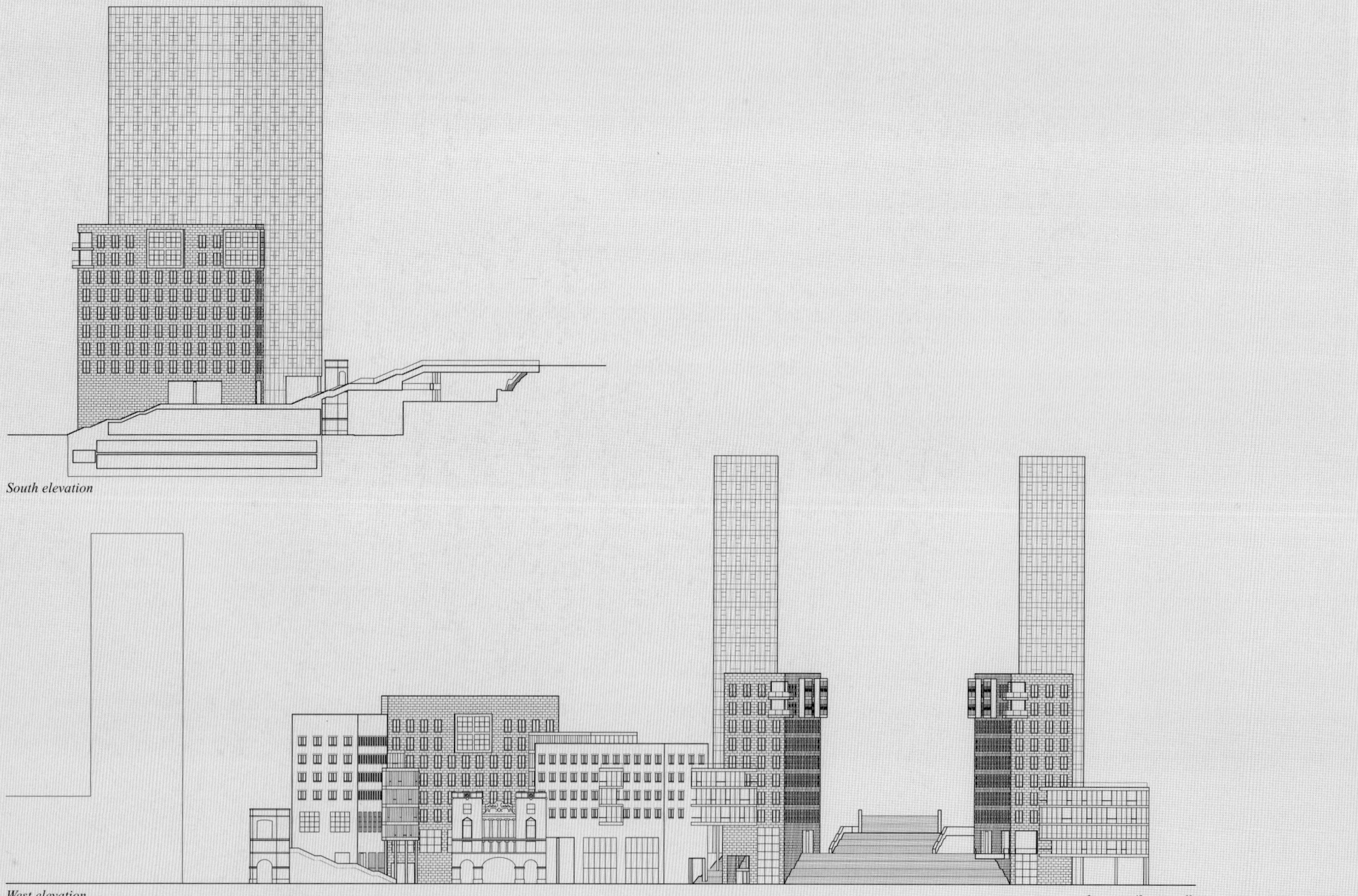

South elevation

West elevation

73 GA PROJECT

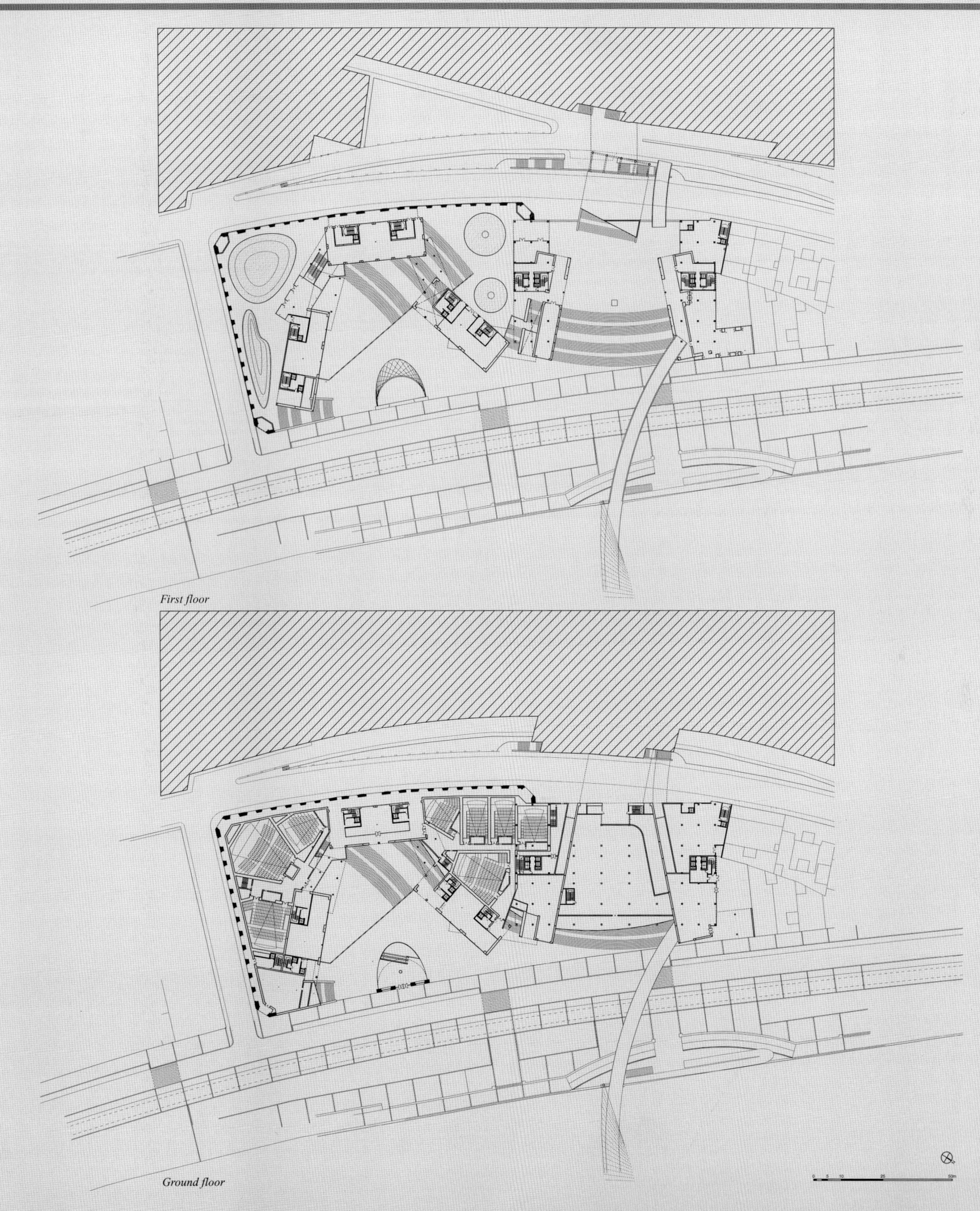

First floor

Ground floor

ERIC OWEN MOSS

PARKING GARAGE & OFFICES
Culver City, California, U.S.A. Design: 1999 Construction: 2000–01

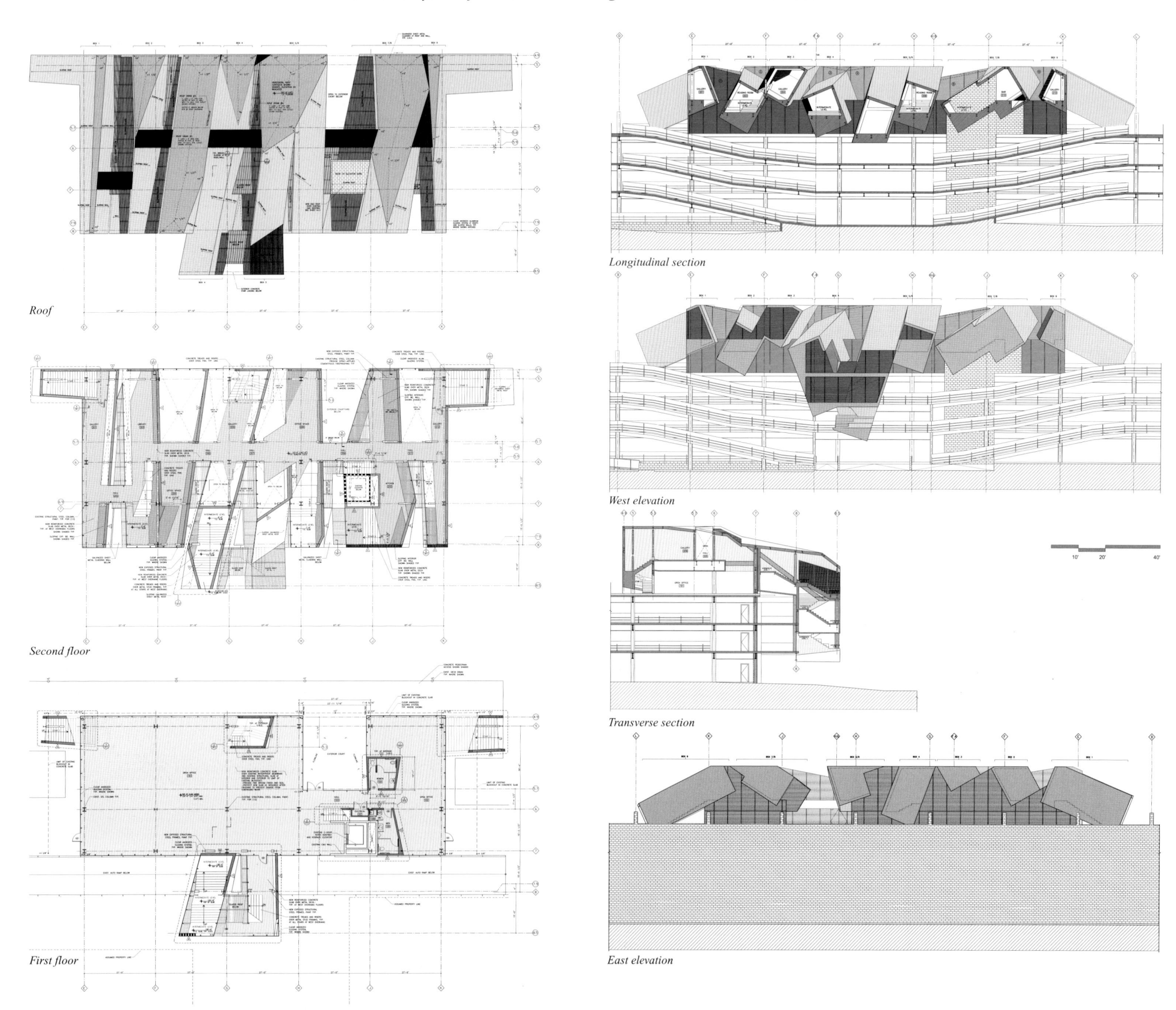

Roof

Second floor

First floor

Longitudinal section

West elevation

Transverse section

East elevation

75

West view

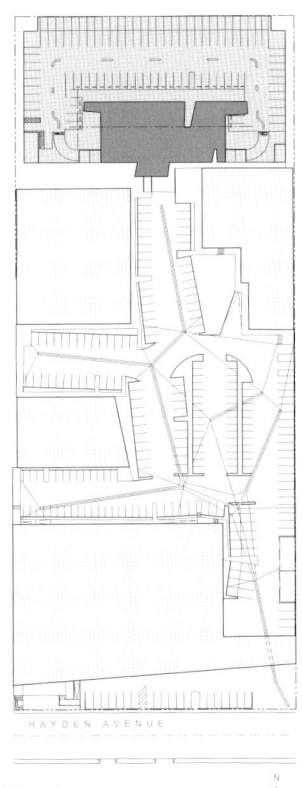

Site plan

Northeast view

GA PROJECT

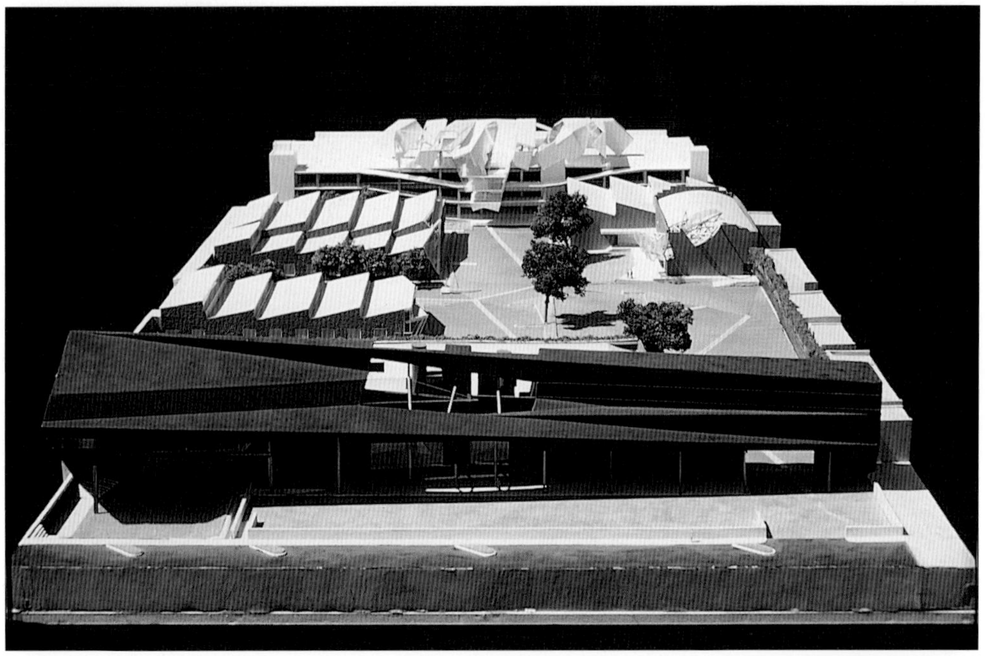

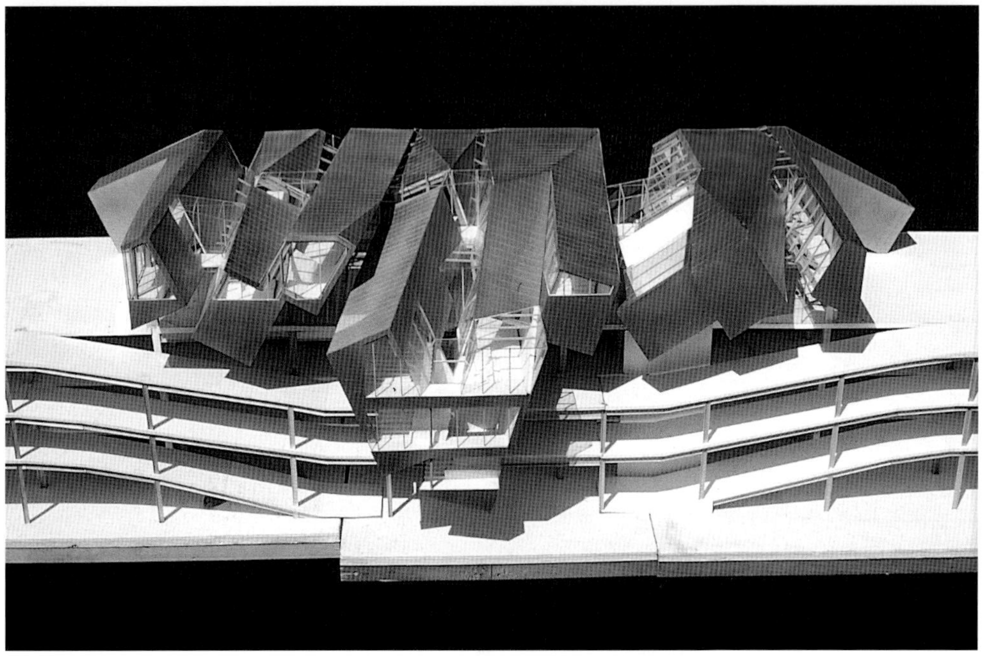

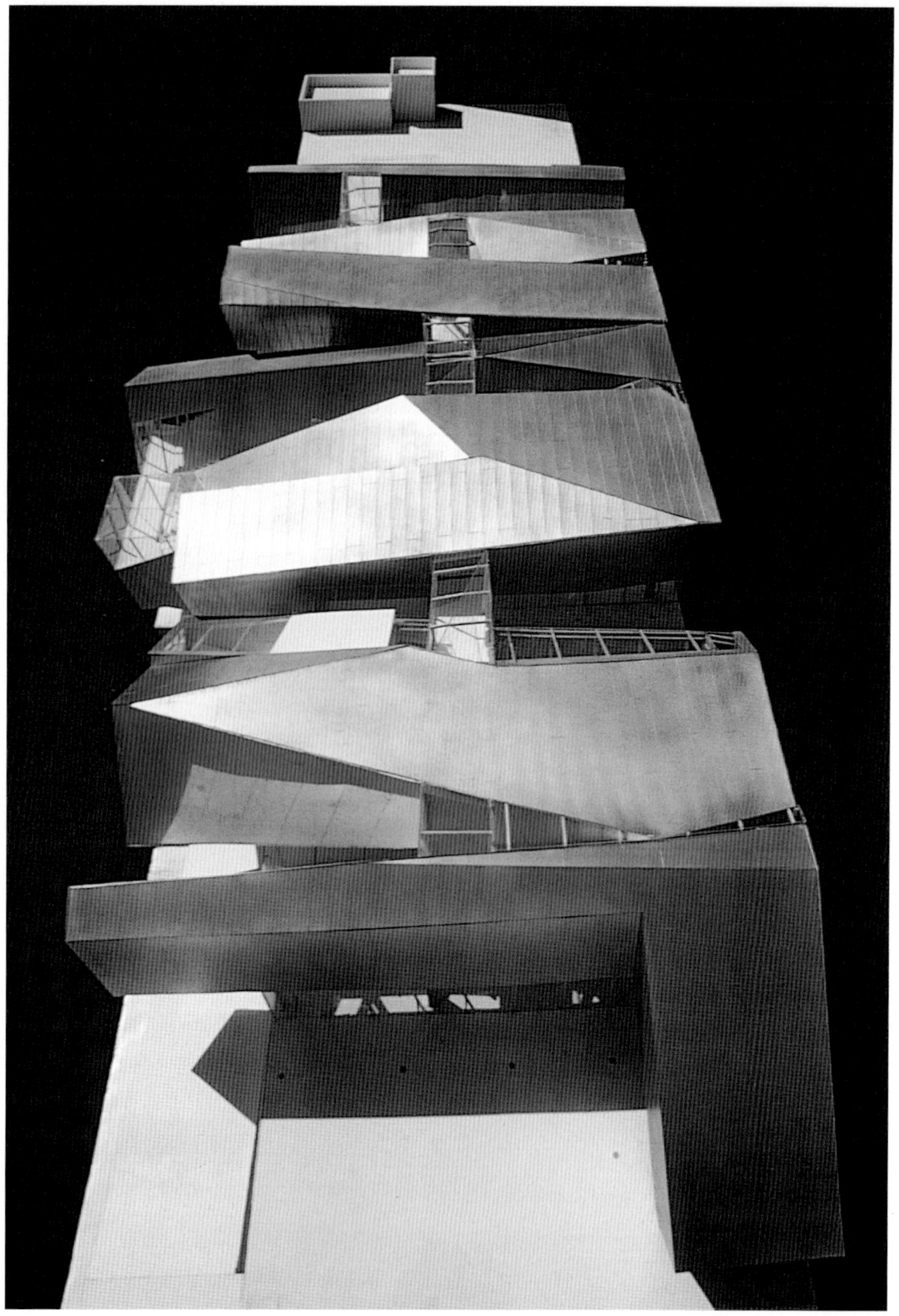

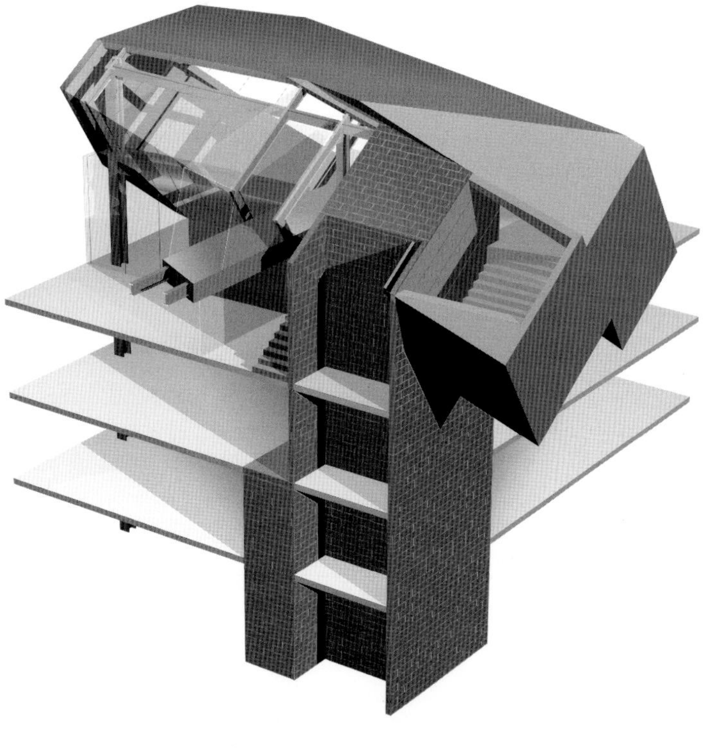

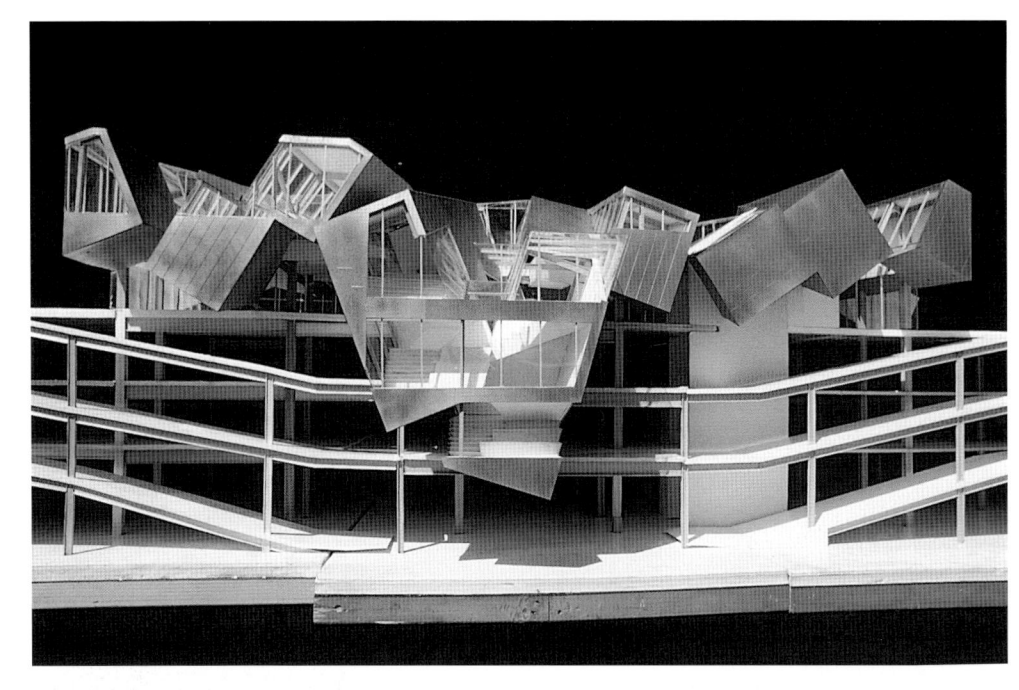

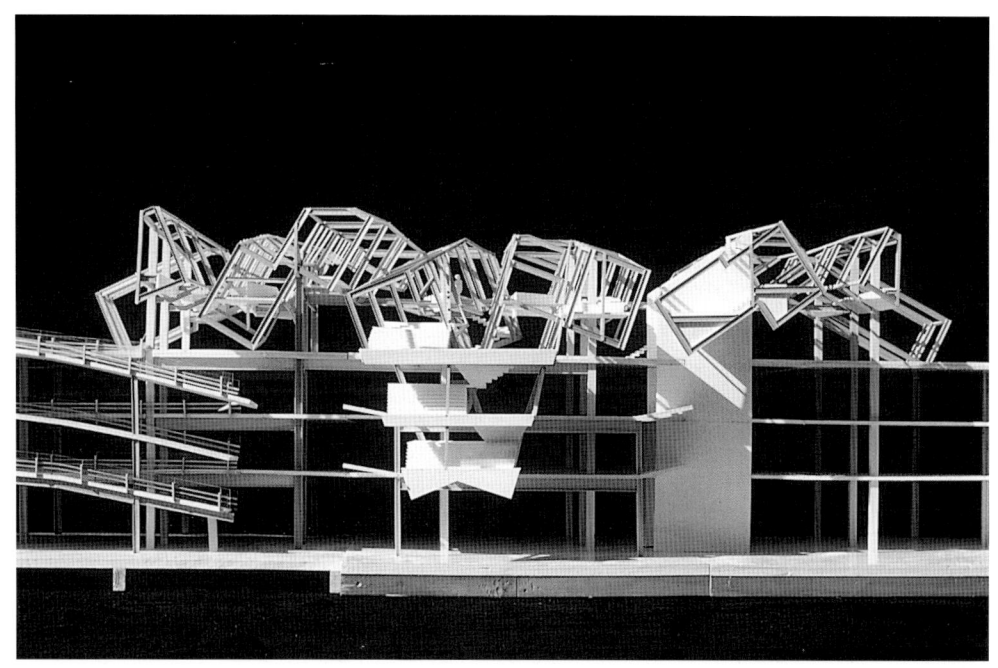

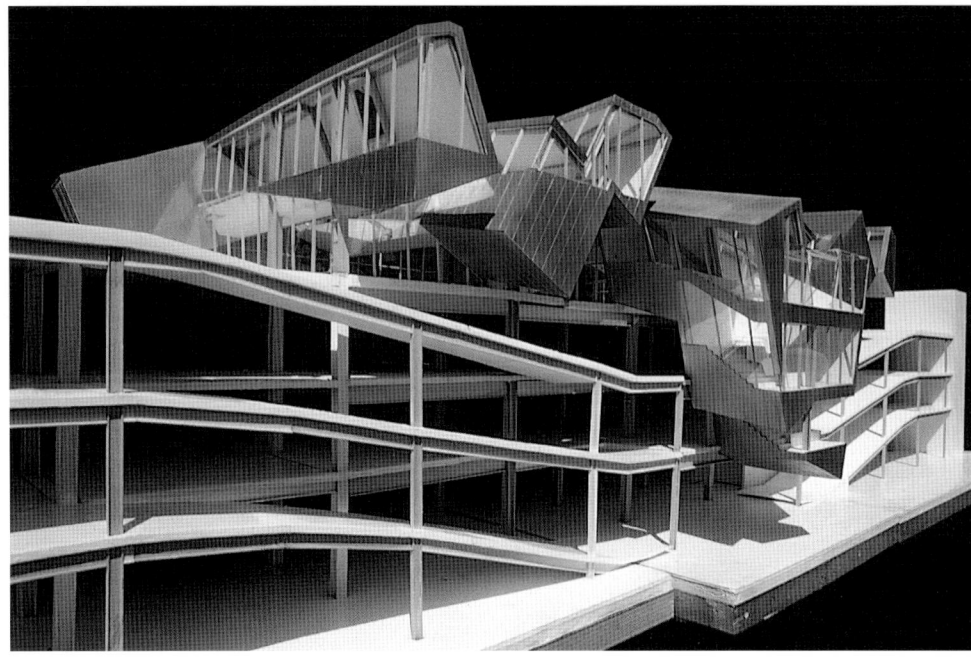

Architects: Eric Owen Moss Architects—Eric Owen Moss, principal-in-charge; John Bencher, project architect; Scott Nakao, Stuart Magruder, Dolan Daggett, Holly Deichmann, Grace Pae, Micah Heimlich, project team (parking garage); Eugene Slobodanyuk, Yi-Hsiu Yeh, Scott Nakao, Dolan Daggett, Holly Deichmann, Corinna Gebert, Frank Geiger, Mark Sallin, Farshid Gazor, Emil Mertzel, Alexandra Rieschl, Jose Fernandes, project team (offices over parking garage)
Owner/developer: Samitaur Constructs—Frederick and Laurie Samitaur Smith
Consultants: Kurily, Szymanski, and Tchirkow—Joe Kurily, structural; Fruchtman and Associates—David Fruchtman, mechanical; Silver, Roth, and Associates—Felix Roth, electrical
General contractor: Samitaur Constructs—Peter Brown, director of field operations; Tim Brown, general superintendent
Site area: 23,00 sq.ft.
Floor area: 11,000 sq.ft.

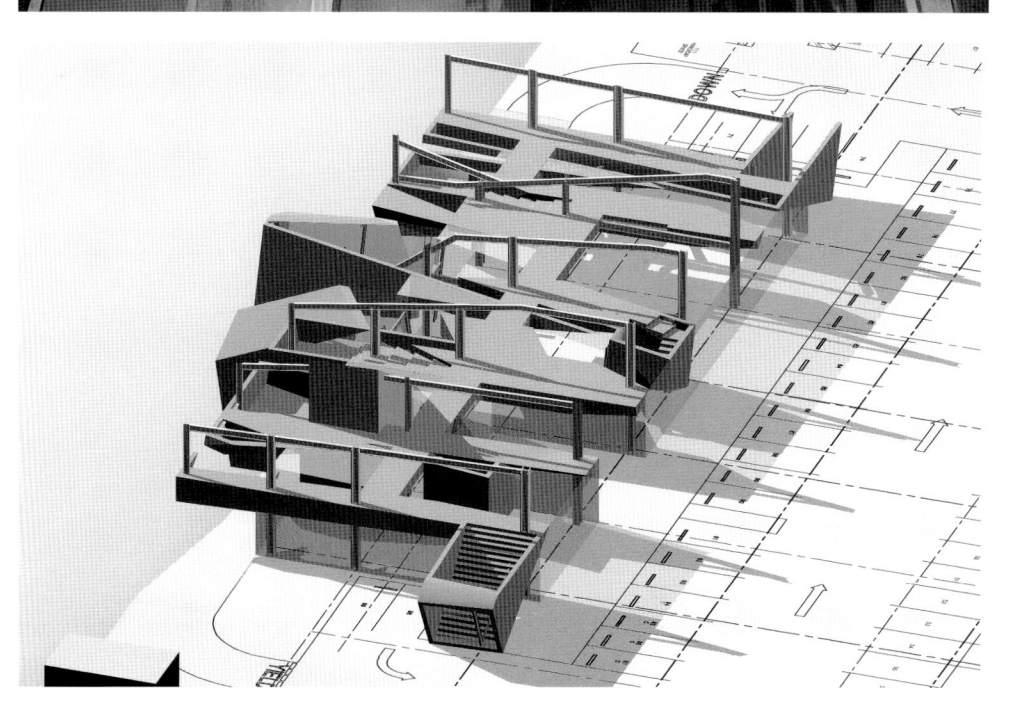

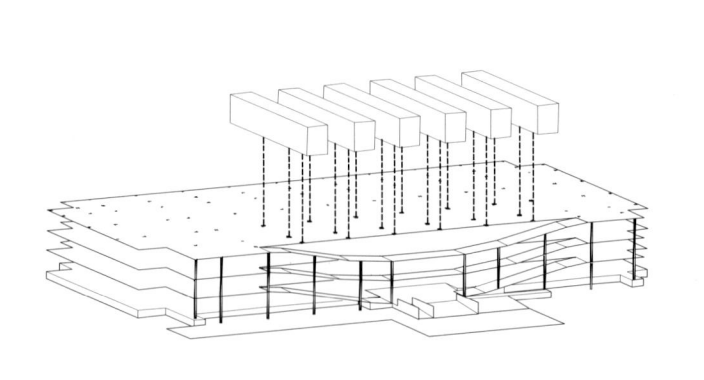

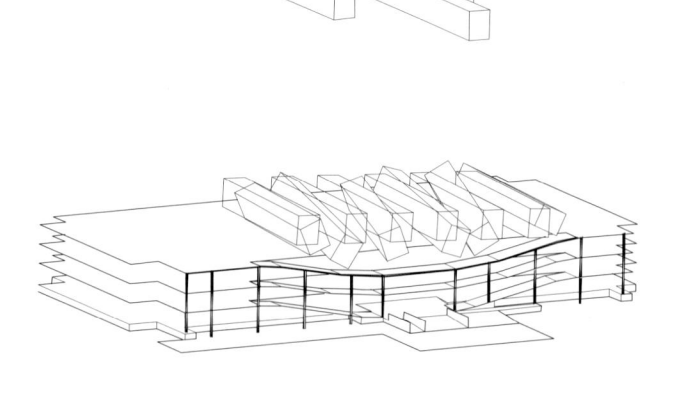

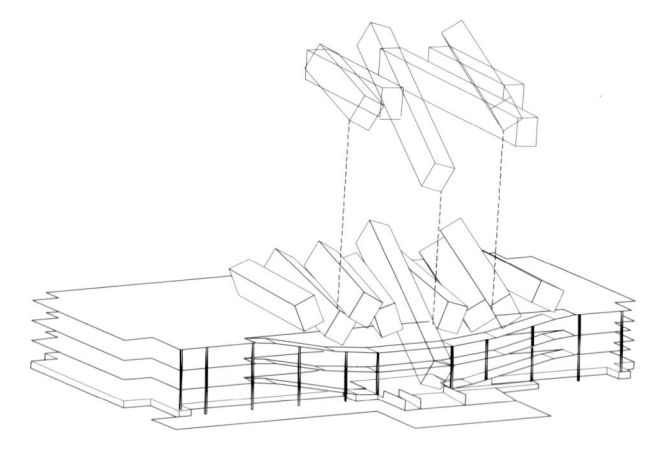

6 BOXES

TILT ALONG RAMP

3 BOXES FILL VOID

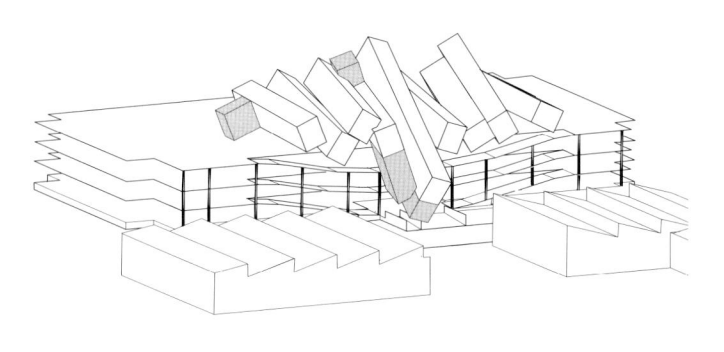

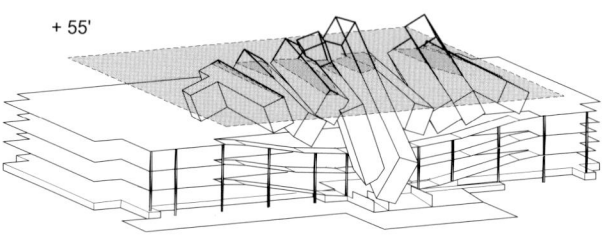

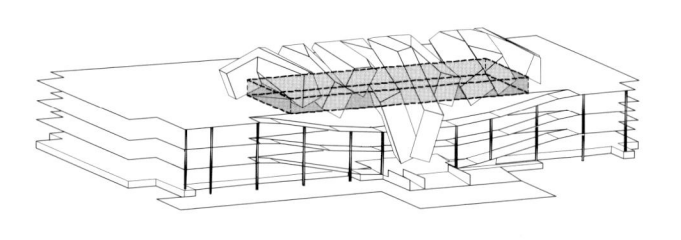

ADDITIONAL PIECES

HEIGHT LIMIT

PLAN CONDITION

The parking garage & offices are located at the east end of the Hayden-National site—a campus-like development of six buildings, offering collectively more than 300,000 square feet of office, production, and post-production facilities. The Hayden-National Site is conceived of as a unified composition of buildings organized around a courtyard, and is entered by driving under and through the Stealth at the complex's west end.

The Wedgewood Holly site is located in a transitional area of deteriorating industrial buildings. The area, which formerly consisted of 1940's era warehouses, is now being transformed into an entertainment and media industry center. Geographically, the site is bounded to the east and north by two major city arteries: the north-south La Cienega Boulevard and the east-west Jefferson Boulevard, and is sited nearly equidistant from downtown Los Angeles and Santa Monica, and between Hollywood and LAX.

The courtyard portion of the Wedgewood Holly site is now used for on-grade parking, but may become a garden and pedestrian-oriented space if adjacent lots can be secured for parking. Additional parking is available in the parking garage & offices, a four level 500-space parking structure with rooftop offices. The parking garage & offices, positioned on a 320' x 170' parcel, are enclosed on the north, east, and south by multi-story warehouse and industrial structures.

The four-level parking structure is straightforward—regular bays formed from steel frames with metal decks. Automobile ramps are attached at opposite ends of the western face. Though the parking structure is essentially invisible to the campus site—the lower garage floors are largely concealed by the surrounding buildings, it serves as a podium for the rooftop office building, which rises substantially higher than adjacent structures.

The offices develop vertically, for two additional levels, as an extension of the steel columns of the parking structure. The main office floor includes open spaces, private offices, and conference areas while the mezzanine level offers a unique arrangement of library, lounge, and private facilities.

Formally, the office is defined by the intersection of nine rectangular boxes, enclosing the mezzanine program and shaping the main floor below. As the boxes are connected, they lose tops, sides, and floors until they are less individual entities and more a combination of roof, wall, and floor planes. The original boxes become residual reference points. In the aggregate, the boxes form a plan rectangle of 140' x 50'. That rectangle is the perimeter of the office building. The walls of the rectangle are glass, extending from the deck to reach the boxes lifted above. The north face of each box is glazed, allowing natural light into the mezzanine spaces and the main office floor. In the center portion of the office space on the western front of the garage/podium, a three tiered lounge space hangs across the west front of the garage, positioned precisely between two existing campus buildings on either side of the garage entry, identifying the office and the entry to the garage.

Construction systems
Parking levels—steel frame primary structure with spray-on fireproofing, concrete over metal deck floors and concrete block wall in rear.
Offices—structural steel frames with concrete over metal deck floors and metal stud walls. Exterior sheet metal cladding on roof walls and glass/mullion system for glazed areas.

| CUT BOX | SHELL | FLOOR | GLASS |

| COLUMNS | FRAMES | BRIDGES | UNION |

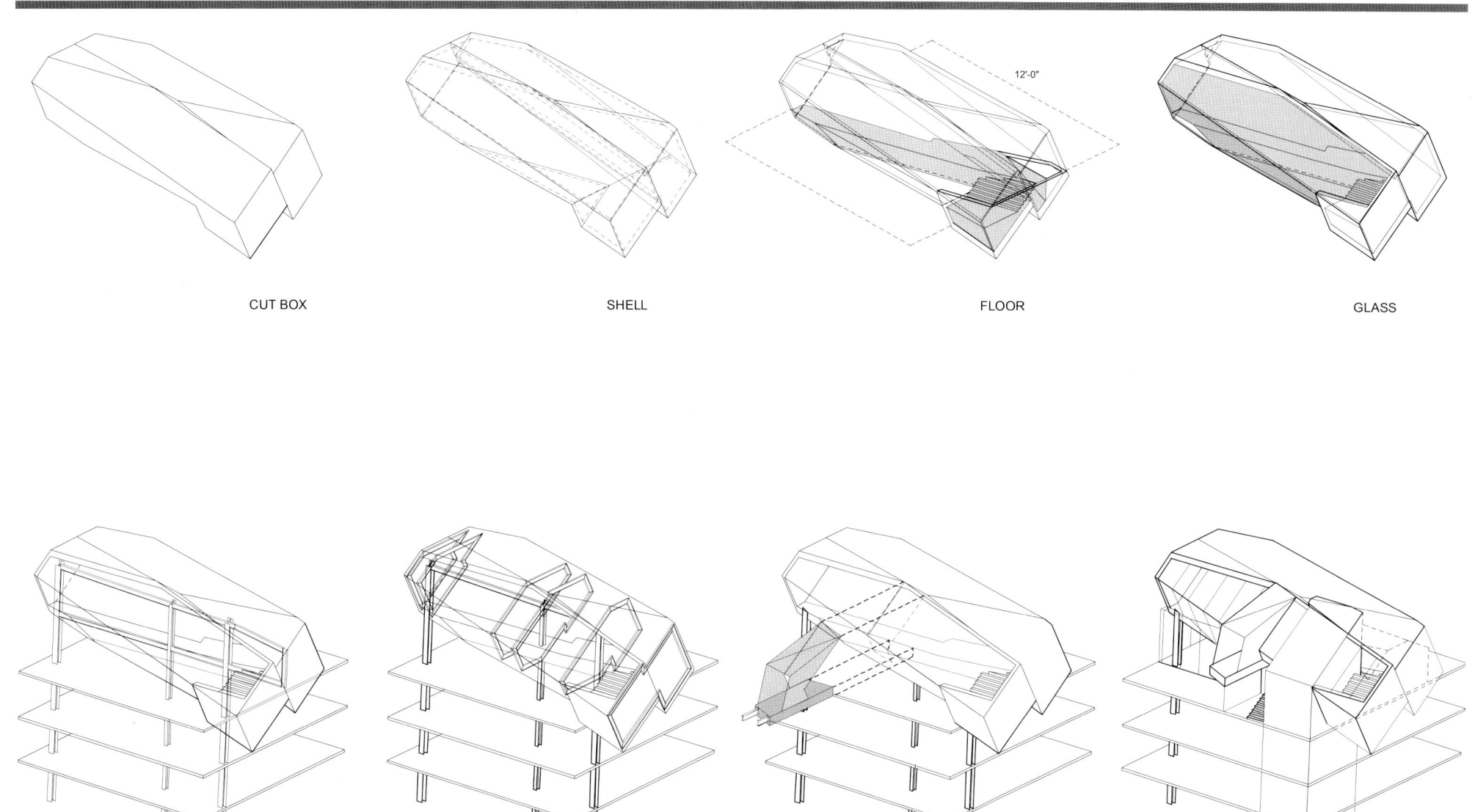

パーキング・ガレージ＆オフィス・ビルは，オフィスをはじめプロダクション，ポストプロダクションなどの施設6棟，計30万平方フィート以上に及ぶ，大学構内のような開発が進行するヘイデン・ナショナル・サイトの東端に位置する。敷地全体は中庭を囲んで一体化する建築群として構想されており，コンプレックス西端にある，ステルス・ビルの足元の開口を車で抜けて入る。

ウエッジウッド・ホリー・サイトは劣化した工場建築群が変貌を続けている地域にある。以前は，1940年代の倉庫が立ち並んでいたこの地域は，目下，エンタテイメント／メディア産業の中心へと変身しつつある。地理的には，敷地の東と西の境界は，街の2つの幹線道路，南北に走るラ・クレネガ大通りと東西に走るジェファーソン大通りに面し，ロサンゼルスのダウンタウンとサンタモニカからほぼ等距離の地点，ハリウッドとLAX（ロサンゼルス国際空港）の間に位置する。

ウエッジウッド・ホリー・サイトは現在，地上駐車場として使われているが，隣接する土地がパーキングとして確保できれば，庭園と歩行者のためのスペースとなるかもしれない。この地上駐車場が一杯になれば，4層，500台収容可能な駐車施設で屋上にオフィスが重なる，このパーキング・ガレージ＆オフィスに収容できるだろう。建物は320×170フィートの区画を占め，北，東，南を多層の倉庫と工場建築に囲まれる。

4階建てのパーキング・ガレージは，鉄骨フレームにメタル・デッキがつくる，単純で規則的な一連の区画で構成されている。車の進入ランプは，西ファサードの反対側に位置する。パーキング・ガレージは基本的にキャンパス・サイトからは見えないが―低層のパーキング階は周囲の建物で大部分が隠される―オフィス棟はこの基壇の上に乗っているので，隣接する建物群よりかなり高く立ち上がる。

オフィス棟は，パーキング・ガレージの鉄骨柱の延長上に2層分を加えて上昇する。その主階はオープン・スペース，個室オフィス，会議エリアなどで構成され，メザニン階は図書室，ラウンジ，個人用設備から成る独特の配置構成を備える。

オフィスは，形態的にはメザニン階の諸プログラムを包含しながら，その下に主階を形づくる9つの矩形の箱の交差からできている。9つの箱は，連結されてゆくにつれて，個としての実体が希薄なものとなるところまで，上面・側面・下面という定義を失い，屋根・壁・床の一つの組合せに姿を変える。元の9つの箱は残存する参照点となる。集合してゆくなかで，箱は140×50フィートの長方形平面を形成する。その長方形はオフィス・ビルの周縁を構成する。長方形の壁はガラス張りで，上の箱に届くまで，デッキから伸び上がる。それぞれの箱の北面にはガラスが嵌められ，メザニン・スペースと主階に自然光を届ける。基壇の役割を持つガレージの西面上方に位置するオフィス・スペースの中央には，ガレージの西面を横断して3段になったラウンジ・スペースが吊り下がり，ガレージ入口の両側に建つ既存のキャンパス・ビル2棟の間に正確に位置し，オフィスとガレージへの入口を明示する。

構造
パーキング階：主構造は防火剤を吹き付けた鉄骨フレーム。メタル・デッキ階の上部にコンクリート。背面の壁はコンクリート・ブロック。
オフィス：基部を構成するメタル・デッキとスタッド・ウォールの上に，鉄骨フレームとコンクリート。屋根／壁の外面はシート・メタル被覆。ガラス面はガラス／マリオン方式。

CHRISTIAN DE PORTZAMPARC

GRANDE BIBLIOTHÈQUE DU QUEBEC
Montreal, Canada Design: 2000

As asked in the programme, we have, with Elizabeth de Portzamparc, conceived the project around and within a vast and pure volume, a public forum, enlightened and heated during the long winters.

Elizabeth de Portzamparc has designed a landscaped urban promenade on two levels, accessible from the streets and from the underground network, opening on a large public garden. This interior street distributes the spaces permanently open: conference halls, exhibitions, newspaper stands, children areas, internet areas and so forth....

Christian de Portzamparc has imagined the above volume of air and light like a aquarium with four "fishes": two of them, the biggest, hang from the ceiling and house the controlled access areas, the other two, smaller, rest on the ground which house the public spaces opened on the promenade.

The interiors of the library are designed by Elizabeth de Portzamparc.

At a time at which we see everywhere that public spaces are generated by business and entertainment, the Big Library of Quebec represents today a chance to imagine a large open space in Montreal, open 24 hours, around a cultural programme.   *Christian de Portzamparc*

プログラムの求めに対し，私たちはエリザベス・ド・ポルザンパルクと共に，このプロジェクトを，巨大で純然たるヴォリュームの周縁や内部に編成され，長い冬の間も暖かい，啓蒙の場所を提供してくれる，パブリック・フォーラムとして考えた。

エリザベス・ド・ポルザンパルクは2層の，景観構成された都市のプロムナードをデザインした。そこは道路や地下のネットワークから簡単に入れ，広い公共庭園に面している。この内部道路は，会議ホール，展示場，新聞閲覧エリア，子供の領域，インターネット・エリアなど，常時開かれているスペースに通じている。

クリスチャン・ド・ポルザンパルクは，大気と光に溢れた前述のヴォリュームを4匹の"魚"のいる水族館のように構想した。大きい方の2匹は天井から吊り下がり，統制されたアクセス・エリアを収め，他の2匹，小さい方は，プロムナードに面した公共空間を収め，地上に休んでいる。

この図書館のインテリアはエリザベス・ド・ポルザンパルクのデザインである。

今，公共空間というものが，どこにおいてもビジネスや娯楽産業の手でつくられている時にあって，ケベック大図書館は，文化的プログラムを持つ，24時間オープンの大公共空間を構想する絶好の機会をモントリオールの地に提示することになる。

(クリスチャン・ド・ポルザンパルク)

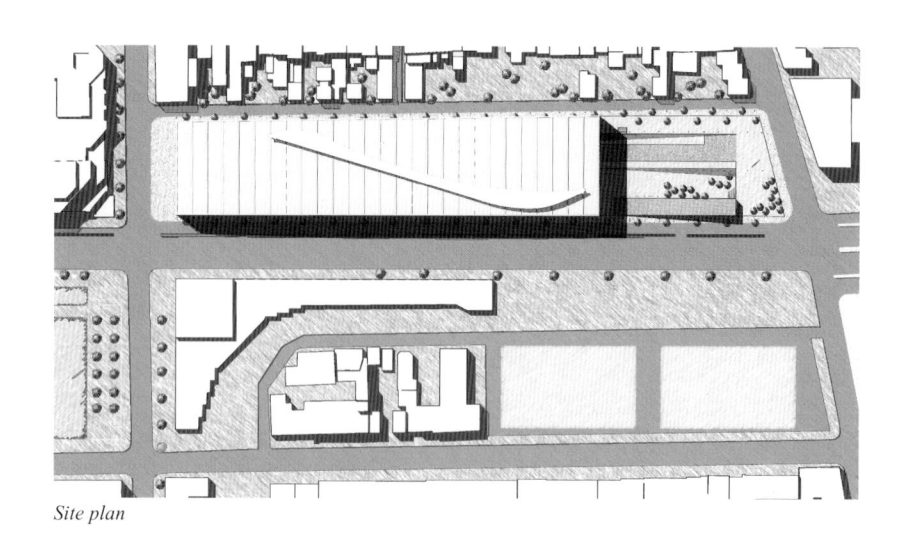

Site plan

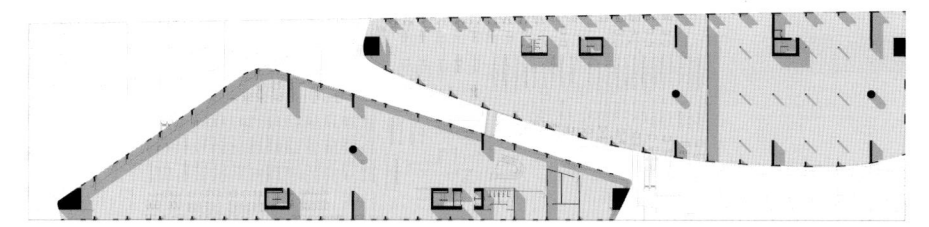

Level +4

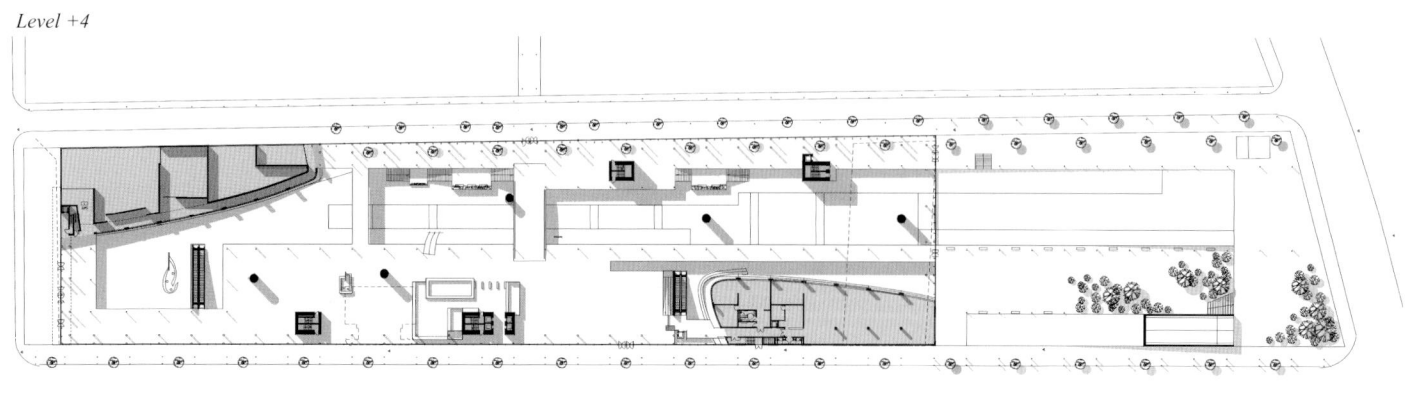

Level 0

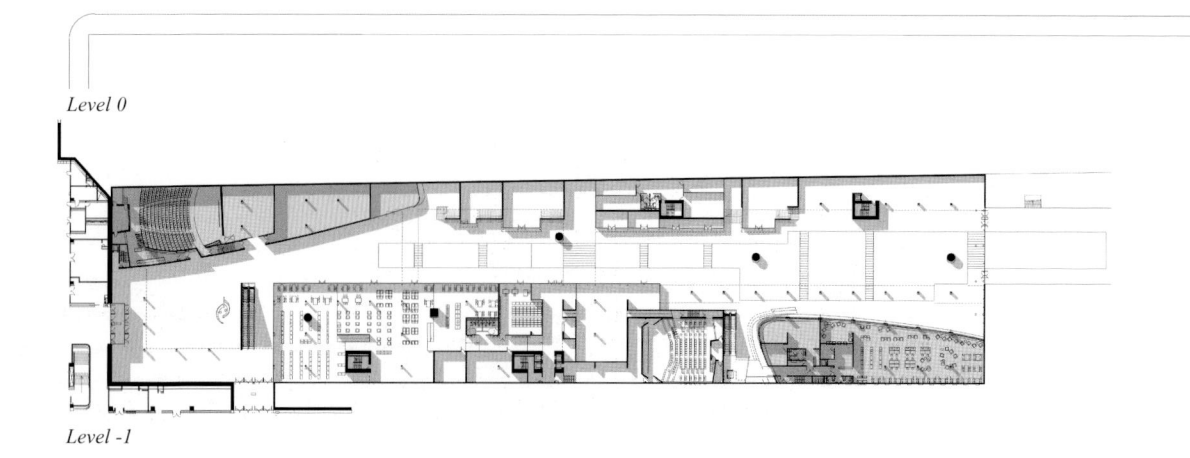

Level -1

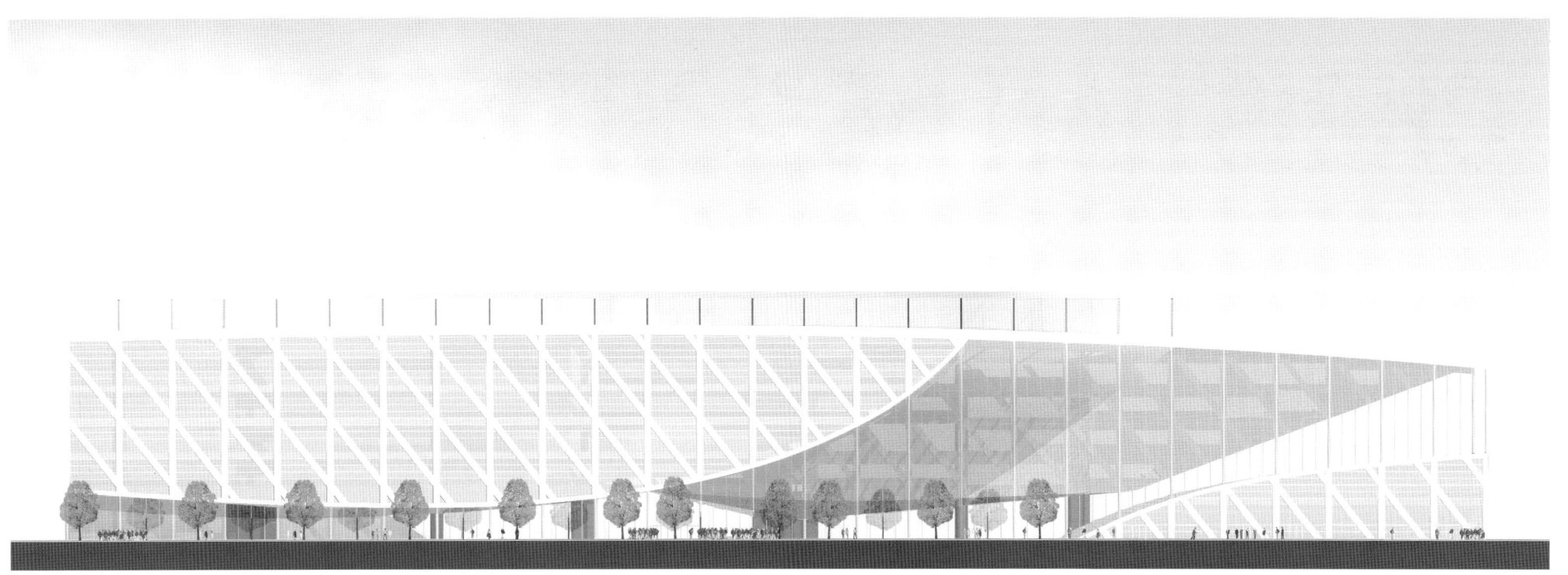

Elevation

Elevation

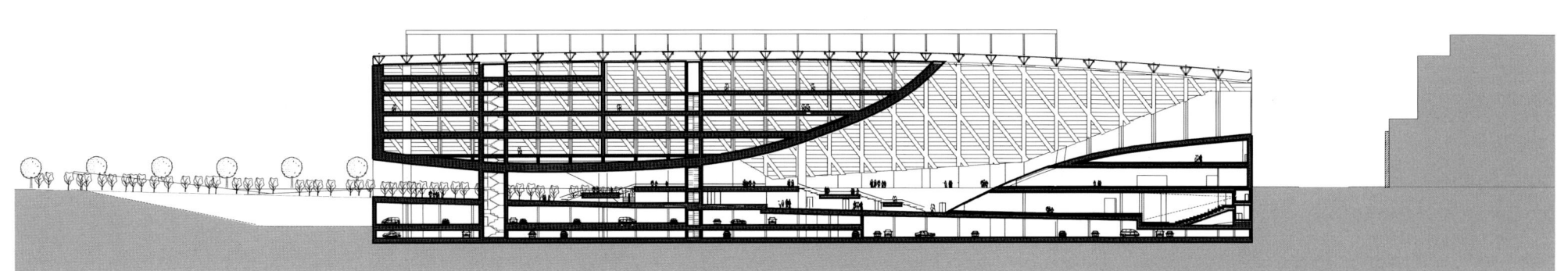

Longitudinal section

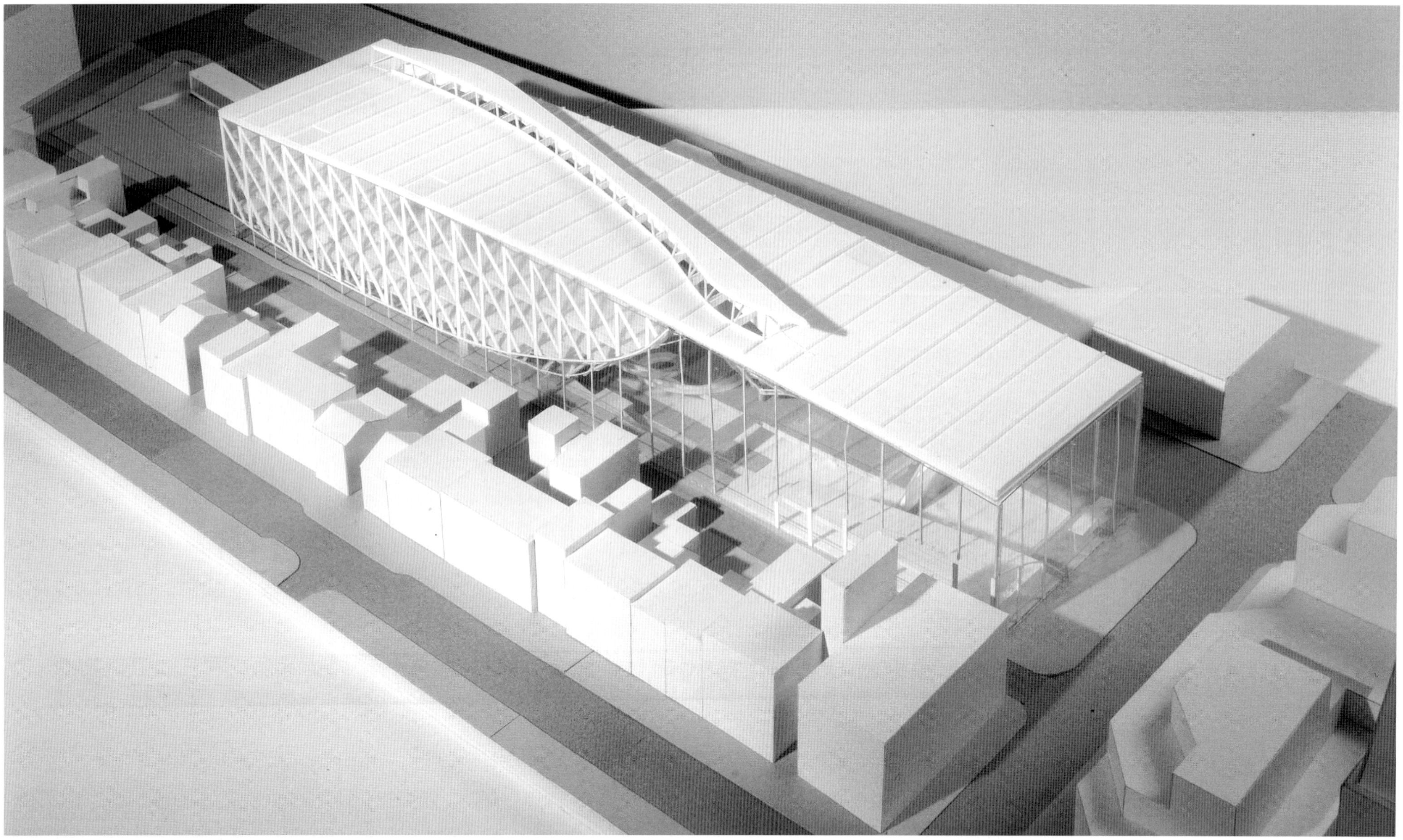

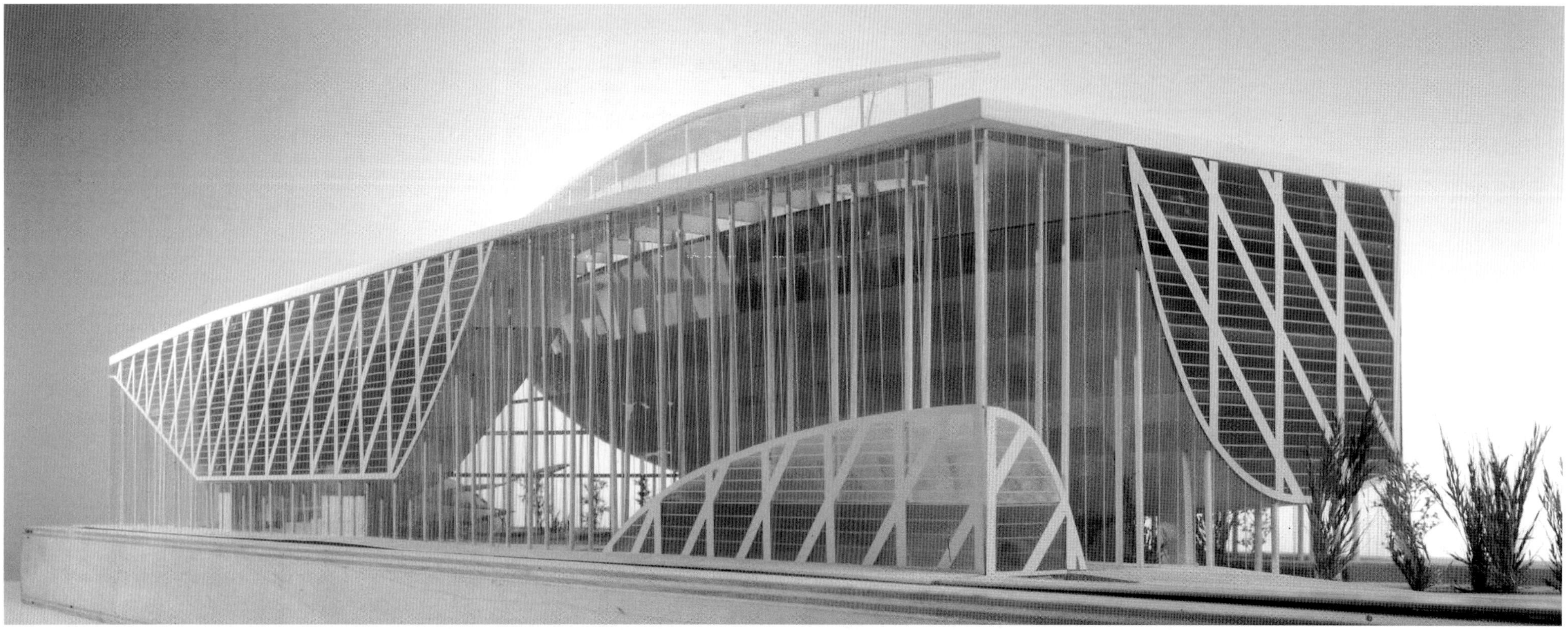

GA PROJECT

Elevation

Elevation

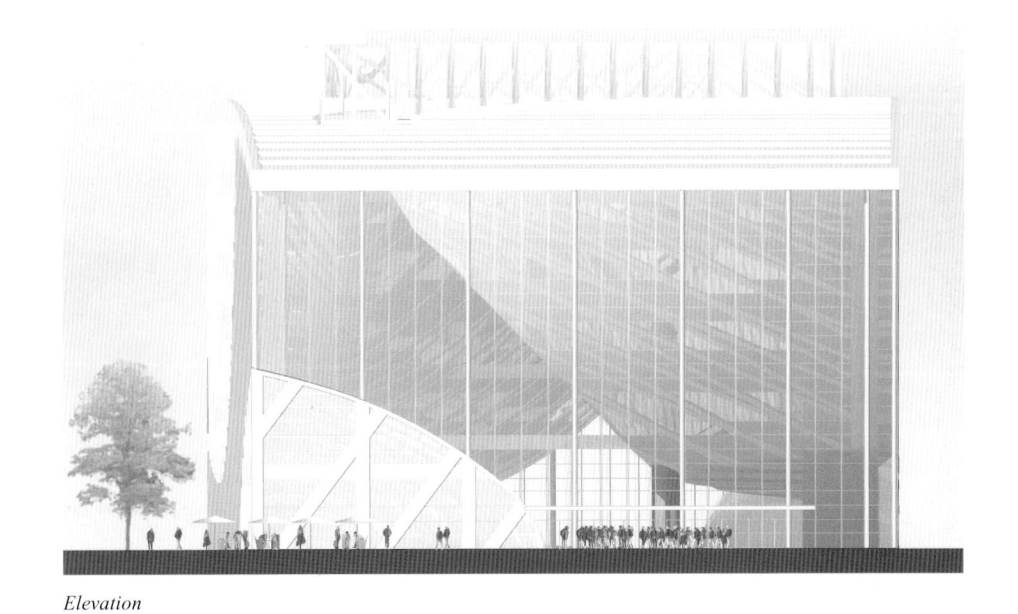

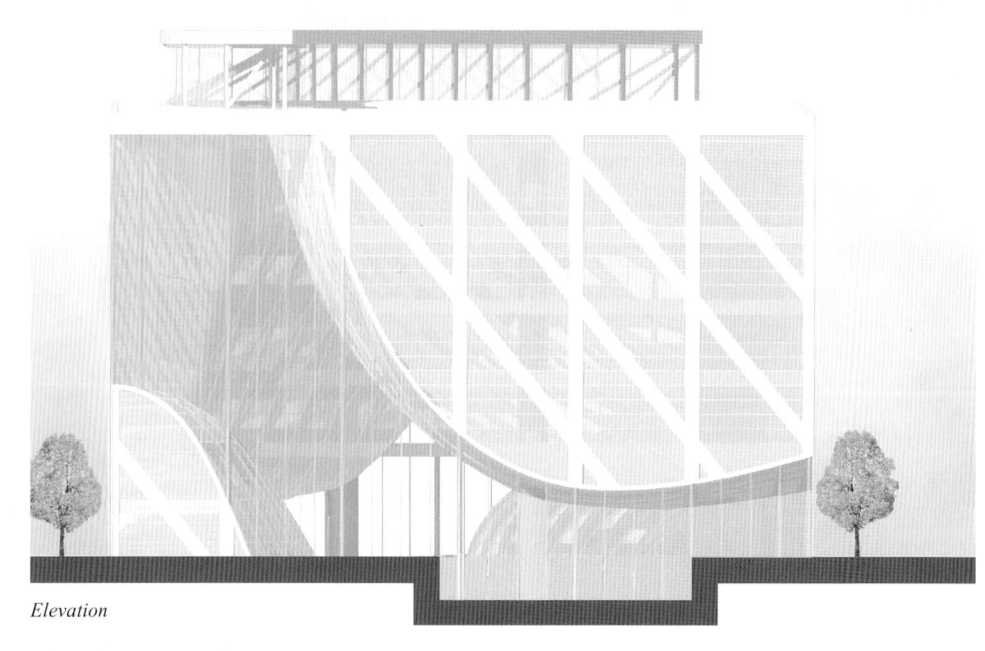

Architect: Atelier de Portzamparc—Christian de Portzamparc, principal-in-charge; Elizabeth de Portzamparc, interior; Jean Marc Venne, designer; Karol Claverie, project architect; Birtz, Bastien, Belanger, Beauchemin, Galienne, Moisan, Plante, associated architects
Client: La Grande Bibliothèque du Québec
Program: library, media library exhibition halls, auditorium, teaching rooms, conference halls, "café-restaurant", book shops
Total floor area: 37,000 m^2

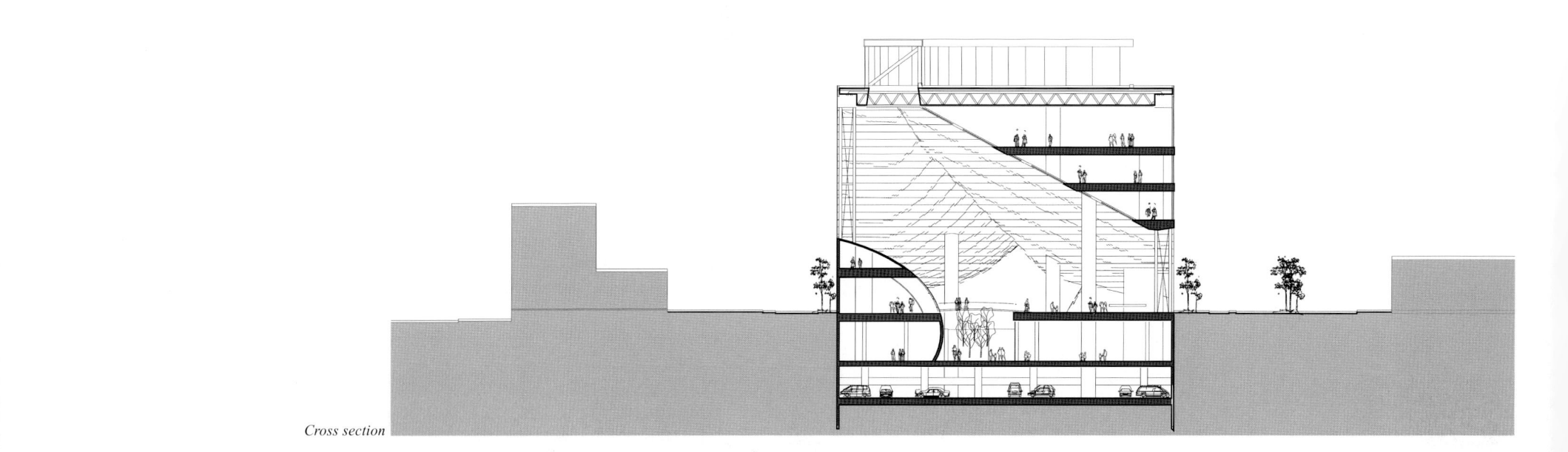

Cross section

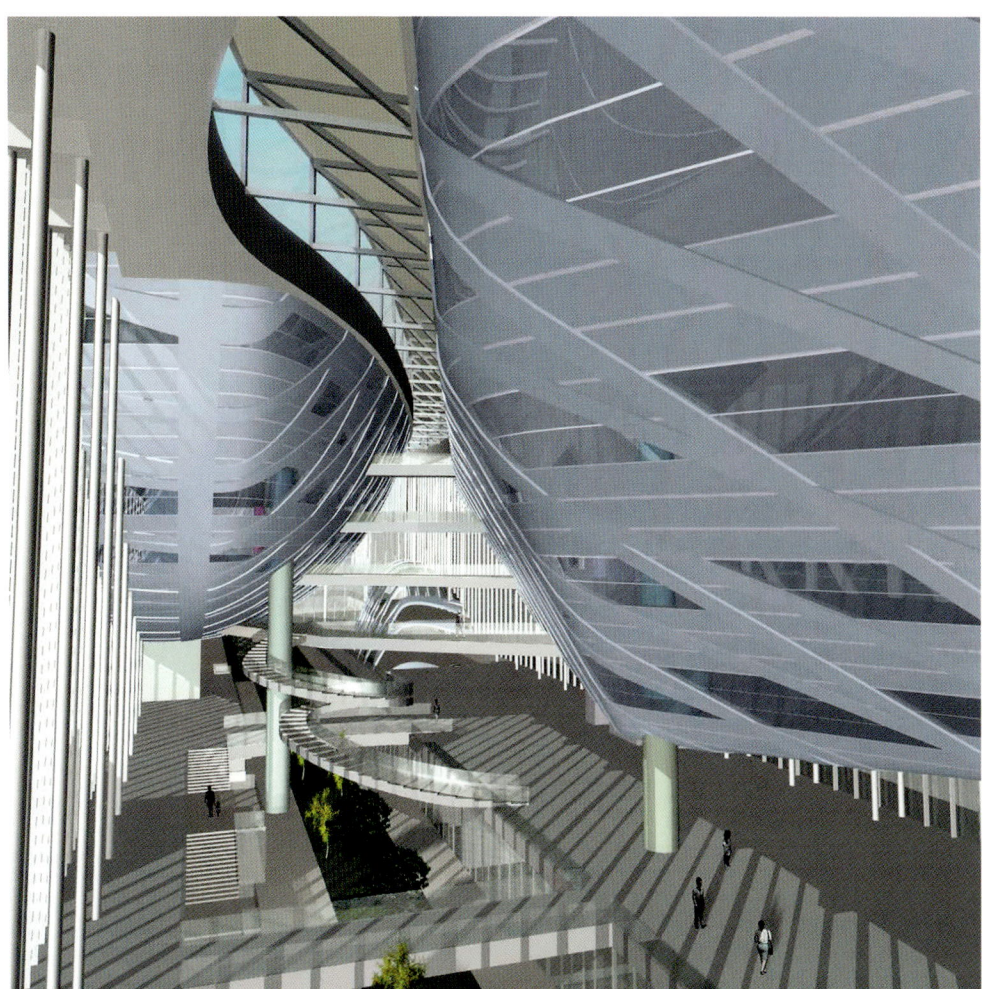

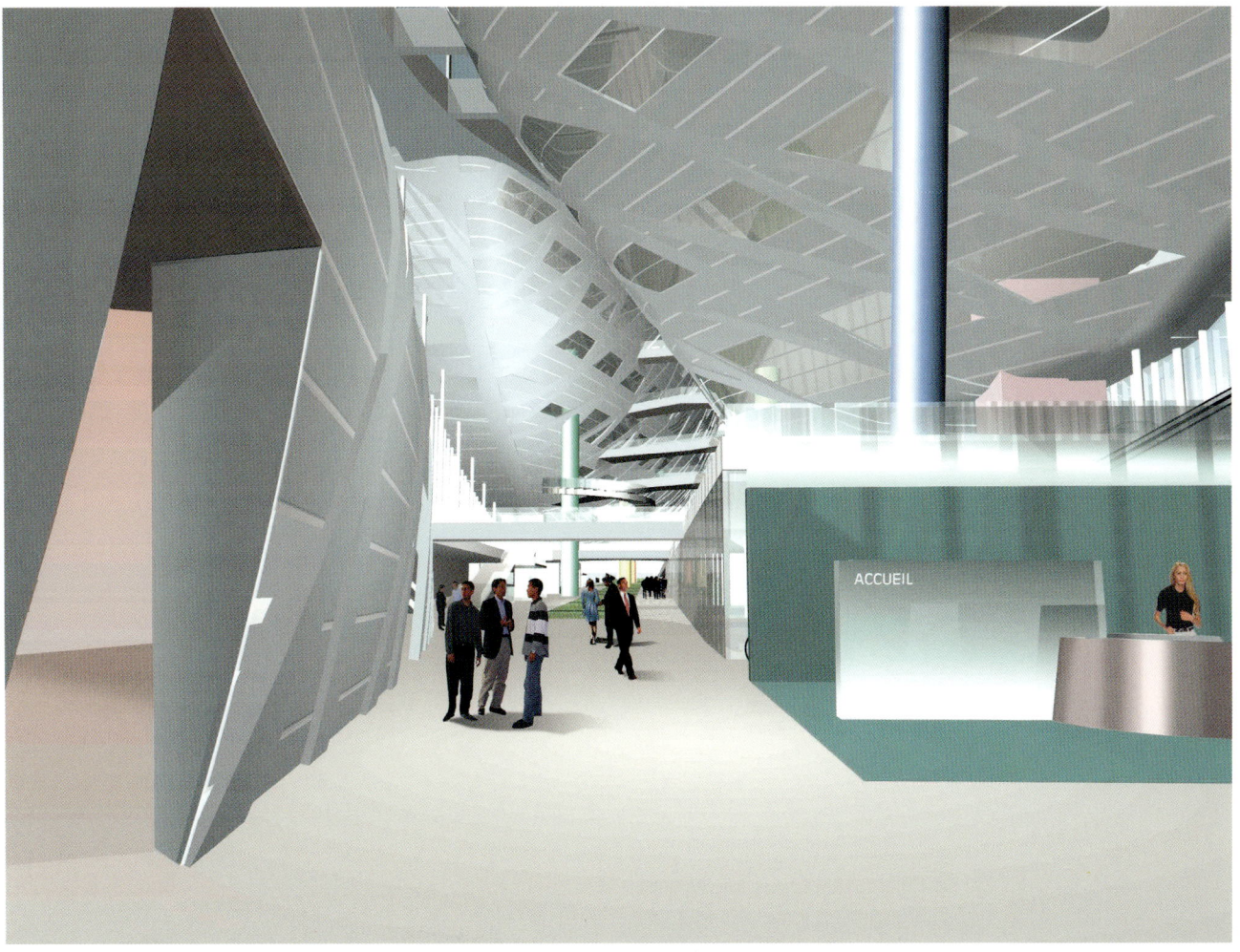

Interior views

NORMAN FOSTER

GREATER LONDON AUTHORITY HEADQUARTERS
London, U.K. Design: 1998–2000 Construction: 2000–02

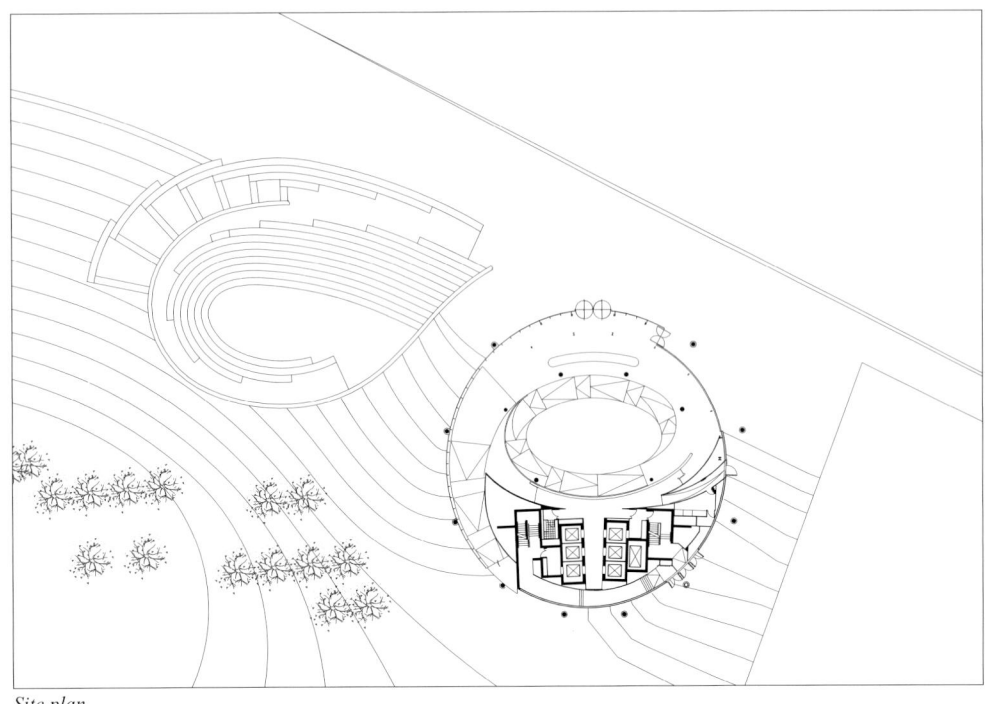

Site plan

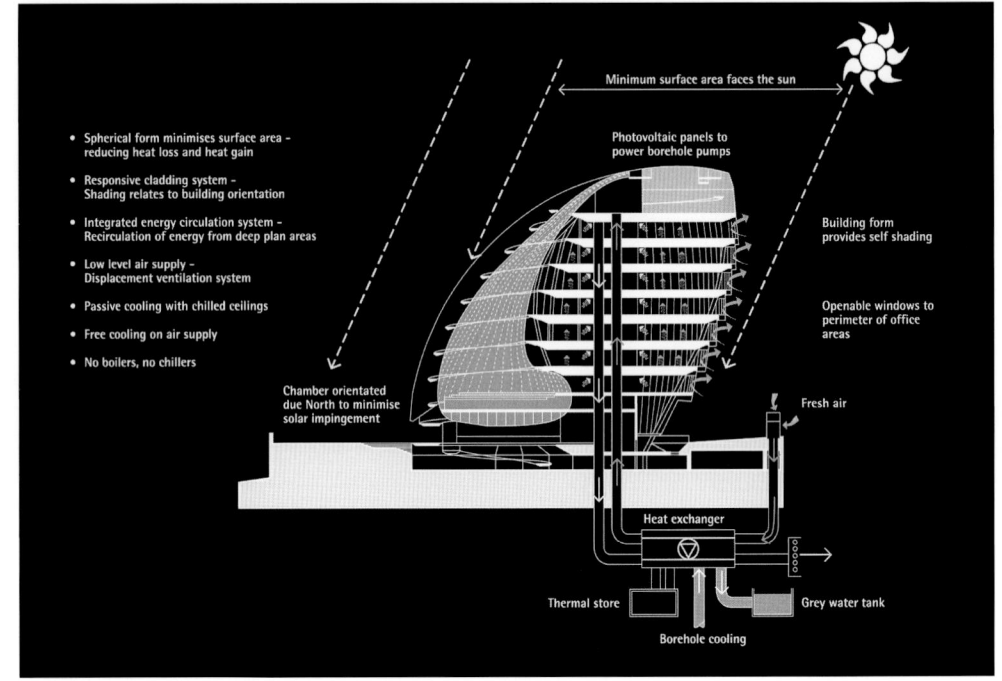

Diagram

Home to the Greater London Authority, this is one of the capital's most symbolically important new buildings. It expresses the transparency of the democratic process and demonstrates the potential for a wholly sustainable, virtually non-polluting public building.

The headquarters occupies a prominent site on the Thames alongside Tower Bridge, adjacent to the new London Bridge City development. The brief comprises an Assembly chamber, committee rooms, and public facilities, together with offices for the Mayor, Assembly members, the Mayor's cabinet, and support staff. It provides 17,000 square metres of accommodation on ten levels.

The Assembly chamber faces north across the river to the Tower of London. Its glass enclosure invites Londoners to watch the Assembly at work. The public is also invited to share the building: a flexible public space on the top floor—'London's Living Room'—can be used for exhibitions or functions for up to 200 guests; and the public commands the rooftop, where a terrace offers unparalleled views across London. At the base is a piazza with a cafe, from which the riverside can be enjoyed. Vertical circulation throughout the building is via lifts and gentle ramps, which allow universal access.

In conventional terms the building has no front or back: its shape is derived from a geometrically modified sphere. This hybrid form achieves optimum energy performance by minimising the surface area exposed to direct sunlight. Analysis of sunlight patterns throughout the year produced a thermal map of the building's surface, which is expressed in its cladding.

A range of active and passive shading devices is employed. The building leans back towards the south, where the floor-plates step inwards to provide shading for the naturally ventilated offices. The building's cooling systems utilise cold ground water pumped up via boreholes from the water table. The combination of these energy-saving techniques means that chillers are not needed and for the majority of the year the building will require no additional heating.

Overall, heating and cooling loads will equate to only one-quarter of the energy consumed by a typical air-conditioned office building.

グレーターロンドン市当局の本部となるこの建物は，首都を象徴する最も重要な新しい建物である。それは，民主主義の透明性を表現し，資源を枯渇させることなく維持し，ほとんど環境を汚さない公共建築を実現することになる。

敷地はテムズ川に面し，タワー・ブリッジのそばという非常に目立つ場所にあり，新しく開発が進んでいるロンドン・ブリッジ・シティーに隣接する。設計概要には，議場，委員会室，公共施設，そして市長・市議会議員・市長の諮問委員及び補佐スタッフのオフィスが含まれている。10階建て，1万7千平米の施設となる。

議場は北に面し，対岸にロンドン塔が見える。議場のガラス壁は，開催中の議会の様子を見物するよう，ロンドン市民に呼びかける。また，一般市民がこの建物を共有するように誘ってもいる。ロンドンのリビング・ルームとも言える最上階のフレキシブルな公共空間は展覧会場や200人以上の集いに使用され，屋上も開放されてテラスからはロンドン市街を一望できる。1階には川岸の眺めを楽しめるカフェを配した広場がある。建物全体の垂直サーキュレーションはエレベータと緩やかなランプで構成され，あらゆる箇所へのアクセスを可能とする。

伝統的用語法に従えば，この建物には正面も背面もない。その形は幾何学的な修正を加えた球体から生まれている。このハイブリッドな形は，直射日光にさらされる表面領域を最小限にすることで，最大のエネルギー効率を達成する。年間を通した日照パターンの分析から建物表面の温度分布図を作成し，その表面被覆に反映させた。

日除けとして，アクティブ，パッシブ両方の方法が広範に採用された。建物は南に向かって上体を反らして行く。その傾斜に沿って床面は内側にセットバックされ，自然換気されるオフィスの日除けの役割を果たす。建物の冷房方式は，地下水面からボーリングであけた穴を通じて汲み上げた冷たい地下水を利用する。これらの省エネルギー対策の組合せによって冷房装置は不要となり，年間の大半は補足的な暖房も必要としない。

全体的に，暖房及び冷房負荷は典型的な空調設備付きの建物が消費するエネルギー量の4分の1に相当するに過ぎないものとなるだろう。

Exploded view

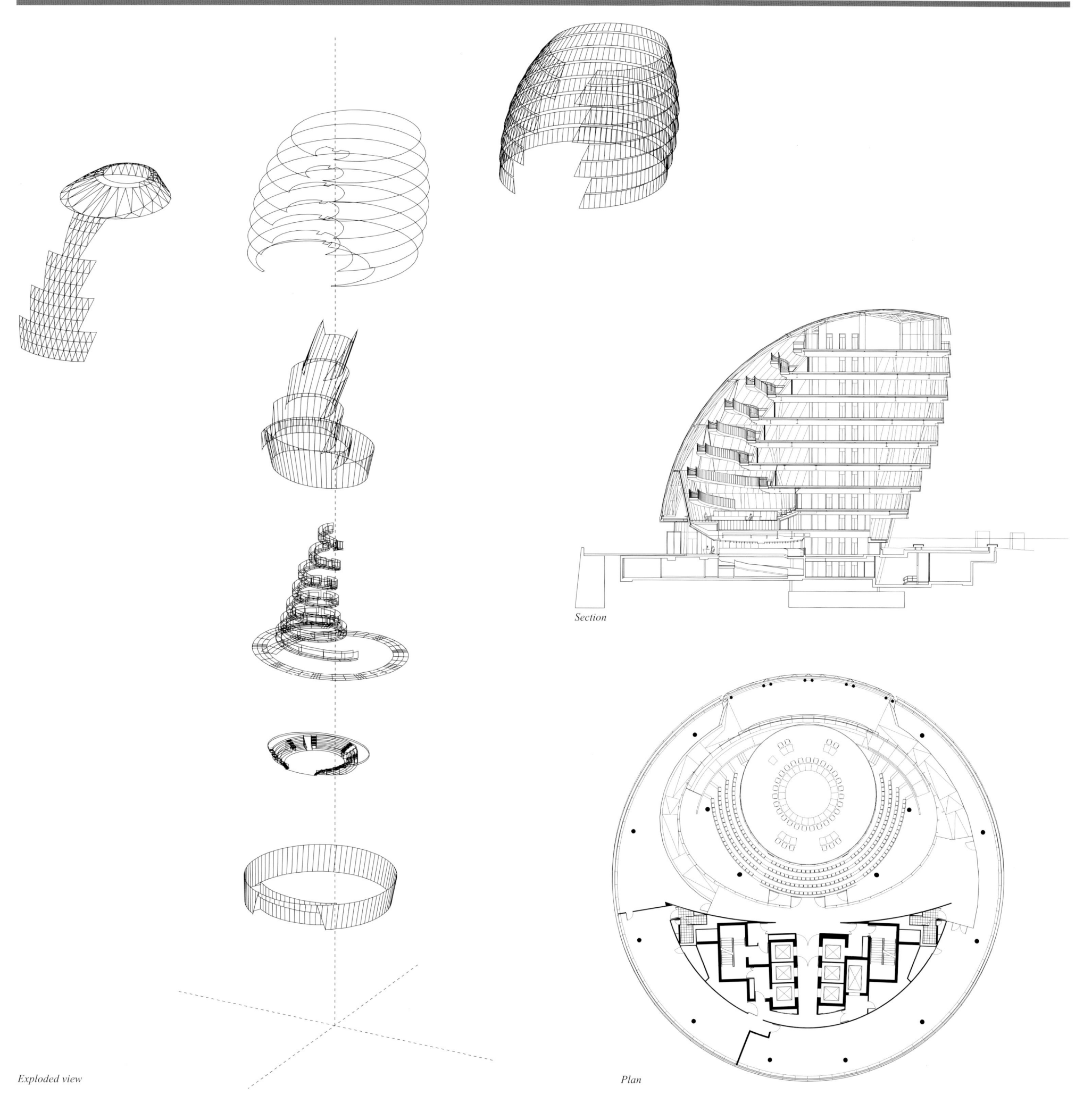

Section

Plan

Montage

Architects: Foster and Partners—Norman Foster, Ken Shuttleworth, Sean Affleck, Richard Hyams, Max Neal, project team
Client: CIT group
Consultants: Ove Arup & Partners, structural/mechanical; Townshend Landscape Architects, landscape; Davis Langdon & Everest, quantity surveyors; Mott Green and Wall, cost consultant
General contractor: Mace Ltd.
Structural Systems: structural steelwork, reinforced concrete core
Major materials: cladding—clear glass with ceramic fit, clear and ceramic low emissivity coated glass incorporating shading devices
Total floor area: 18,000 m^2
Stories: 9 floors above ground

Assembly chamber

RENZO PIANO

PAUL KLEE MUSEUM
Bern, Switzerland Design: 1999–

The Paul Klee Museum in Bern, Switzerland, was designed to pay true homage to the artist. It is located on a site outside the city on gently rolling hills with the Alps as backdrop. The idea was to capture the "spirit of the countryside" while working the land directly. Thus the museum will take the exact shape of the hills, while integrating with the countryside as closely as possible so that the sense of beauty and boundlessness evoked by the mountains is not disturbed.

A suite of three large rooms—artificial hills—will house a portion of Klee's large body of work. The majority of the works that cannot be exhibited for reasons of preservation will be made available to researchers and specialists.

At the museum entrance is a section open to access by the general public, containing an auditorium. Visitors will gradually walk inside "hills" as they move to the inner sanctum of the "exhibition" section before finally arriving at a research and study center on Klee and his works. The various wings will be connected by a path that is clearly intended to recall the image of a saber suddenly thrust into the hillsides. The museum will be located along a pre-existing motor way that will give the impression of cutting the "hills" into sections.

Unlike other museums we have designed, this one could not benefit from the brightest light because Klee's works must be protected from sunlight to preserve them. Constructed from wood inspired by boat construction in olden days, the museum will be illuminated by a series of openings made through the roof through which light will pour in and be spread through the rooms by a system of translucent screens, creating softer light.
Aymeric Lorente

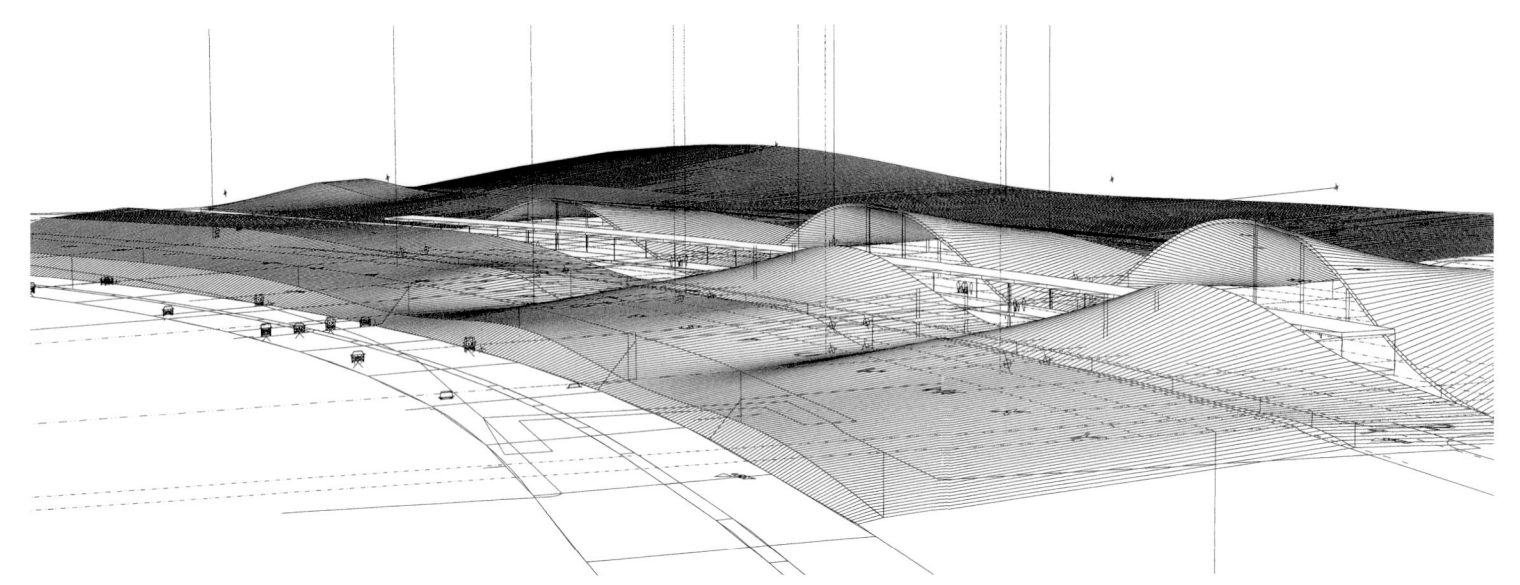

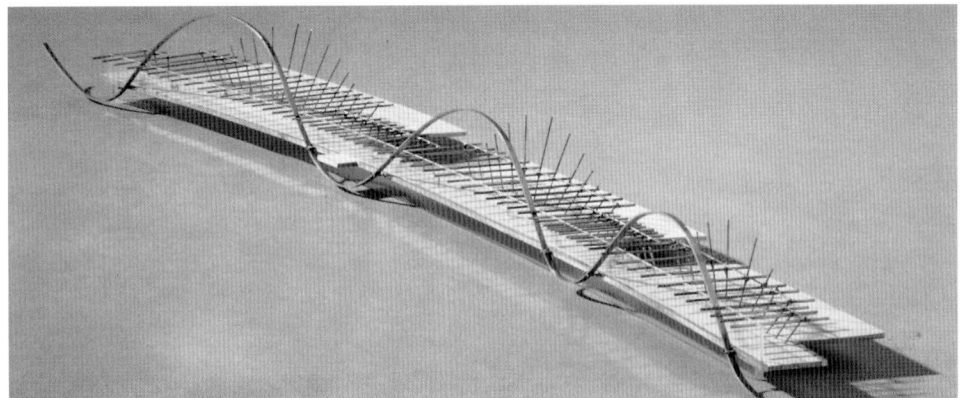

Structural model

スイス，ベルンに計画されているパウル・クレー美術館のデザインは，クレーへ，心からの敬意を捧げたものである。敷地は，背景にアルプスが広がる郊外の緩やかな丘にある。基本的な考えは，この地形そのものと直接取り組みながら，"田園の雰囲気"を捕縛することだった。こうして，美術館は丘の形を正確になぞり，田園風景にできるだけ身を寄せ，融け込むものとなり，山並みから生まれている美しさと無限な広がりは損なわれることはない。

人工の丘を構成しながら連なる3つの大きな部屋に，膨大なクレーの作品の一部が納められる。作品保護のため展示できない絵画の大部分を，研究者や専門家が見られるようになるだろう。

一般入場者のアクセスとなる美術館のエントランスにはオーディトリアムが置かれている。来館者はゆっくりと"丘"の内部を進み，"展示場"のある内部聖域へ向かい，最後にクレーとその作品の研究センターに至る。様々なウィングが，丘に突然突き刺されたサーベルを連想させようと明らかに意図した通路で結ばれる。美術館は既存の高速道路に沿って配置される。高速道は"丘"を断片に切り分けているような印象を与えるだろう。

われわれが今までに設計してきた美術館とは異なり，ここでは，明るい光の恩恵を享受させることはできない。クレーの絵画は陽光から保護する必要があるからだ。昔の船舶構造から啓示を得た木造の美術館は，屋根を貫き連続する開口から照明されるが，差し込んだ光は，半透明のスクリーンによって柔らげられ，展示場全体に拡散してゆく。（A・ロレント）

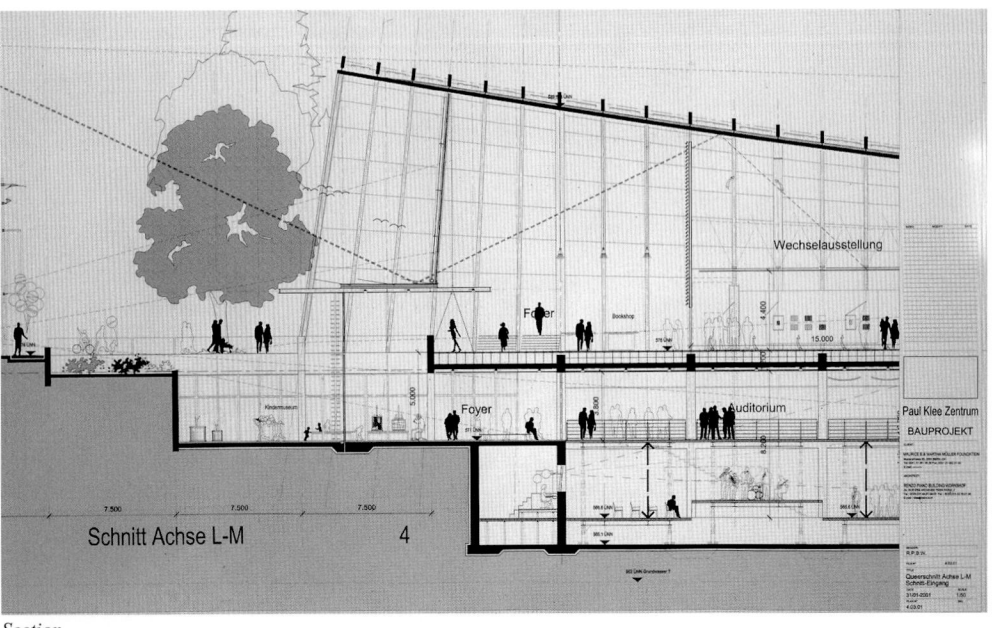

Section

GA PROJECT

Architects: Renzo Piano Building Workshop
Client: Maurice E. and Martha Foundation
Consultants: Ove Arup & Partners, GEC Ingénierie, ARB

Model photos: M. Denance ©RPBW

GA DOCUMENT

92

Section

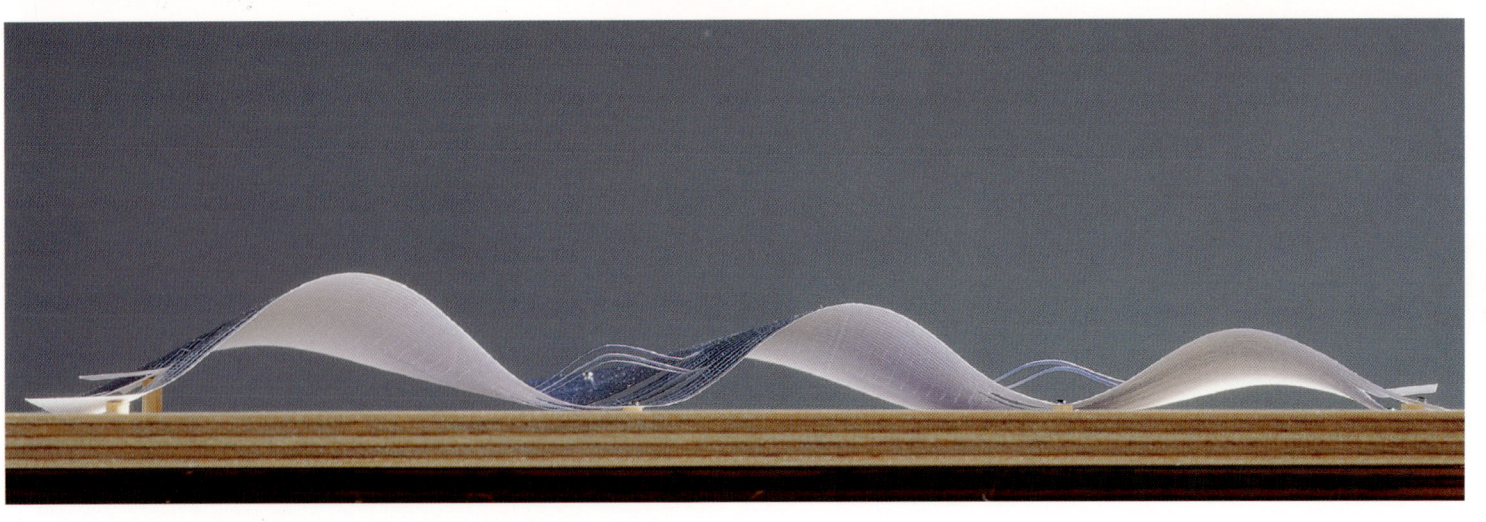

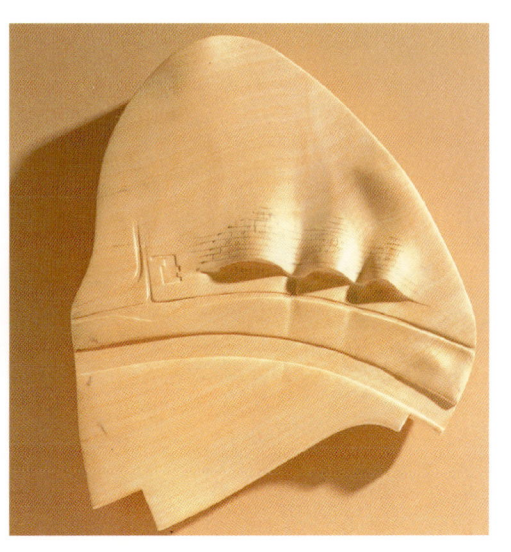

Plan

Section

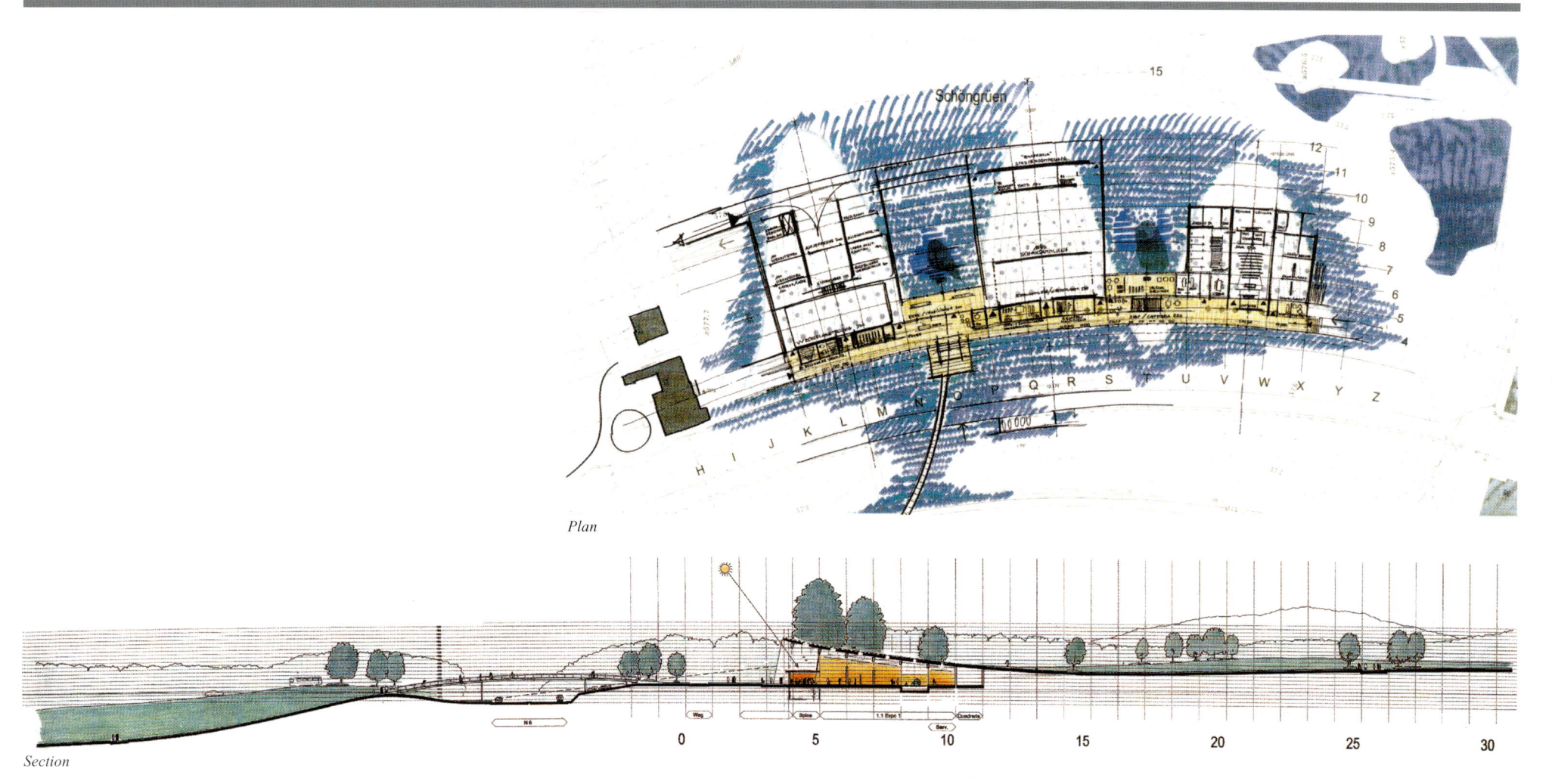

Sketch

Plan

TOYO ITO

HÔPITAL COGNACQ-JAY
Paris, France Design: 1999–2002 Construction: 2002–2004

The project was a first-prize winner to a design competition which took place in October 1999, involving designated participants from five different companies. The site is located in the southern part of the 15th district in Paris where middle-rise apartment buildings line the streets of a rather quiet residential quarter. The existing hospice was built in 1922 as a hospital, and was later turned into a hospice for terminal care in 1978. The present 72-bed ward can no longer stand the age, nor provide sufficient accommodation. The competition's program consisted of increasing the number of beds to 152, and of establishing new rehabilitation facilities for children suffering from various handicaps such as stammering.

Our proposal has focused on creating harmony between this hospice and its surrounding Parisian townscape, along with spaces and places where not only the patients but their families, care-takers, doctors and local residents all get to relax and feel psychological and physical comfort.

The original hospice is equipped with a patio of a moderate size. The variety of plants that grows there delights everyone's eyes. Tables and chairs complete the scenery, so that anyone can take meals in open-air on days of fine weather. Our planning has begun with the idea of reproducing this patio's tranquil atmosphere as much as possible, inside and outside the building. First, the alleys were rearranged so that they would surround the patio.

Since the existing building is completely independent from them, the new building would extend from the one bordering two streets. In this manner, the patio would be enclosed by buildings. Also, a program to be the core of services would be arranged on the first basement floor, so that basement levels would be as open as possible. Then, the building's side faces would fold in pleats to gain maximum surface area adjacent to the outside, ensuring a view over the patio to all rooms.

This pleated structure would produce external spaces that may be looked upon as patios with unique characters, to be put to use as integral parts of the building.

Various changes of program have arisen from the part of the hospital after the competition. The facade has gone through a long process of presentations, and many local laws and regulations had to be cleared pertaining to problems such as height or tree-planting. As of now, the actual planning has only just begun.
Jun Yanagisawa/Contemporaries

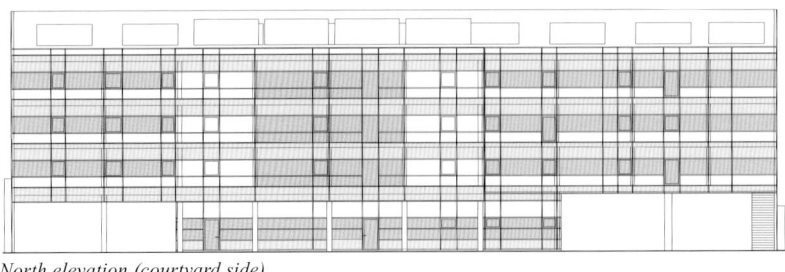

North elevation (courtyard side)

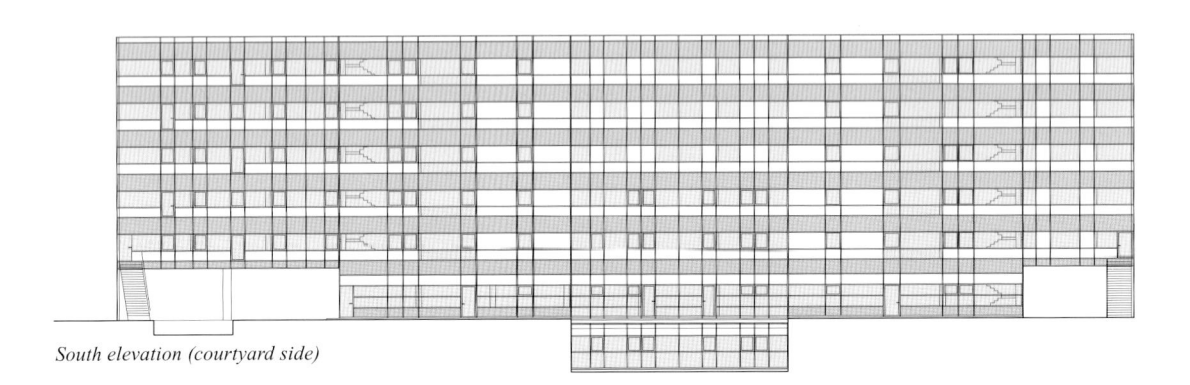

South elevation (courtyard side)

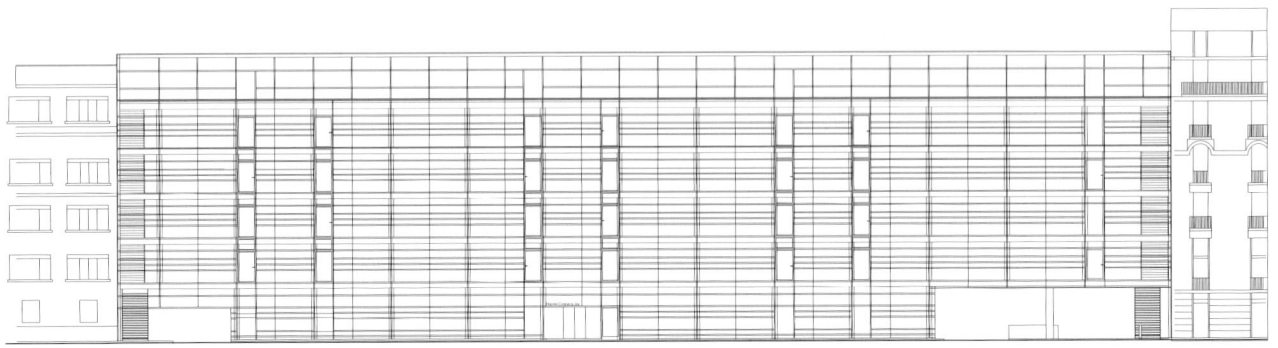

North elevation (rue millon side)

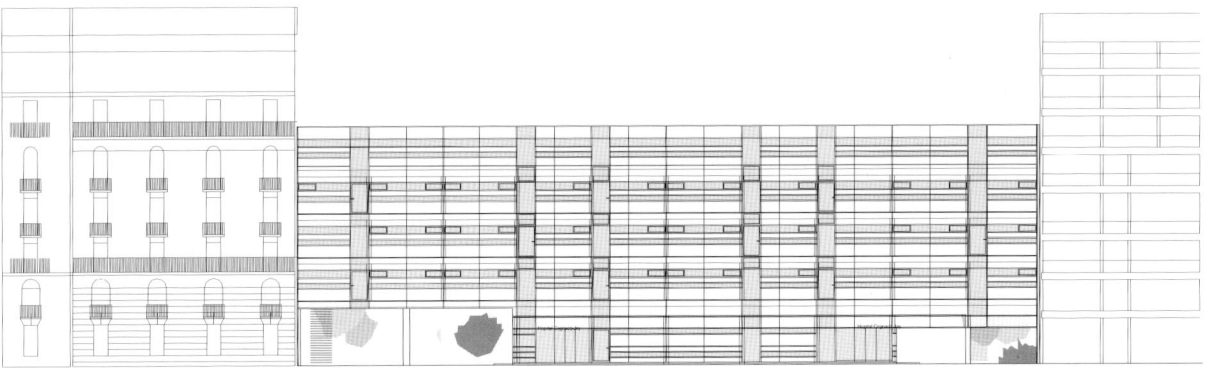

South elevation (rue blomet side)

Ground floor

Third floor

Basement floor

First floor

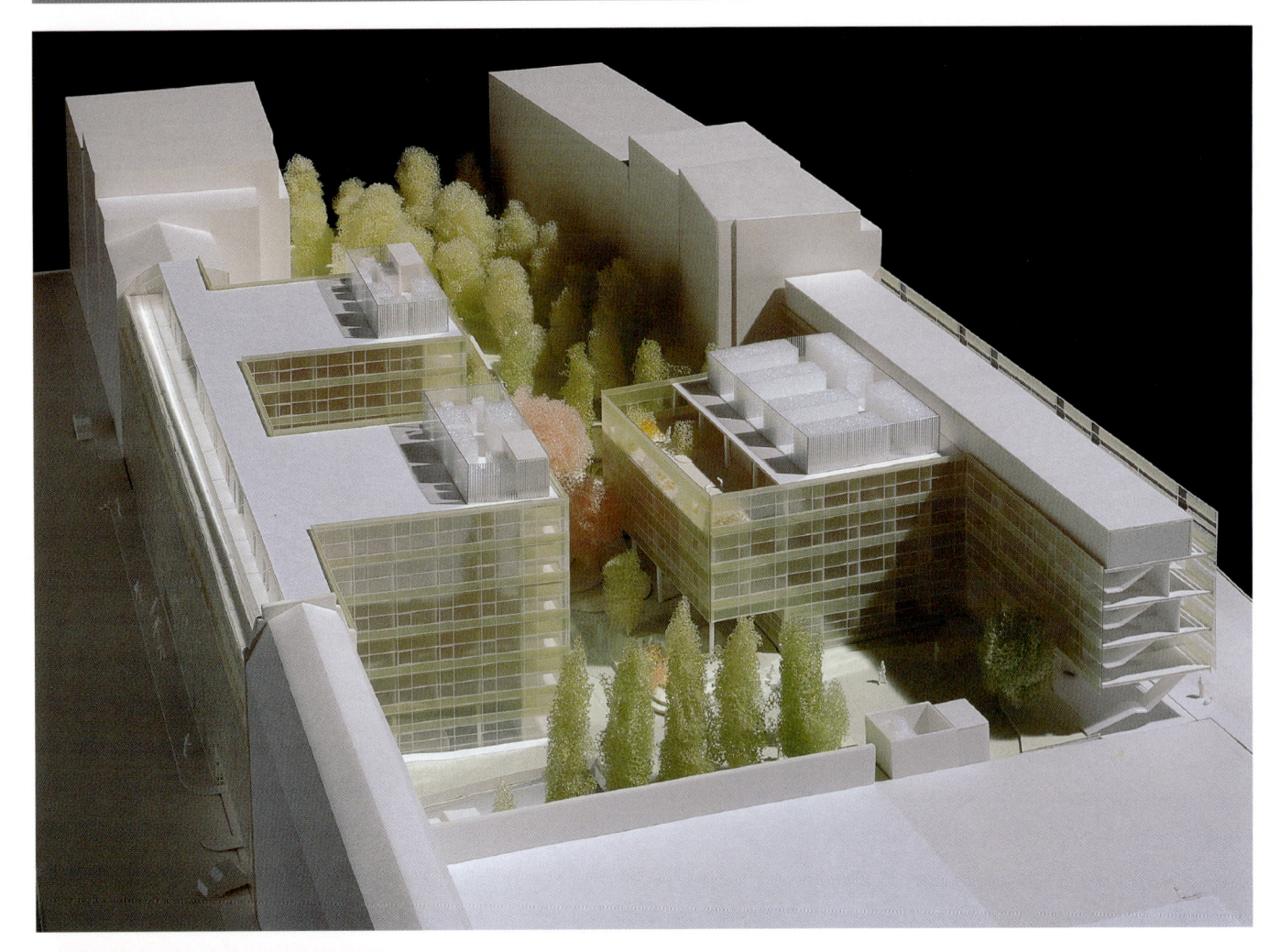

Model photos: K. Takada

1999年10月に5社による指名設計競技での1等案。計画地はパリ15区のやや南，周辺は中層の集合住宅が立ち並ぶ比較的閑静な住宅街である。現存するホスピスは1922年に建設され，当初は病院であったが，1978年からターミナルケアの施設としてホスピスに移り変わった。現在，72床の病室数は老朽化も進みまた規模も不足しているために，病床数を倍以上の152床に増やし，更に吃音などのハンデを背負った児童のためのリハビリテーション施設をも新たに設立したいというのがコンペティションのプログラムであった。

私たちの課題はこのターミナルケアの施設に対してパリの町並みとの調和をはかりながら，いかに患者のみならずその家族，看護する人々，医者あるいは周辺の住民にとって精神的にも肉体的にもくつろげる空間や場所を提案出来るかということであった。

現存するホスピスにはさほど大きくはないが中庭がひとつあり，そこでは多様な植物が生育し，見るものの目を楽しませ椅子やテーブルなどもさりげなく置かれている。そうした植物に囲まれて，気候の良いときなどは誰もが外で食事をしたり出来るような雰囲気を醸し出している。私たちは，この中庭のように穏やかな雰囲気をもった場所を出来るだけ建物の内外を問わず作り出したいというところから設計を始めた。そのためにまず街区を整理し，中庭を取り囲むような構成を選択した。

現存の建物は，街区に対して完全に独立しているので，私たちは2本の通りに対して隣接する建物に連続するようにしながら建物によって囲まれる中庭を作り出した。同時に地上のレベルを出来るだけ開放的にするために，サービスの核となるプログラムを地下1階のレベルに配置している。更には，全ての病室を中庭側に向けさせるために，建物は凸凹型の構成をとり，襞のように外部に接する面積をかせいでいる。

こうした凸凹の構成によって生まれた外部空間は，それぞれ特徴のある中庭として位置付けられ，建物と一体となって利用されることを目論んでいる。

コンペティション以降の病院側の様々なプログラムの変更，ファサードの度重なるプレゼンテーション，パリにおける斜線や緑化などの法規的な問題等を経ながら，現在ようやく実施設計に差し掛かっている。　柳沢潤／コンテンポラリーズ

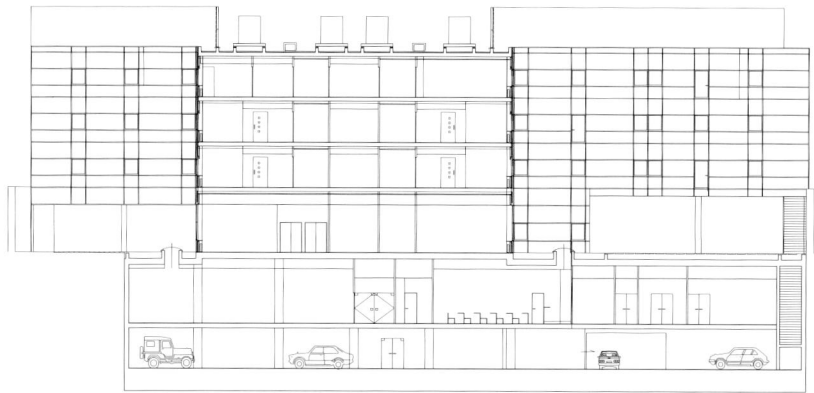

Section 1

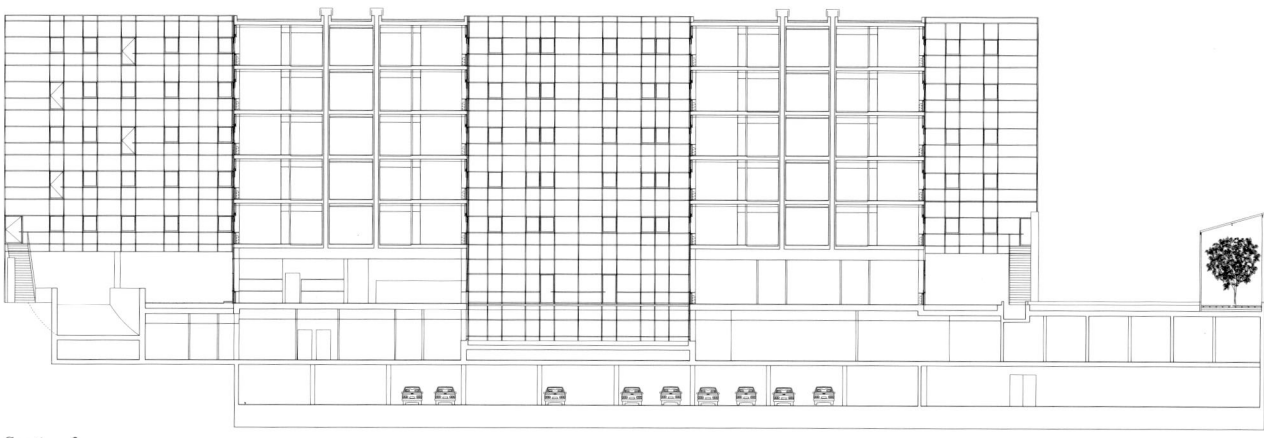

Section 2

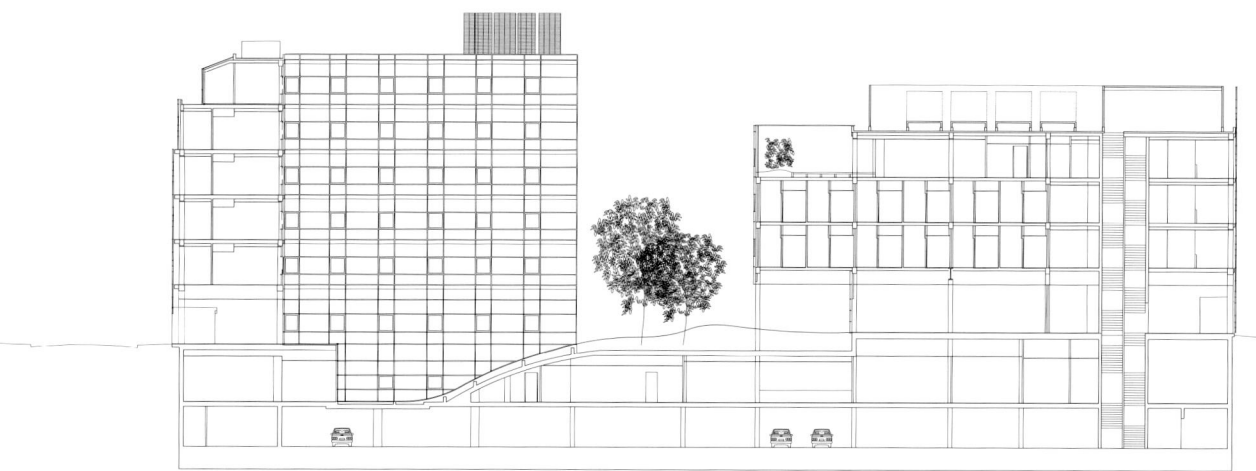

Section 3

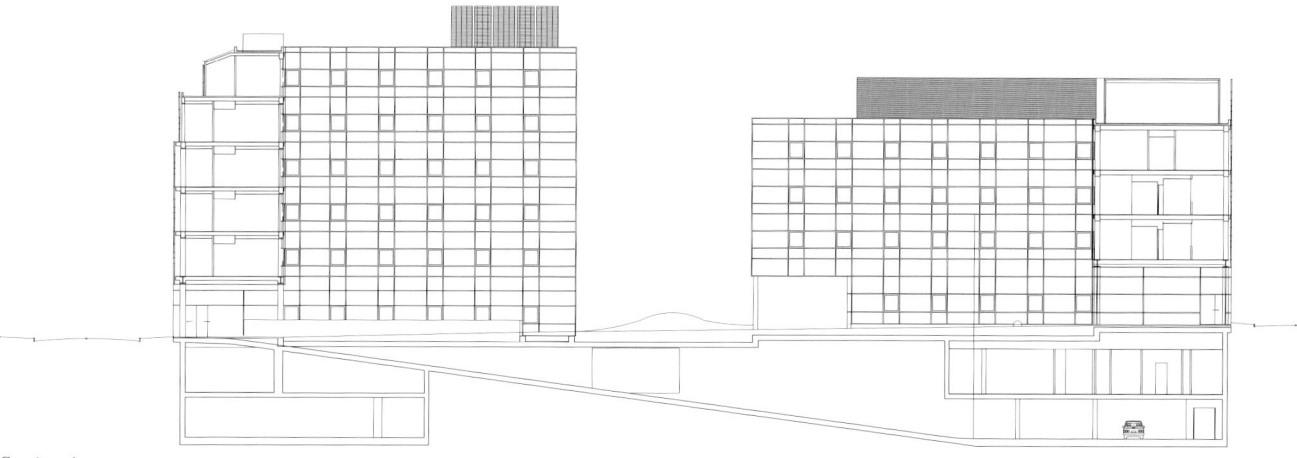

Section 4

Main Architects: Toyo Ito Associates, Architects—Toyo Ito, Takeo Higashi, Akio Takatsuka
Cooperated Architects: Jun Yanagisawa/Contemporaries, Manuel Tardits/MIKAN, Extra Muros
Client: Cognacq-Jay Foundation
Consultants: Mutsuro Sasaki, SETEC, structural; Environmental engineering, mechanical; SODECSET, economist; Hiroyasu Shoji, lighting
Structural system: reinforced concrete, steel
Major materials: glass sandwich panel, exterior; linoleum, plaster board, interior
Site area: 4,976 m²
Total floor area: 14,754 m²

DOMINIQUE PERRAULT

HOTEL AND CONGRESS CENTER
Barcelona, Spain Design: 2000–01 Construction: 2001–03

Night view

Street view

99 | GA PROJECT

Lobby

Restaurant

Guest room

Park

One can 'read the city of Barcelona' as a horizontal city, built according to geometric rules of CERDA's plan, but also as a vertical city with architectural landmarks such as the Sagrada Familia, the buildings of Olympic Village, and especially the hill-side district with the telecommunication tower, the Tibidao.

This reading of Barcelona's constructed substance has lead us to imagine a building whose base fits itself into the horizontal city and whose bodies and crown form a part of the vertical city. This morphology organizes an exercise of volumes, with a 'cubic' building behind the Tower as a balance weight, or for the tower itself, a rectangular parallelepiped cut in two lengthwise, one half of which being shifted toward the sky. This rupture of a 'perfect geometric block' creates a movement of form and volume that gives an urban sense to the insertion of the Tower into the horizontal city:
—a cantilever at a height of 25 meters provides an entrance hall for the Tower
—an emergence in the form of volume projection creates a 'crest' among the outline of the vertical city.

Such layout of elementary forms produces location marks for the edifice:
—a cantilever to show the entrance of the hotel, but also PERE IV Street,
—the cube pushed backwards to make some room for an open terrace looking over LOPE de VEGA Street.
—The crust that pulls itself away into the sky, standing as a new landmark along the new section of Diagonal.

Altogether, these urban signs furnish the Tower with a real capacity of architectural interaction with the site's present and future contexts. The organization of functions is a logical consequence of its architectural situation:
—at the foot of the building: activities related to moving and regrouping such as the hotel's lobby, restaurants, auditorium, swimming pool, and daytime and night lounges.
—within the body of the building: single, double or suite rooms opening to the sea or to the mountain with view to the Sagrada Familia.

The principle of design and of comfort inside the hotel is to have in each room a large and full view to the exterior like a huge screen plugged onto the cityscape. This huge screen is comprised visually of a series of smaller screens such as television sets that form a 'wall of images'. In fact, the building is dressed with a shell of aluminium plates dotted with big, round holes. This protective, finishing skin is inalterable because it is made of thick, lightweight aluminium plates that are thus dense, rigid and noncorrosive. This envelope is alive, since it 'plays' with light—shiny on one side and dark on the other, transparent at the angles of the Tower, opaque and almost closed along the gables, and finally bordered with lace at the edge of terraces.

Like a metallic needle, the tower sparkles in Barcelona's skyline. This 'jewel' is joyous and cheerful, with pieces of glass tinted in red, yellow, blue and green, scattered randomly over the facade like stained-glass. During the night, the tower transforms itself into an 'urban lamp', a luminous sign planted along the Diagonal.

A Tower-Hotel is a singular building in a city—its identity, style and brand have to be 'unforgettable', in the sense of memory, for those who pay frequent visits as well as for those who discover it. Such will of belonging to a place, of participating to activities of the place, has lead us to introduce a notion of a lobby trespassed as if it were a public road. One approaches the hotel entrance hall through a small footbridge overhanging a garden, like a piece of nature that extends the presence of the 'urban park' located on the opposite side of the Diagonal. Next, one crosses the lobby to the other side, to the south, over the piazza-terrace opening to district 22a. This layout is highly interactive with respect to the urban functions of the area. The Hotel becomes a place of passage and of welcome, a friendly spot. This fresh and actual characteristic in motion corresponds to the evolution of this 'start-up district' that is Barcelona's techno-business future—between the sea and the mountain, between history and geography.

バルセロナを、セルダが計画した幾何学的な規則に従って建設された水平な都市と考えてもよい。しかしここはまた、サグラダ・ファミリアやオリンピック村の建築群、そして特に通信塔の立つティビダオの山腹地区が示すように、建築的ランドマークのある垂直な都市でもある。

バルセロナの現実の都市構成に対するこうした見方から、基部は水平都市に適合し、中間部と頂部は垂直都市の一角を担うような建物をイメージした。この形態学に基づいてヴォリュームによる演習を行った。重さを均衡させるため、背後に"キュービック"なブロックを従えたタワー、あるいは直角平行6面体を2つに長く切り分け、その一方を空に向けて転換させたタワー。"完璧な幾何学形"を壊すことで、形態とヴォリュームに動きが生まれ、平板な広がりに都市的感覚が付与される。
——25メートルの高さに設置されたカンティレヴァーがエントランス・ホールを提供する。
——屹立するヴォリュームから浮上する頂部が、垂直都市の輪郭のなかに"最高峰"となって聳える。

こうした基本形態による構成は、この建物が立つ場所の標識をつくりだす。
——カンティレヴァーはホテルのエントランスと同時にペレ4世通りも示す。
——ロペ・デ・ヴェガ通りを見晴らす開放的なテラスをつくるために、キューブを押し下げる。
——空に向かって仰向いたその堅い面は、ディアゴナル通りの新しい地区に沿った新たなランドマークとなる。

これらの都市サインは一体となって、このタワーに、敷地の現在そして未来のコンテクストと建築的に相互交流し得る実際的能力を与える。諸機能の空間配置はその建築的状況の論理的帰結である。
——建物の足元：ホテルのロビー、レストラン、オーディトリアム、昼間及び夜間のラウンジ関連の動きや再編に関わる諸活動領域。
——建物の中間部：海あるいはサグラダ・ファミリアと山の眺めに向いた、シングル、ダブル、スィートの各客室。

ホテル内部の快適性に基づいたデザイン原則は、都市景観に向けて巨大スクリーンを取り付けたかのように、各部屋から広々と外の眺めが見えることである。この巨大スクリーンは、"イメージの壁"を形づくるテレビジョン・セットのような一連の小スクリーンで視覚的に構成されている。実際に、建物は大きな丸い穴が点々とあいたアルミ・プレートの殻で包まれる。この保護的な被膜は他に代えられない。それは厚い軽量アルミ・プレートでつくられ、密度があり、堅く、腐食しないからである。この被膜は生きている。光と"遊ぶ"からである。片側が輝くときは他方は暗く、タワーの角度によって透明となり、切妻に沿っては不透明でほとんど閉ざされ、最後に、テラスの端がレースで縁取られる。

金属の針のように、タワーはバルセロナのスカイラインのなかできらきら光る。この"宝石"は、ステンドグラスのようにファサードに無作為に散らされた、赤、黄、青、緑に染められたガラスの小片で飾られ、陽気で、喜びに溢れたものになる。夜の間、それは"都市のランプ"、ディアゴナル通り沿いに設置された輝くサインに変身する。

タワー・ホテルは比類のない都市建築となる。その個性、スタイルと質は、記憶という意味で、頻繁にこの街を訪れる人にも、初めての人にも"忘れられない"ものでなければならない。場所に所属し、場所の活性化に参加するというこうした意志は、公道であるかのように侵入されるロビーを取り入れる気持ちにさせた。ディアゴナルの反対側にある"公園"の延長として自然の断片を思わせる庭園の上に吊られた、小さなブリッジを渡りホテルのエントランス・ホールに入る。次に、ロビーを反対側、南の22@地区に面したピアッツァ・テラスに向かって横切る。この配置は、地区の都市機能と双方向的に関わる。ホテルは、通路であり人を歓迎する場所、心地よいスポットになる。この新鮮で、動的な性格は、海と山の間、歴史と地理の間にあって、バルセロナのテクノ・ビジネスの未来に向かって"歩み始めた地区"の発展と同調する。

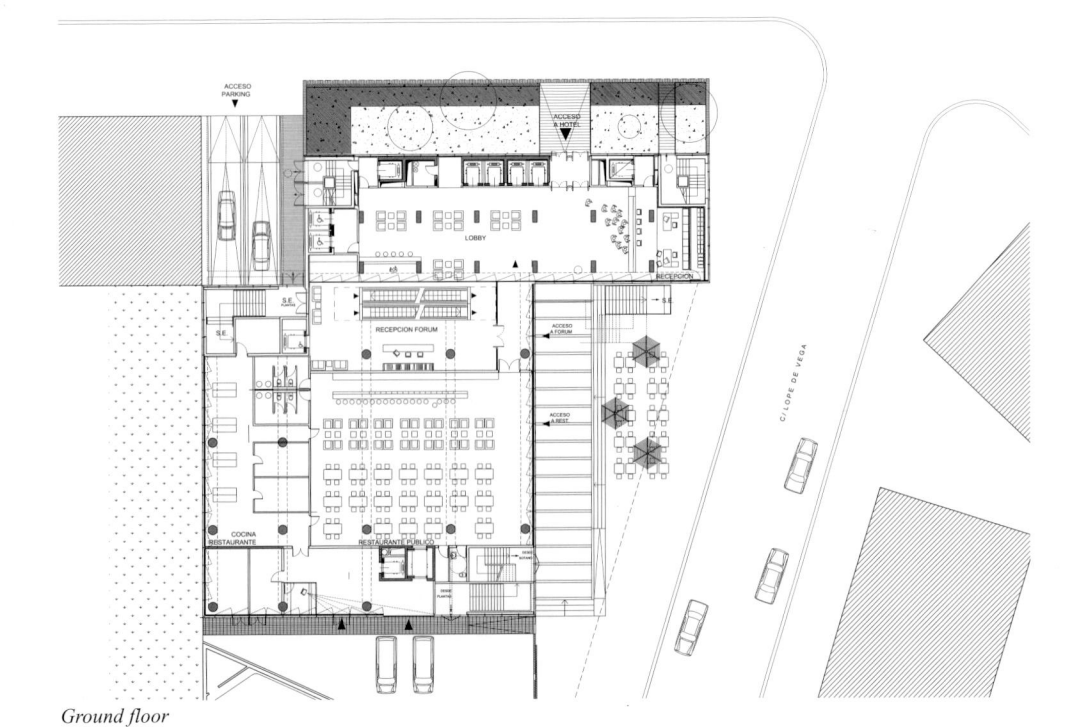

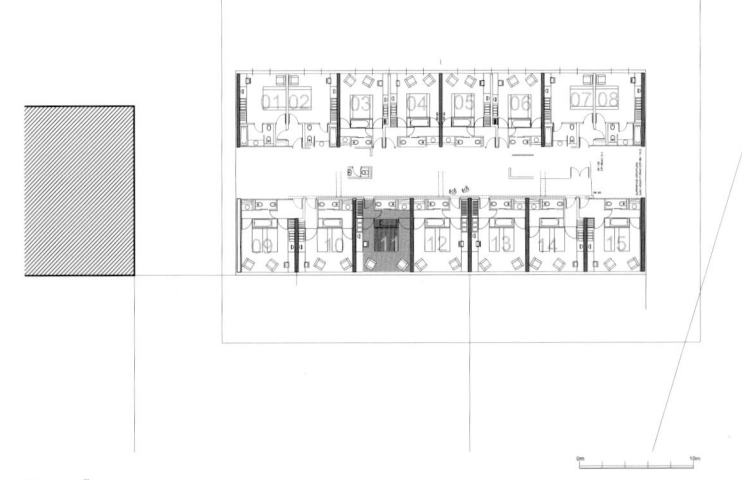

Ground floor

Upper floor

101 GA PROJECT

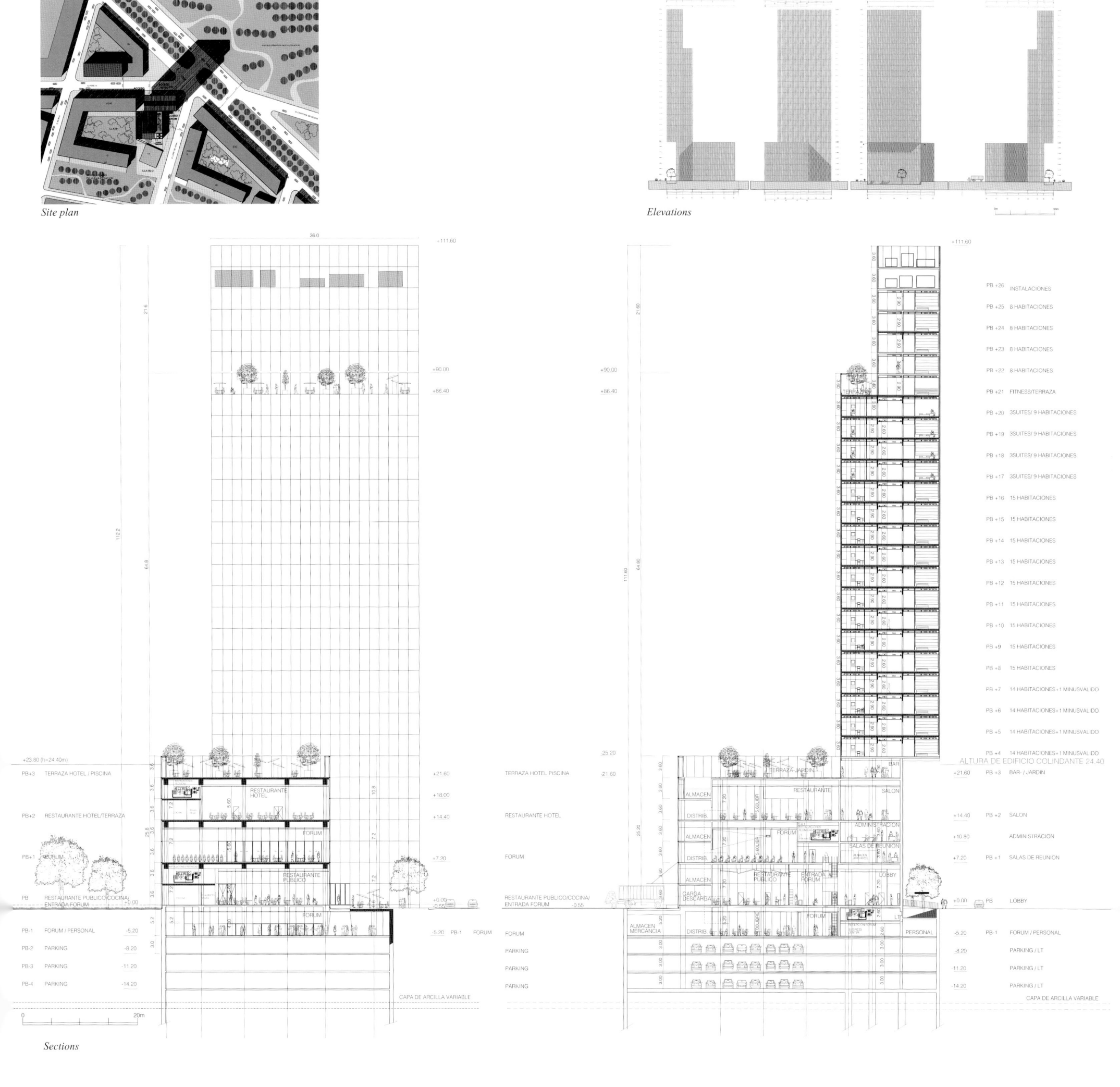

Site plan

Elevations

Sections

LEGORRETA+LEGORRETA

COMMUNITY CENTER BUILDING FOR THE UNIVERSITY OF CALIFORNIA, MISSION BAY CAMPUS

San Francisco, California, U.S.A. Design: 1999–2000 Construction: 2001–02

A high quality campus life promotes optimal learning and efficient work performance, enhances the recruitment and retention of faculty staff and students, and makes the campus a desirable place to work, learn and visit.

Located in one of the largest developments of San Francisco, the UCSF Mission Bay Campus Community Center has been conceived to be the heart of the campus, where students, faculty and community will come together to enjoy, socialize, and interact.

Projected to have about 2,000 people in the first phase, and about 9,100 when completed, the four story 156,000 gross sq.ft. building will combine a variety of uses in a single structure. The diverse program, combines such facilities as a fitness complex, a conference center with an auditorium for 400 people, a gymnasium with basketball and volleyball courts, swimming pools (one indoors and the others outdoors), dining and food facilities, offices, and retail space, all of which are organized around an atrium.

質の高いキャンパス・ライフは，学習意欲を高め，効率的な仕事を促し，教職員や学生の募集や定着にも好い結果をもたらし，キャンパスを，働き，学び，訪れるに望ましい場所としてくれるだろう。

サンフランシスコにおける大規模開発地区の一つに計画されている，UCSFミッション・ベイ・キャンパス・コミュニティ・センターは構内の中心となり，学生，教職員そして周辺住民が一緒になって楽しみ，互いに交流し，社会活動を行う場である。

第1期計画で約2,000人，最終的には約9,100人に対応できる，4階建て，延べ156,000平方フィートの建物には，様々な用途のエリアが統合される。プログラムには，フィットネス・コンプレックス，400席のオーディトリアムが付属する会議センター，バスケットボール及びバレーボール・コートのあるジム，水泳プール（屋内1，屋外1），食堂とカフェテリア，オフィス，店舗などの施設が含まれ，このすべてがアトリウムの周囲に編成される。

Architects: Legorreta + Legorreta—Ricardo Legorreta, Victor Legorreta, Noe Castro, Miguel Almaraz, Adriana Ciklik, principals-in-charge; Miguel Almaraz, project architect; Juan Carlos Nolasco, Gabriel Merino, Noe Baez, project team
Client: University of California at San Francisco
Consultants: Forell/Elsesser, structural; NBA, mechanical; Hortonlees, lighting; Peter Walker & Partners, landscape
General contractor: Swinerton & Walbert
Structural system: steel & concrete slabs
Major material: plaster (EIFS), travertine marble, metal

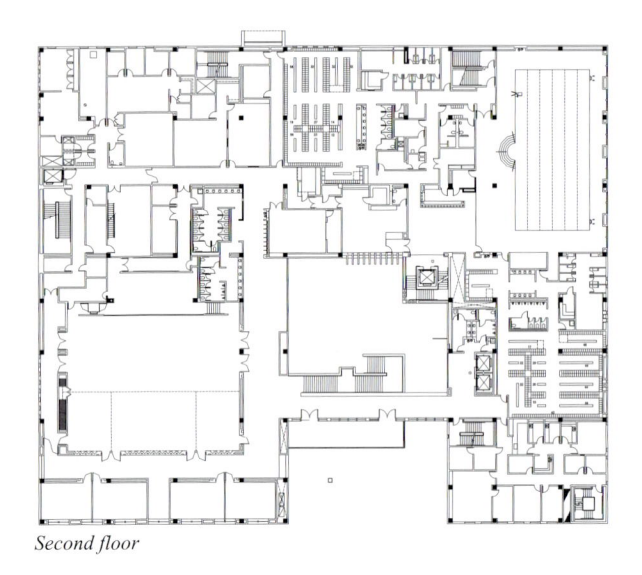

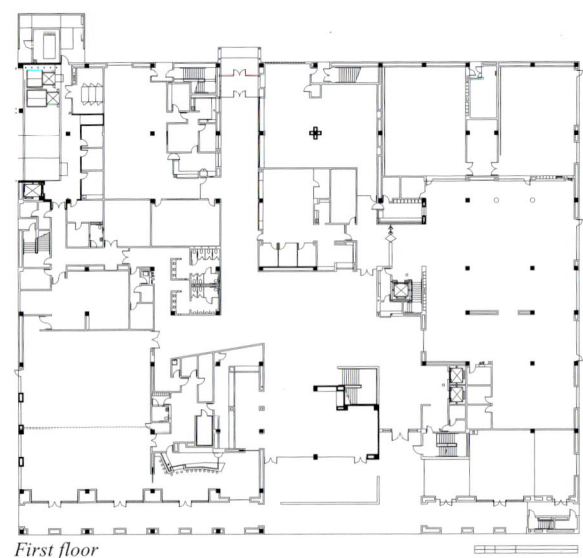

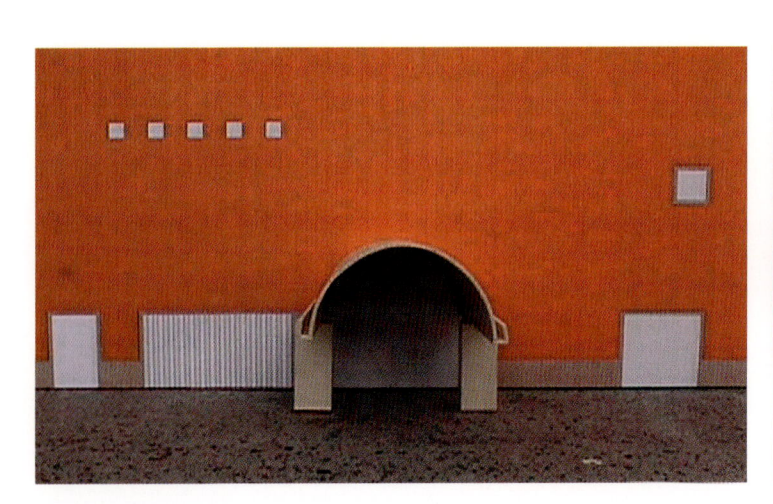

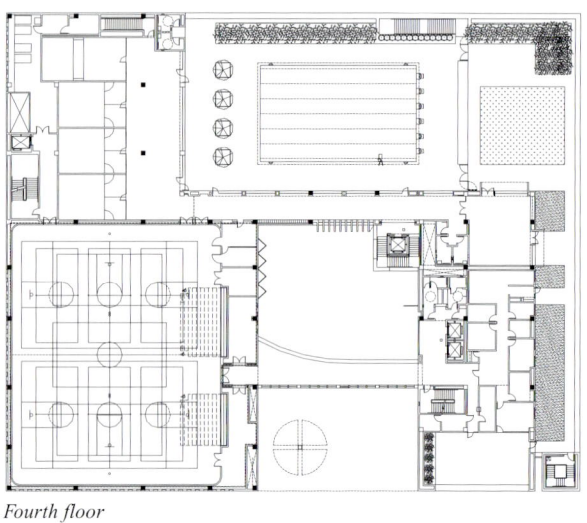

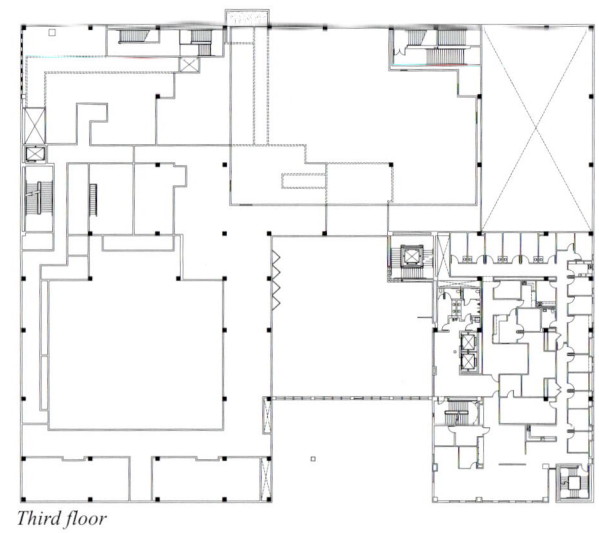

Second floor

Fourth floor

First floor

Third floor

Model: aerial view

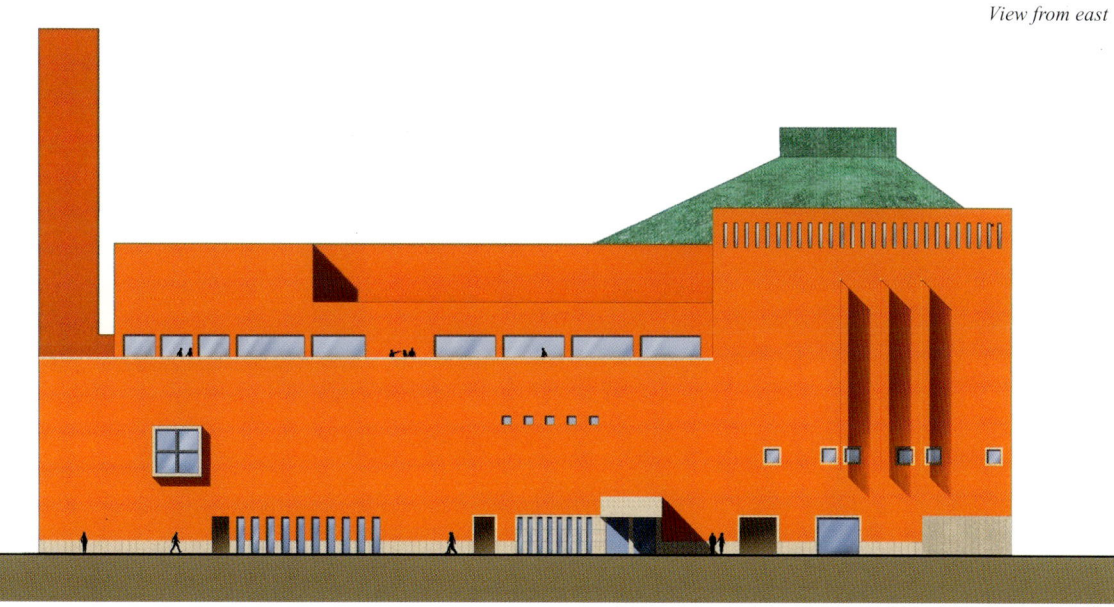

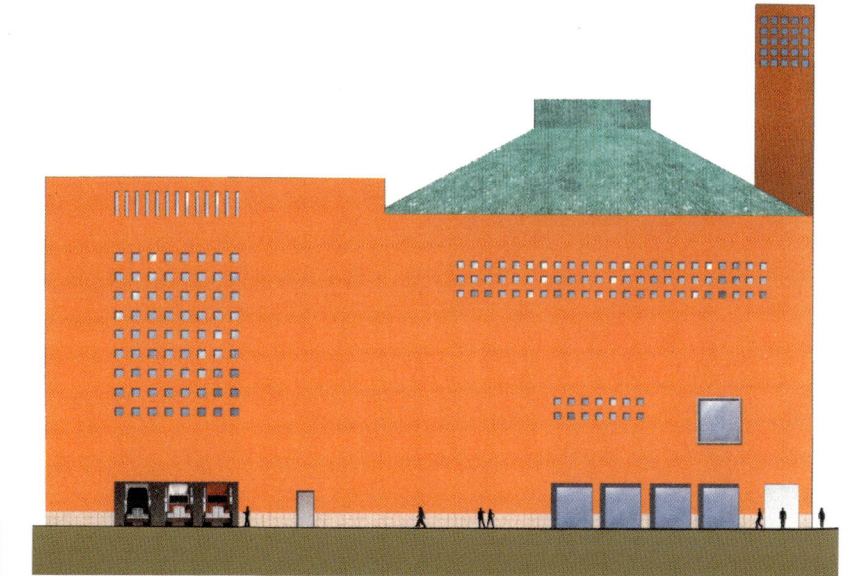

View from east

West elevation

South elevation

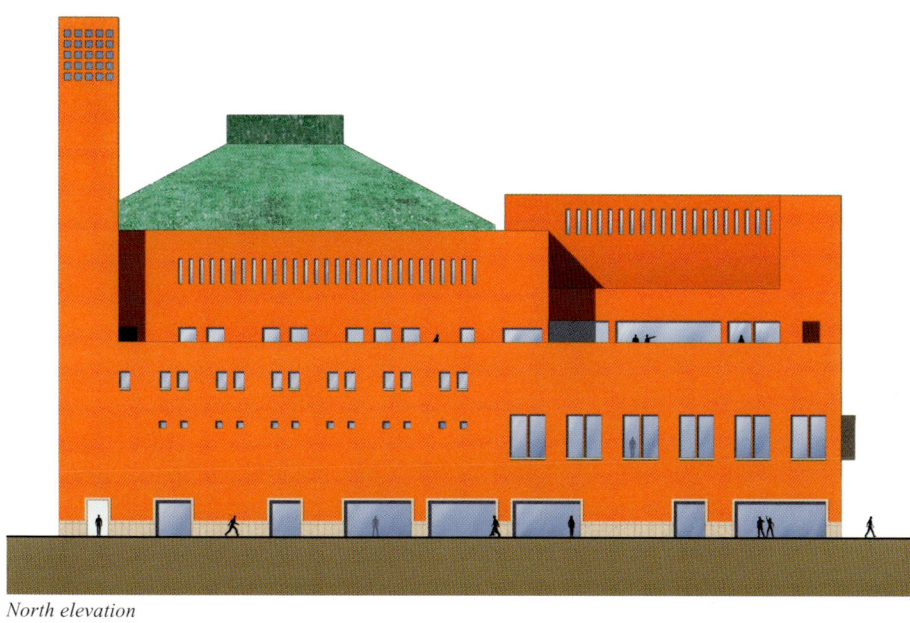

North elevation

East elevation

TADAO ANDO DETAILS
安藤忠雄ディテール集

Overlayered plans, sections and perspectives, with various details in different scales, Ando's drawing has unique three dimensional character. The drawings represent not only the literal information of details, but also his philosophy of architecture.
From "Row house in Sumiyoshi" to recent projects, these two volumes contain Ando's architectural details of major projects and embody the spirits of Ando, who is the evangelist of the essence of architecture.

平面や断面，パースが重ね合わされ，スケールの異なるディテールが挿入された三次元性を持つ独自の図法。その図面には，あらゆる事象を捉えながら結晶化させた建築理念が投影され，建築を創造することの意志が凝縮される。
住吉の長屋から現在まで，主要作品を網羅するこのディテール集の中に，時代に流されず，建築の本質を求めて止まないもう一つの安藤空間が展開する。

1
Size: 300×307mm / 168 total pages / ¥4,806

EDITED BY YUKIO FUTAGAWA
CRITICISM BY PETER EISENMAN
企画・編集：二川幸夫
論文：ピーター・アイゼンマン
翻訳：渡辺洋（英訳），丸山洋志（和訳）

2
Size: 300×307mm / 148 total pages / ¥4,714

EDITED BY YUKIO FUTAGAWA
CRITICISM BY FRANCESCO DAL CO
企画・編集：二川幸夫／論文：フランチェスコ・ダル・コ

表記価格には消費税は含まれておりません。

LIGHT & SPACE 光の空間
MODERN ARCHITECTURE

企画・撮影＝二川幸夫
序文＝パオロ・ポルトゲージ
文＝三宅理一

Edited and Photographed by Yukio Futagawa
Introduction by Paolo Portoghesi Text by Riichi Miyake

空間を構成する根源的な要素である光。
あふれる自然の光をとらえ，絞り込み，屈折させ，形を与えて内部に導き入れる。
近代建築の黎明期から現代にいたる，光と影を主役として織りなされてきた建築空間の集大成。

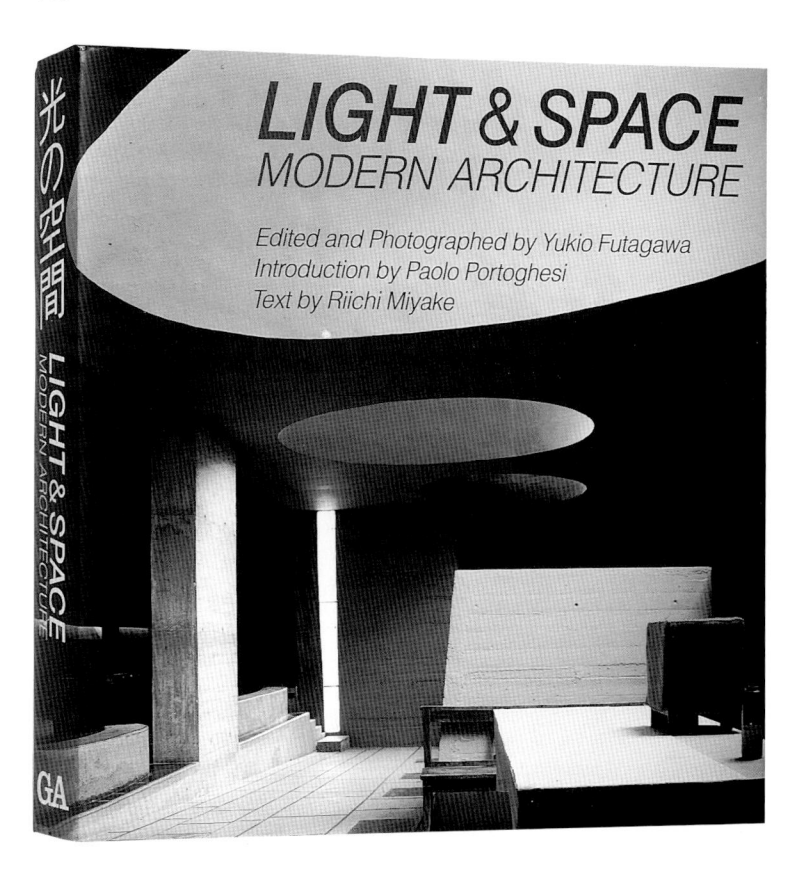

Light is a fundamental element of architecture.
Through the finest examples
from the beginning of Modernism to the present,
this compendium examines
the way natural light is captured, and shaped
in architectural space.

Size: 300×297mm

vol.1

The Myth of Iron and Glass 鉄とガラスの神話	Window to the Womb 胎内への窓
Usurpation of the Sky 空の簒奪	The Texture of Transparency 透明な質感
Allegory of Trees 樹木のアレゴリー	Metaphysical Light 形而上学的な光
Light and Shadow in the Fin-de-Siècle 世紀末の光と影	

vol.2

The Shining Brow 輝く額	Light without Shadow 影のない光
The Pleasure of Architecture 建築の快楽	Primitive Light 始原の光
Travel to the Orient 東方への旅	Sticky Space ねばっこい空間
The Myth of the Glazed Box ガラスの箱の神話	The Mechanical Sky メカニカルな空
See-Through Architecture 透視できる建築	Architecture of Membrane 被膜の建築

Vol.1 (paperback)　98 Works by 67 Architects　216 total pages, 30 in color　¥5,806　　Vol.2 (paperback)　130 Works by 62 Architects　216 total pages, 24 in color　¥5,806
Combined Issue (hard cover)　426 total pages, 54 in color　合本上製：¥14,369

表記価格には消費税は含まれておりません。

GA DOCUMENT
Global Architecture

GA DOCUMENT presents the finest in international design, focusing on architecture that expresses our times and striving to record the history of contemporary architecture. Striking black-and-white and vibrant color photographs presented in a generous format make for a dynamic re-presentation of spaces, materials and textures. International scholars and critics provide insightful texts to further inform the reader of the most up-to-date ideas and events in the profession.

多様に広がり、変化を見せる世界の現代建築の動向をデザインの問題を中心に取り上げ、現代建築の完全な記録をめざしつつ、時代の流れに柔軟に対応した独自の視点から作品をセレクションし、新鮮な情報を世界に向けて発信する唯一のグローバルな建築専門誌。掲載する作品をすべて現地取材、撮影することで大型誌面にダイナミックに表現し、その空間、ディテールやテクスチャーを的確に再現する。

Vols. 1, 16, 18, 20, 23, 25, 28, 29, 32, 36, 47 are out of print.
Size: 300 × 297 mm

1, 16, 18, 20, 23, 25, 28, 29, 32, 36, 47号は絶版。(17, 19, 21号は在庫僅少)

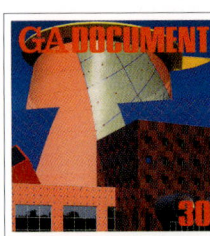

30
作品：磯崎新、ティーム・ディズニー・ビルディング／M・グレイヴス、ウォルト・ディズニー・ワールド・ドルフィン＆スワンホテル／H・ホライン、ハース・ハウス ケェーラーガッセの小学校／安藤忠雄、姫路文学館／M・ボッタ、WATARI-UM ルガーノのオフィス・アパートタワー／A・プレドック、ラスベガス図書館・ディスカバリーミュージアム／他
Works: A. Isozaki *Team Disney Building*; M. Graves *Walt Disney World Dolphin and Swan Hotels*; H. Hollein *Haas-Haus, Elementary School*; T. Ando *Museum of Literature, Himeji*; M. Botta *Watari-um, Residential and Offices Building in Via Ciani*; A. Predock *Las Vegas Library/Discovery Museum*; and others
120 total pages, 48 in color ¥2,903

31
作品：フォスター・アソシエイツ、サックラーギャラリー、クレッセント・ウィング（セインズベリー・センター）、センチュリータワー、スタンステッド空港ターミナル・ゾーン、ITN本社ビル／R・マイヤー、ゲッティセンター／H・ホライン、フランクフルト現代美術館／ベーニッシュ＆パートナーズ、郵便・通信博物館／M・カガン、パリ市都市警備局
Works: Foster Associates *Royal Academy Sackler Galleries, Sainsbury Center Crescent Wing, Century Tower, Stansted Airport Terminal Zone, ITN Headquarters*; R. Meier *Getty Center*; H. Hollein *Museum for Modern Art*; Behnisch & Partners *Post Museum*; M.W. Kagan *Cité Technique et Administrative de la Ville de Paris*
120 total pages, 36 in color ¥2,903

33
特集：GA JAPAN '92 第4回＜現代日本の建築家＞展
安藤忠雄／藤井博巳／原広司／長谷川逸子／早川邦彦／石山修武／磯崎新／伊東豊雄／北川原温／黒川紀章／槇文彦／毛綱毅曠／妹島和世／篠原一男／高松伸／谷口吉生／山本理顕／葉祥栄
Special Feature: "GA JAPAN '92" Exhibition at GA Gallery
T. Ando, H. Fujii, H. Hara, I. Hasegawa, K. Hayakawa, O. Ishiyama, A. Isozaki, T. Ito, A. Kitagawara, K. Kurokawa, F. Maki, K. Mozuna, K. Sejima, K. Shinohara, S. Takamatsu, Y. Taniguchi, R. Yamamoto, S. Yoh
100 total pages, 42 in color ¥2,525

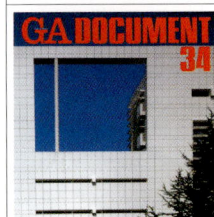

34
作品：リチャード・マイヤー、カナル＋テレヴィジョン本社屋、オランダ王立製紙会社本社屋、ヴァイスハウプト・フォーラム／アンリ・E・シリアニ、世界大戦記念館／ボレス＋ウィルソン、フランクフルト市立幼稚園／ベーニッシュ＆パートナーズ、アルベルト・シュヴァイツァー学校／H＆B・ゴーダン、フランス・スポーツセンター
Works: R. Meier *Canal+Television Headquarters, Royal Dutch Papermills Head-quarters, Weishaupt Forum*; H.E. Ciriani *Historial de la Grande Guerre*; Bolles-Wilson *Kindergarten Frankfurt*; Behnisch & Partners *Special School "Albert-Schweitzer-Schule"*; H. and B. Gaudin *Maison du Sport Français*
120 total pages, 30 in color ¥2,903

35
作品：J・スターリング、ブラウン本社屋および工場施設／R・ピアノ、自動植物繊維構造体研究所、ジェノヴァ万博、トムソンCSF社工場／安藤忠雄、真言宗本福寺水御堂、姫路市立星の子館、大手前女子大学アートセンター／M・ボッタ、ルガーノとベリンゾーナの商業・アパート／P・モッティーニ、ル・グラマ小学校
Works: Stirling Wilford Nägeli *Braun Headquarters and Production Building*; R. Piano *UNESCO-BW Laboratory, Columbus International Expo '92, Thomson CSF Factory*; T. Ando *Water Temple, Children's Seminar House, Otemae Art Center*; M. Botta *Two multiuse residential buildings*; P. Mottini *Le Gramat Elementary School*
120 pages, 42 in color ¥2,903

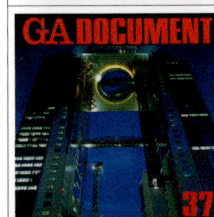

37
評論：P・L・ピネル 作品：Z・ハディド、ヴィトラ社消防署／フォスター・アソシエイツ、カレ・ダール／原広司、梅田スカイビル／P・アイゼンマン、コロンバス・コンベンションセンター、布谷ビル／H＆B・ゴーダン、サン・ルー大学増築／伊東豊雄、下諏訪町立諏訪湖博物館・赤彦記念館／Ch・ド・ポルザンパルク、ブールデル美術館
Essay: Patrick L. Pinnel Works: Z. Hadid *Vitra Fire Station*; Foster Associates *Carré d'Art*; H. Hara, *Umeda Sky Building*; P. Eisenman *Greater Columbus Convention Center*; H. and B. Gaudin *Université de Saint-Leu Extension*; T. Ito *Shimosuwa Lake Suwa Museum and Akahiko Memorial Museum*; Ch. de Portzamparc *Bourdelle Museum*
120 total pages, 36 in color ¥2,903

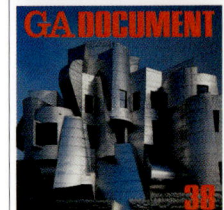

38
作品：F・O・ゲーリー、ミネソタ大学美術館、アイオワ大学先端技術研究所、トリード大学芸術学部／スコーギン・エラム・ブレイ、アリゾナ州立大学法学部図書館、コーニング児童センター／A&T・スカルパ、ベネトン社工場／E・ミラージェス、アリカンテのスポーツセンター、オスタレッツ文化センター／A・シザ、ガリシアン現代美術センター、ポルト大学建築学部
Works: F.O. Gehry *Univ. of Minnesota Art Building and Teaching Museum, Iowa Advanced Technology Laboratories Building, Univ. of Toledo Art Building*; Scogin Elam and Bray *Arizona State Univ. Law Library, Corning Incorporated Child Center*; A. and T. Scarpa *New Benetton Factory*; E. Miralles *National Center for Rhythmic Gymnastics, Civic Center*; A. Siza *Galician Center for Contemporary Art, School of Architecture*
120 pages, 42 in color ¥2,903

表記価格には消費税は含まれておりません。

39
特集：GA JAPAN '94 第5回＜現代日本の建築家＞展
安藤忠雄／原広司／長谷川逸子／早川邦彦／石山修武／磯崎新／伊東豊雄／北川原温／黒川紀章／槇文彦／妹島和世／篠原一男／高松伸／山本理顕／葉祥栄／日建設計
Special Feature: "GA JAPAN '94" Exhibition at GA Gallery
T. Ando, H. Hara, I. Hasegawa, K. Hayakawa, O. Ishiyama, A. Isozaki, T. Ito, A. Kitagawara, K. Kurokawa, F. Maki, K. Sejima, K. Shinohara, S. Takamatsu, R. Yamamoto, S. Yoh, Nikken Sekkei
120 total pages, 24 in color ¥2,903

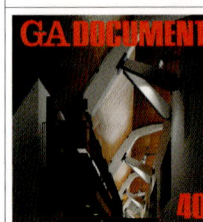

40
作品：R・マイヤー、ダイムラー・ベンツ研究センター、ウルム市観光センター、ヒポルックス銀行／J・クーネン、オランダ建築会館／F・O・ゲーリー、パリのアメリカン・センター、ヴィトラ社新本社屋／ボレス＝ウィルソン、ミュンスター市立図書館／M・ボッタ、カイマー社オフィスビル／B・ドーシ、フセイン＝ドーシ美術館／R・レヴァル、教育メディア研究センター
Works: R. Meier *Daimler Benz Research Center, Exhibton and Assembly Building, Hypolux Bank Building*; J. Coenen *The Netherlands Architecture Institue*; F.O. Gehry *American Center, New Headquarters for Vitra International AG*; Bolles-Wilson *New City Library Münster, two projects*; M. Botta *Caimato Office Block*; B. Doshi *Hussain-Doshi Gufa*; R. Rewal *Central Institute of Educational Technology*
120 pages, 42 in color ¥2,903

41
作品：サンティアゴ・カラトラヴァ、TGVリヨン・サトラス空港駅／ニコラス・グリムショウ、ウォータールー国際ターミナル／SNCF、リール・ヨーロッパ駅／OMA、リール・グラン・パレ／レンゾ・ピアノ、関西国際空港旅客ターミナルビル／ジャン・ヌヴェル、カルティエ財団、トゥール会議場、ダクス・ホテル
S. Calatrava *Gare de Satolas TGV*; Nicholas Grimshaw *Waterloo International Terminal*; SNCF *Gare de Lille-Europe*; OMA *Lille Grand Palais*; R. Piano *Kansai International Airport Passenger Terminal Building*; J. Nouvel *Fondation Cartier, Centre des Congrès, Dax Les Thermes*
120 pages, 36 in color ¥2,903

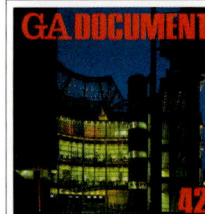

42
古典：ファテプール・シークリー（インド） 論文：ジョセフ・ジョヴァニーニ
作品：リチャード・ロジャース、チャンネル4テレビ局本社／エンリック・ミラージェス、ウエスカ・スポーツ・ホール／アンリ・ゴーダン、パリのスタジアム／ギュンター・ベーニッシュ、フランクフルトの学校増改築／シュタイドゥル＋パートナー、ウルム大学西キャンパス
Classic: Fathepur Sikri (India) Critic: Joseph Giovannini
Works: R. Rogers *Channel 4 Television Headquarters*; E. Miralles *Huesca Sports Hall*; H. & B. Gaudin *Le Stade Charléty*; G. Behnisch *The Geschwister Scholl School*; Steidle + Partner *Ulm University West Site*
120 pages, 48 in color ¥2,903

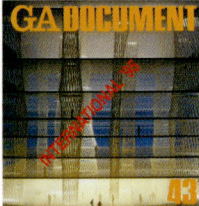

43
特集：GA INTERNATIONAL '95 第5回＜現代世界の建築家＞展
Special Feature: "GA INTERNATIONAL '95" Exhibition at GA Gallery
Tadao Ando, Günter Behnisch, Santiago Calatrava, Coop Himmelblau, Norman Foster, Frank O. Gehry, Hiroshi Hara, Zaha M. Hadid, Steven Holl, Hans Hollein, Arata Isozaki, Toyo Ito, Ricardo Legorreta, Daniel Libeskind, Richard Meier, Enric Miralles, Morphosis, Eric Owen Moss, Jean Nouvel, Renzo Piano, Christian de Portzamparc, Richard Rogers, Scogin Elam and Bray, Kazuo Shinohara, Bernard Tschumi, Bolles + Wilson
120 pages, 24 in color ¥2,903

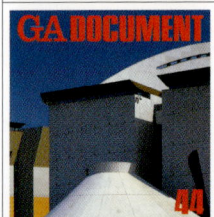

44
古典：マヤ＝ウシュマル、カバー、サイール テキスト：ギジェルモ・エギアルテ
作品：Ch・ド・ポルザンパルク、音楽都市東棟／R・ロジャース、新ヨーロッパ人権裁判所／E・ノルテン、ドラマ・センター／磯崎新、ラ・コルーニャ人間科学館／H・ホライン、サンタンデール銀行／D・ペロー、フランス国立図書館／A・シザ、ポルト大学建築学部図書館
Classic: Maya-Uxmal, Kabah, Sayil Text: Guillermo Eguiarte
Works: Ch. de Portzamparc *Cité de la Musique*; R. Rogers *New European Court of Human Rights*; E. Norten *Drama Center*; A. Isozaki *Domus*; H. Hollein *Banco Santander*; D. Perrault *Bibliothèque Nationale de France*; A. Siza *Library, University of Oporto*
120 pages, 48 in color ¥2,903

45
作品：ノーマン・フォスター、ケンブリッジ大学法学部棟／フランク・O・ゲーリー、EMR情報・技術センター／コープ・ヒンメルブラウ、フローニンヘン美術館東館／メカノ、ユトレヒト工科大学 経済経営学部棟、アルメロ市立図書館／アンリ・シリアニ、アルル考古博物館／マリオ・ボッタ、エヴリーの教会
Works: N. Foster *Cambridge Law Faculty*; F. O. Gehry *EMR Communication and Technology Center*; Coop Himmelblau *The Groninger Museum, East Pavilion*; Mecanoo *Utrecht Polytechnic Faculty for Economy & Management, Public Library Almelo*; Henri Ciriani *Arles Archaeological Museum*; M. Botta *Cathedral in Evry*
120 pages, 48 in color ¥2,903

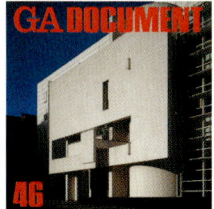

GA DOCUMENT 46
作品：R・マイヤー, バルセロナ現代美術館／ハーグ・シティ・ホール＆中央図書館／スイス北アメリカ本社／ガゴシアン・ギャラリー／ブルダーDWLアーキテクツ, フェニックス中央図書館／リカルド・レゴレッタ, サウス・チュラ・ヴィスタ図書館, プラザ・レフォルマ／プロジェクト：リカルド・レゴレッタ, 科学博物館
Works: R. Meier *Barcelona Museum of Contemporary Art, Hague City Hall & Central Library, Swissair North American Headquarters, The Gagosian Gallery*; bruder DWL architects *Phoenix Central Library*; Ricardo Legorreta *South Chula Vista Library, Plaza Reforma*, Project: Ricardo Legorreta *Tech Museum of Innovation*
120 pages, 36 in color ¥2,903

GA DOCUMENT 48
作品：ジャン・ヌヴェル, ギャラリー・ラファイエット, ベルリン／ラファエル・ヴィニオリ, 東京国際フォーラム／ポール・アンドリュー, シャルル・ド・ゴール空港TGV駅／フランク・O・ゲーリー, ティーム・ディズニー社屋他／ボレス＋ウィルソン, 州政府オフィス・ビル／コープ・ヒンメルブラウ, ザイバースドルフのリサーチ・センター／他　プロジェクト：ボレス＋ウィルソン, ニュー・ルクソール劇場
Works: Jean Nouvel *Galeries Lafayette, Berlin*; Rafael Vinoly *Tokyo International Forum*; Paul Andreu *The Exchange Module and TGV Station*; Frank O. Gehry *Team Disney Administration Building*; Bolles+Wilson *Government Office Building*; Coop Himmelblau *Office and Research Center*; and others Project: Bolles+Willson *New Luxor Theater*
120 pages, 54 in color ¥2,903

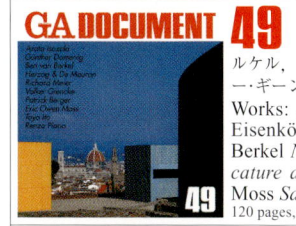

GA DOCUMENT 49
作品：磯崎新, フィレンツェ・ビエンナーレ'96: Time and Fashion／ギュンター・ドメニック＆ヘルマン・アイゼンコックル, カール・フランツェンス大学学部棟他／ベン・ファン・ベルケル, トゥエンテ国立美術館増改築／ヘルツォーク＆ド・ムーロン, 風刺漫画美術館／フォルカー・ギーンケ, 植物園の温室／エリック・オーエン・モス, サミトール／伊東豊雄, 長岡Lホール／他
Works: A. Isozaki *Biennale di Firenze '96: Time and Fashion*; G. Domenig and H. Eisenköck, *Karl Franzens University RESOWI Faculty, extension of the Library*; B. V. Berkel *National Museum Twenthe, extension and conversion*; Herzog & De Meuron *Caricature and Cartoon Museum*; V. Giencke *Glasshouses at the Botanical Gardens*; E. O. Moss *Samitaur*; Toyo Ito *Nagaoka L Hall*; and others
120 pages, 48 in color ¥2,903

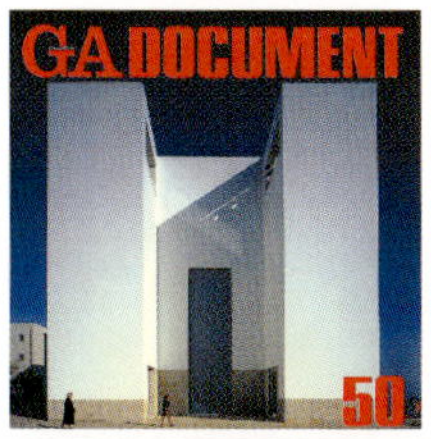

GA DOCUMENT 50
インタヴュー・作品・プロジェクト：トッド・ウィリアムズ＆ビリー・ツィン　作品：アルヴァロ・シザ, マルコ・ドゥ・カナヴェーゼスの教会, アヴェイロ大学機械工学科棟／J・マヌエル・ガリェゴ, コルーニャの美術館／磯崎新, 岡山西警察署／エンリケ・ノルテン, テレビ局の複合施設／リカルド・レゴレッタ, メキシコシティ芸術都市／他
Interview, Works & Projects: T. Williams & B. Tsien *The NSI, Phoenix Art Museum, Cranbrook Athletic Complex*; and others Works: A. Siza *Church of Marco De Canavezes*; A. Dias *University of Aveiro, Department of Mechanical Engineering*; J. M. Gallego *Museum of Fine Art, La Coruña*; A. Isozaki *Okayama-Nishi Police Station*; E. Norten *Televisa Mixed Use Building*; R. Legorreta *The City of the Arts*; and others
120 pages, 48 in color ¥2,848

GA DOCUMENT 51
特集：GA INTERNATIONAL '97 第6回〈現代世界の建築家〉展
Special Feature: "GA INTERNATIONAL '97" Exhibition at GA Gallery
Tadao Ando, Coop Himmelblau, Peter Eisenman, Norman Foster, Frank O. Gehry, Zaha M. Hadid, Hiroshi Hara, Steven Holl, Hans Hollein, Arata Isozaki, Toyo Ito, Rem Koolhaas, Daniel Libeskind, Ricardo Legorreta, Fumihiko Maki, Richard Meier, Enric Miralles, Morphosis, Jean Nouvel, Eric Owen Moss, Renzo Piano, Christian de Portzamparc, Richard Rogers, Álvaro Siza, Shin Takamatsu, Bernard Tschumi, Peter Wilson, Tod Williams & Billie Tsien
120 pages, 24 in color ¥2,848

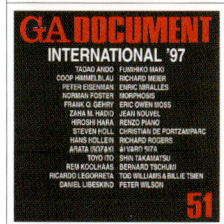

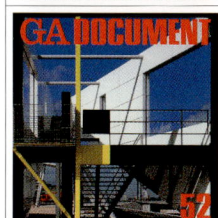

GA DOCUMENT 52
作品：E・O・モス, オフィス・コンプレックス／A・プレドック, アリゾナ・サイエンス・センター／槇文彦, 風の丘葬祭場／ボレス＋ウィルソン, ロッテルダムの埠頭広場, 他／H・ホライン, ロワー・オーストリア展示場, 他／原広司＋アトリエ・ファイ, 京都駅ビル／N・フォスター, ビルバオ市地下鉄駅／P・シメトフ, エヴルーの図書館／R・ボフィル, オリンピック・プール
Works: E.O. Moss *Pittard Sullivan*; A. Predock *Arizona Science Center*; F. Maki *Kaze-no-Oka Crematorium*; Bolles + Wilson *Quay Building, Light Forum, Albeda College*; H. Hollein *Lower Austrian Exhibition Hall, Light Forum*; Hiroshi Hara+Atelier Φ *Kyoto Station Building*; N. Foster *Bilbao Metro*; P. Chemetov & B. Huidobro *Library in Evreux*; R. Bofill *Olympic Swimming Pool*
120 pages, 48 in color ¥2,848

GA DOCUMENT 53
作品：OMA, ユトレヒト大学・エデュカトリアム／S・ホール, シアトル大学・聖イグナティウス礼拝堂／N・フォスター, コメルツバンク本社屋, 他／R・ロジャース, テームズ・ヴァレー大学・LRC／W・P・ブルーダー, リッデアドヴォケイティング＆デザイン／B・チュミ, ル・フレノワ国立現代芸術スタジオ／C・ド・ポルザンパルク, ナシオナル通りのハウジング／他
Works: OMA *Educatorium, Utrecht University*; S. Holl *Chapel of St. Ignatius*; N. Foster *Commerzbank Headquarters, American Air Museum in Britain*; R. Rogers *L.R.C. Thames Valley University*; C. de Portzamparc *Paris, Rue Nationale*; F. Soler *Suite Sans Fin, Rue Emile Durkheim*; Studios Architecture *North Charleston Campus, Silicon Graphics Computer System*
120 pages, 54 in color ¥2,848

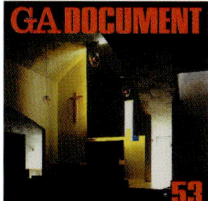

GA DOCUMENT 54
フランク・O・ゲーリー　ビルバオ・グッゲンハイム美術館
Frank O. Gehry Guggenheim Bilbao Museoa
96 pages, 42 in color ¥2,848

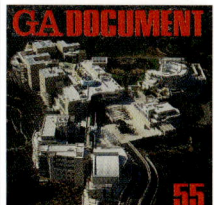

GA DOCUMENT 55
作品：R・マイヤー, ゲッティ・センター／R・ピアノ, バイエラー財団美術館／磯崎新, 群馬県立近代美術館現代美術棟／安藤忠雄, 綾部工業団地交流プラザ／安藤忠雄, TOTOセミナーハウス／MZRC, フランス・スタジアム／メカノ, デルフト工科大学図書館／原広司, 宮城県図書館／サン・アントニオ中央図書館
Works: R. Meier *Getty Center*; R. Piano *Beyeler Foundation Museum*; A. Isozaki *Museum of Modern Art, Gunma—Contemporary Art Wing*; T. Ando *Ayabe Community Center*; T. Ando *TOTO Seminar House*; MZRC *Stade de France*; Mecanoo *Library of the Delft University of Technology*; H. Hara *Miyagi Prefectural Library*; and others
132 pages, 54 in color ¥2,848

GA DOCUMENT 56
作品：S・ホール, ヘルシンキ現代美術館／S・フェーン, 氷河博物館／S・フェーン, アウクルト・センター／コープ・ヒンメルブラウ, UFAシネマ・センター／P・アンドルー, シャルル・ド・ゴール空港2・ホールF／S・カラトラヴァ, アラメダ橋と地下鉄駅／S・カラトラヴァ, 貿易センター／S・カラトラヴァ, カンポ・ボランティン歩道橋
Works: S. Holl *Kiasma, Museum of Contemporary Art*; S. Fehn *Glacier Museum*; S. Fehn *The Aukrust Centre*; Coop Himmelblau *UFA Cinema Center*; P. Andreu *CDG 2—Hall F*; S. Calatrava *Alameda Bridge and Underground Station*; S. Calatrava *Alameda Bridge and Underground Station*; and others
120 pages, 42 in color ¥2,848

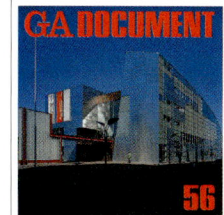

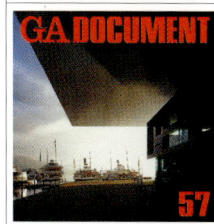

GA DOCUMENT 57
作品：ジャン・ヌヴェル, ルツェルン・コンサートホール／アルヴァロ・シザ, アリカンテ大学管理・教室棟／アーキテクチュア・スタジオ, ヨーロッパ連合議事堂／磯崎新, 秋吉台国際芸術村　静岡県コンベンションアーツセンター「グランシップ」　なら100年会館　論文：磯崎新「パノプティコンからアーキペラゴへ」
Works: J. Nouvel *Lucerne Culture and Convention Centr*; Á. Siza *Rectory of The University of Alicante*; Architecuture Studio *European Parliament*; A. Isozaki *Akiyoshidai International Art Village, Shizuoka Convention & Arts Center "Granship", Nara Centennial Hall* Essay: A. Isozaki *"From Panopticon to Archipelago"*
132 pages, 54 in color ¥2,848

GA DOCUMENT 58
特集：GA INTERNATIONAL '99 第7回〈現代世界の建築家〉展
Special Feature: "GA INTERNATIONAL '99" Exhibition at GA Gallery
Tadao Ando, Coop Himmelblau, Peter Eisenman, Norman Foster, Zaha M. Hadid, Hiroshi Hara, Steven Holl, Hans Hollein, Arata Isozaki, Toyo Ito, Ricardo Legorreta, Fumihiko Maki, Mecanoo, Richard Meier, Enric Miralles, Rafael Moneo, Morphosis, Eric Owen Moss, Dominique Perrault, Renzo Piano, Christian de Portzamparc, Richard Rogers, Álvaro Siza, Bernard Tschumi, Tod Williams/ Billie Tsien
108pages, 24 in color ¥2,848

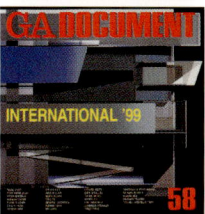

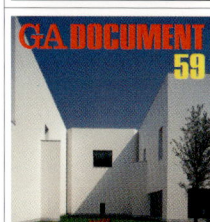

GA DOCUMENT 59
作品：アルヴァロ・シザ, ポルト現代美術館／黒川紀章, ヴァン・ゴッホ美術館新館／ダニエル・リベスキンド, フェリックス・ヌバウム美術館　ユダヤ美術館／妹島和世＋西沢立衛, 飯田市小笠原資料館／ノーマン・フォスター, ドイツ新議事堂, ライヒスターク／フレデリック・ボレル, ペリポール通りの集合住宅
Works: Á. Siza *Contemporary Art Museum of Oporto*; K. Kurokawa *New Wing of Van Gogh Museum*; D. Libeskind *Felix Nussbaum Haus, Berlin Museum with the Jewish Museum*; K.Sezima+R. Nishizawa *O-Museum*; N. Foster *New German Parliament, Reichstag*; F. Borel *Housing Building, Rue Pelleport*
120 pages, 48 in color ¥2,848

GA DOCUMENT 60
フォーカス・オン・アーキテクト①：E・ミラージェス　作品：B・チュミ, 建築学校　アルフレッド・ラーナー・ホール／H・ホライン, ドナウ・シティの小学校／S・ホール, クランブルック科学研究所／Ch・d・ポルザンパルク, ポルト・マイヨーの会議場増築／UNスタジオ, ヘット・ヴァルクホフ美術館／モーフォシス, ヒポ・アルプ・アドリア・センター
Focus on Architect 1: E. Miralles B. Tagliabue Works: B. Tschumi *School of Architecture, Alfred Lerner Hall at Columbia University*; H. Hollein *Bilingual Elementary School*; S. Holl *Cranbrook Institute of Science*; Ch. de Porzamparc *Extention of the Paris des Congrés*; UN Studio *Museum Het Valkhof*; Morphosis, *Hypo Alpe-Adria-Center*
132 pages, 54 in color ¥2,848

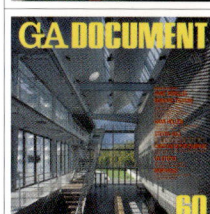

GA DOCUMENT 61
特集：GA INTERNATIONAL 2000 第8回〈現代世界の建築家〉展
Special Feature: "GA INTERNATIONAL 2000" Exhibition at GA Gallery
Tadao Ando, Peter Eisenman, Norman Foster, Zaha M. Hadid, Hiroshi Hara, Steven Holl, Arata Isozaki, Toyo Ito, Ricardo Legorreta, Fumihiko Maki, Richard Meier, Enric Miralles Benedetta Tagliabue, Morphosis, Eric Owen Moss, Jean Nouvel, Dominique Perrault, Renzo Piano, Christian de Portzamparc, Richard Rogers, Álvaro Siza, Bernard Tschumi, Tod Williams Billie Tsien
108pages, 48 in color ¥2,848

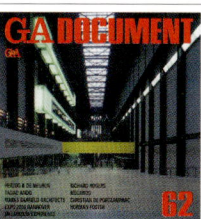

GA DOCUMENT 62
作品：ヘルツォーク＆ド・ムーロン, テート・モダン／安藤忠雄, FABRICA（ベネトン・アートスクール）, 淡路夢舞台／エキスポ2000ハノーバー／ミレニアム・エクスペリエンス／R・ロジャース, ウッドストリートのオフィス／メカノ, ナショナル・ヘリテイジ・ミュージアム／C・ド・ポルザンパルク, グラス市裁判所／N・フォスター, カナリー・ウォーフ駅／他
Works: Herzog & de Meuron *Tate Modern*; T. Ando *FABRICA*; T. Ando *Awaji-Yumebutai*; Marks Barfield Architects *Millennium Wheel*; EXPO 2000 Hannover; Millennium Experience; R. Rogers, *88 Wood Street, London EC2*; Mecanoo *National Heritage Museum*; Ch. de Portzamparc *Grasse Courts of Justice*; N. Foster *Canary Wharf Station*
132 pages, 66 in color ¥2,848

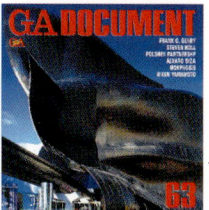

GA DOCUMENT 63
作品：F・O・ゲーリー, E・M・P, コンデ・ナスト, ヴォンツ分子科学センター／S・ホール, サルファティ通りのオフィス／ポルシェック・パートナーシップ, アメリカ自然史博物館ローズ・センター／A・シザ, サンチャゴ大学情報科学学部／モーフォシス, ロングビーチの小学校, ダイヤモンド・ランチ・ハイスクール／山本理顕, 公立はこだて未来大学, 埼玉県立大学
Works: F. O. Gehry *E. M. P., Condé Nast, Vontz Center*; S. Holl *Sarphatistraat Offices*; Polshek Partnership *Rose Center, American Museum of Natural History*; A. Siza *Faculty of Information Science*; Morphosis *International Elementary School, Diamond Ranch High School*; R. Yamamoto *Future University of Hakodate, Saitama Prefectural University*
120 pages, 60 in color ¥2,848

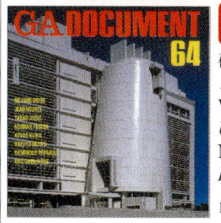

GA DOCUMENT 64
作品：R・マイヤー, イスリップ連邦裁判所, フェニックス連邦裁判所／J・ヌヴェル, ナント裁判所／安藤忠雄, 南岳山光明寺／N・フォスター, スタンフォード大学医療科学研究センター／隈研吾, 馬頭町広重美術館／妹島和世, hhstyle.com／D・ペロー, オリンピック・ヴェロドローム／スイミング・プール／E・O・モス, ステルス, ビルディング1／2, アンブレラ
Works: R. Meier *United States Courthouse & Federal Building, Sandra Day O'Connor United States Courthouse*; J. Nouvel *Palais de Justice de Nantès*; T. Ando *Komyoji, Temple*; N. Foster *Center for Clinical Science Reseach, Stanford University*; K. Kuma *Bato Machi Hiroshige Museum*; K. Sejima *hhstyle.com*; and others
120 pages, 54 in color ¥2,848

表記価格には消費税は含まれておりません。

GA HOUSES

GA HOUSES documents outstanding new residential architecture from all over the world. Included in each issue also are retrospective looks at residential works of the past which are now considered epoch-making. This magazine is essential not only for architects and architectural students but for those who wish to master the art of living.

世界各国の住宅を現地取材により次々に紹介してゆくシリーズ。最近の作品はもちろん、近代住宅の古典の再検討、現代建築家の方法論、集合住宅のリポートなど、住宅に関わる問題点を広い範囲にわたってとりあげてゆく。

Vols. 1–16, 18–24, 28, 31, 34, 37 are out of print.
1–16, 18–24, 28, 31, 34, 37号は絶版。　Size: 300×228mm

---

32 特集：ジョン・ロートナー　作品：ソットサス／プリンス／ナイルズ／プレドック／PAPA
Lautner; Sottsas; Prince; Niles; Predock; PAPA
160 pages, 48 in color. ¥2,903

33 作品：レゴレッタ／マック／キャピー／エリクソン／グワスミー＆シーゲル／ヒューバート＆ゼルニオ／葉／村上／他
Legorreta; Mack; Kappe; Gwathmey & Siegel; Hubert & Zelnio; Yoh; Murakami; and others
160 pages, 56 in color. ¥2,903

35 作品：オーブレリー／モーフォシス／ウォルドマン／ノタ／デニソン＆ルキーニ／エリクソン／安藤／斎藤
Oubrerie; Morphosis; Waldman; Nota; Denison Luchini; Erickson; Ando; Saito
160 pages, 56 in color. ¥2,903

36 作品：クールハース／ボッタ／ロトンディ／プリンス／イスラエル／アルキテクトニカ／BAM／安藤／他
OMA; Botta; Rotondi; Prince; Israel; Arquitectonica; BAM; Ando; and others
160 pages, 64 in color. ¥2,903

38 連載：巨匠の住宅—ル・コルビュジエ1　作品：ホール／シゴル＆コールマン／モス／石田／ナイルズ／早川／他
Essays on Residential Masterpieces—Le Corbusier 1; Holl; Moss; Niles; Standing; Hayakawa; and others
168 pages, 56 in color. ¥2,903

39 連載：巨匠の住宅—ル・コルビュジエ2　作品：マック／ノタ／レゴレッタ／シュヴァイツァー／安藤／ボッタ／他
Essays on Residential Masterpieces—Le Corbusier 2; Ando; Botta; Mack; Schweitzer; Legorreta; and others
160 pages, 64 in color. ¥2,903

40 連載：巨匠の住宅—フランク・ロイド・ライト1　作品：フライ／プレドック／ソットサス／クイグリー／ブルーダー／他
Essays on Residential Masterpieces—F. L. Wright 1; Frey; Predock; Quigley; Sottsass; Bruder; and others
160 pages, 56 in color. ¥2,903

41 特集号：プロジェクト1994
Special Issue: Project 1994
168 pages, 20 in color. ¥2,903

42 連載：巨匠の住宅—フランク・ロイド・ライト2　作品：村上／早川／妹島／飯田／レゴレッタ／ミラージェス／プレドック／他
Essays on Residential Masterpieces—F. L. Wright 2; Murakami; Legorreta; Miralles; Predock; and others
160 pages, 48 in color. ¥2,903

43 連載：巨匠の住宅—フランク・ロイド・ライト3　作品：OMA／クイグリー／グワスミー＆シーゲル／石田／北山／ヌヴェル／他
Essays on Residential Masterpieces—F. L. Wright 3; OMA; Quigley; Ishida; Kitayama, Nouvel; and others
160 pages, 48 in color. ¥2,903

44 連載：巨匠の住宅—ルイス・I・カーン　作品：ブルーダー／プリンス／岸／北川原／ロートナー／他
Essays on Residential Masterpieces—Louis I. Kahn; Lautner Bruder; Waldman; Koenig; Prince; and others
160 pages, 56 in color. ¥2,903

45 特集号：プロジェクト1995
Special Issue: Project 1995
184 pages, 24 in color. ¥2,903

46 連載：巨匠の住宅—ジョン・ロートナー　作品：カラチ／ノルテン／イスラエル／近藤／北川原／ミラージェス／他
Essays on Residential Masterpieces—John Lautner; Kalach; Norten; Israel; Niles; Rotondi; and others
160 pages, 64 in color. ¥2,903

47 特集号：日本の現代住宅　第4集　論文：原広司　エッセイ：石山修武　座談会：山本理顕、岸和郎、妹島和世
Special Issue: Japan Part IV
176 pages, 48 in color. ¥2,903

48 特集号：プロジェクト1996
Special Issue: Project 1996
176 pages, 32 in color. ¥2,903

49 作品：ザパタ／フォスター／イスラエル／ビール／ナイルズ／伊東／有馬／ローマックス／塩田／アーリック／窪田
Zapata; Foster; Israel; Beel; Niles; Ito; Arima; Lomax; Shioda; Erhlich; Kubota
160 pages, 72 in color. ¥2,903

50 作品：イスラエル／ノタ／ホルバーグ／クルック＆セクストン／ヴァレリオ／セイトウヴィッツ／ベルケル／坂本／他
Israel; Nota; Hallberg; Krueck & Sexton; Valerio; Saitowitz; Berkel; Sakamoto; and others
160 pages, 72 in color. ¥2,903

51 ロト・アーキテクツ／マイヤー／ウォルドマン／ヒルドナー／マック／テン・アルキテクトス／ジョイ
Roto Architects; Meier; Waldman; Hildner; Mack; Ten Arquitectos; Joy
160 pages, 72 in color. ¥2,903

52 特集号：プロジェクト1997
Special Issue: Project 1997
176 pages, 32 in color. ¥2,848

53 連載：世界の村と街—西アフリカ・セネガル／巨匠の住宅—R・M・シンドラー　作品：モーフォシス／ナイルズ／他
Villages & Towns—Senegal; Essays on Residential Masterpieces—R. M. Schindler; Morphosis; Niles; and others
158 pages, 64 in color. ¥2,903

54 連載：世界の村と街—イエメン　作品：コーニッグ／キャピー／ロックフェラー／フリカク／マック／齋藤／妹島／他
Villages & Towns—Yemen; Koenig; Kappe; Rockefeller/Hricak; Mack; Saito; Sejima; and others
160 pages, 72 in color. ¥2,848

55 特集号：プロジェクト1998
Special Issue: Project 1998
144 pages, 24 in color. ¥2,848

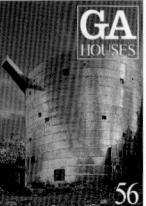

56 連載：世界の村と街—西アフリカ、ガーナ　作品：ブルーダー／アーリック／スコーギン／イーラム／プレイ／マイヤー／ザパタ／他
Villages & Towns—West Africa; Bruder; Ehrlich; Scogin/Elam/Bray; Meier; Zapata; and others
160 pages, 72 in color. ¥2,848

57 連載：世界の村と街—インドネシア　作品：安藤忠雄／コールハース／ペリアン／カラチ＆アルヴァレス／レゴレッタ／他
Villages & Towns–Indonesia; Ando; Koolhaas; Perriand; Kalach & Alvarez; Legorreta; and others
160 pages, 72 in color. ¥2,848

58 作品：レゴレッタ／原広司／スコーギン／イーラム／プレイ／村上徹／岸和郎／中東壽一／マック／他
Works;Legorreta; Hara; Scogin/ Elam/Bray; Murakami; Kishi; Nakahigashi; Mack; and others
160 pages, 72 in color. ¥2,848

59 特集号：プロジェクト1999
Special Issue: Project 1999
176 pages, 32 in color. ¥2,848

60 住宅デザインのコツ—安藤忠雄　作品：マイヤー／入江経／ブルーダー／ジョイ／伊東豊雄／ナイルズ／八木敦司／他
Tips on House Design: Tadao Ando Works;Meier; Irie; Bruder; Joy; Ito; Niles; Yagi; and others
160 pages, 72 in color. ¥2,848

61 住宅デザインのコツ：スコーギン／イーラム／プレイ　作品：マイヤーズ／ミラージェス／ソウト・デ・モウラ／レゴレッタ／他
Tips on House Design: Scogin/ Elam/Bray Works; Myers; Miralles; Legorreta; Aoki; and others
160 pages, 72 in color. ¥2,848

62 住宅デザインのコツ：トッド・ウィリアムズ ビリー・ツィン　作品：カラチ／テン・アルキテクトス／ノタ／マック／他
Tips on House Design: Williams/Tsien Works; Kalach; Ten Arquitectos; Nota; Mack; Ehrlich; and others
160 pages, 72 in color. ¥2,848

63 特集号：プロジェクト2000
Special Issue: Project 2000
176 pages, 40 in color. ¥2,848

64 住宅デザインのコツ：ファーナウ＆ハートマン　作品：シザ／ホール／スミス＝ミラー＋ホーキンソン／レゴレッタ／他
Tips on House Design: Fernau & Hartman Works; Siza; Holl; Smith-Miller+Hawkinson; and others
144 pages, 24 in color. ¥2,848

65 巨匠の住宅—リナー・ボ・バルディ　作品：ブルーダー／セイトウヴィッツ／妹島和世／キャピー／岸和郎／他
Residentietial Masterpieces: Rina Bo & P.M. Bardi Works; Bruder; Saitowitz; Sejima; Kappe; and others
144 pages, 72 in color. ¥2,848

表記価格には消費税は含まれておりません。